1956

POWER DEFIED

Nikita Khrushchev challenged Soviet orthodoxy
with a savage attack on the memory of Josef Stalin

French settlers in Algeria successfully defied the French Prime Minister,
Guy Mollet, but in the end it was the native population of Algeria
who saw off France's authority

King Hussein of Jordan dismissed the British commander
of the Arab Legion, on which his throne depended

Archbishop Makarios threatened British authority in Cyprus
and was deported to the Seychelles

Gamal Abdel Nasser seized the Suez Canal and defied the Western world

Poland's Gomulka faced down Khrushchev's anger and the might of
the Red Army

The Hungarian people challenged the Kremlin and went down to defeat,
with Imre Nagy and the uprising's leaders later going to the scaffold

Britain, France and Israel attacked Egypt, in defiance of the United States

Israel held on to its gains in Gaza and Sinai, rejecting
the authority of the United Nations

Fidel Castro landed in Cuba at the start of fifty years'
defiance of the United States

1956

POWER DEFIED

Peter Unwin

MICHAEL RUSSELL

The right of Peter Unwin to be identified
as the author of this work has been asserted by him
in accordance with the Copyright, Designs
and Patents Act, 1988

First published in Great Britain 2006
by Michael Russell (Publishing) Ltd
Wilby Hall, Wilby, Norwich NR16 2JP

Page makeup in Sabon by Waveney Typesetters
Wymondham, Norfolk
Printed and bound in Great Britain
by Biddles Ltd, King's Lynn, Norfolk

Indexed by the author

FOR PAUL AND STEPHEN
SONS AND FELLOW SCRIBBLERS

Contents

I

The Year and I

This is a book about a year. When it opened, 1956 promised to be nothing remarkable, just another in a procession of years leading away from the traumas of the Second World War towards hopeful or despondent, prosperous or penurious, peaceful or dangerous destinations. Britain was broke, the United States complacent, the Soviet Union stirring after the death of Stalin. The East Europeans were beginning to be cautiously hopeful that the worst of their postwar troubles might be over, while the Middle East was seething with the frustrated emotion of people who know that they want something but cannot identify what it is nor see their way to getting it. You could say as much of many of the territories that made up what was left of Western Europe's colonial empires.

No one in January 1956 anticipated war, revolution, crisis, rupture. Twelve months later the world had experienced each of these things and was the wiser for it, and the events of the year had violently shaken every kind of kaleidoscope. Aggression in Egypt, revolution in Hungary, American intervention to dash the last hopes of the European empires, the appearance of the first shoots that would flower in time as the European Union, all this and more had changed the world for good. 1956 had turned out to be a year as significant as 1914, 1929, 1939 and 1945.

The year cast its shadow forward also. It is clear now that the events of those astonishing few months marked a watershed between the postwar era and the modern world. Their consequences have played out over all the decades since. Half a century later they are with us still, just as the parallels between events then and events today are manifest. We can see, in short, that 1956 was a year in which the earth moved, one of the most significant years of our lives.

For me, there is something else about 1956. It was the year I really came of age. Two years earlier my father had given me a key of my own to his front door, just as a friend had presented me with a bowler hat to mark my entry into man's estate. But a hiatus followed, and I spent two years as a temporary soldier, parked in a siding of life, everyday military routine interrupted only by my marriage (celebrated, rather

unpromisingly, on the tenth anniversary of the bombing of Hiroshima).
In 1956 my life seemed to resume its forward march. I became a father.
We bought a house. I embarked on a diplomatic career.

When I started work in the Foreign Office in the summer of 1956 I
was unequivocally consigned to the shallow end of the pool of world
events. For eighteen months my efforts to be useful were only distrac-
tions to the colleagues who bustled so purposefully around me. But the
great happenings of world affairs were no longer remote abstractions;
they were live issues, with which men I knew were grappling for a
living, and with which I too would grapple when I got the hang of
them. I began to persuade myself that, given time, I could become an
insider like the people around me.

The attitudes I began to learn then permanently shaped my thinking
about world events. The Iraq tragedy today is as real to an old man in
retirement as the Suez fiasco ever was to the tyro when he started work
in its shadow. Today the Poles challenge their more powerful European
Union partners with the same insouciant bravado with which, in October 1956, they defied Nikita Khrushchev. The Hungary for which I
grieved in November 1956 has won the freedom for which it fought
then. Britain and France still differ about how best to deal with the
American arrogance and indispensability which were then so vigorously
displayed. The European Union which has grown over the decades out
of the lessons of that year still struggles to decide what political use it
should make of its economic and social power. The empires which
Britain and France thought they were defending have gone the way of
Nineveh and Tyre, but Western troops are still taking casualties at the
hands of men convinced that the United States is intent on building a
new empire in the Middle East. Israel's plot with France to humble
Gamal Abdel Nasser turned out to be the worst way to find the peace
and security among its Arab neighbours which still eludes it. And all the
world's potentates are still not agreed on the right road to Jerusalem..

So this is the story of one year as I remember it, and of how its legacy
has played out over the fifty that have followed it.

On 6 July our first child was born. We took her home from hospital in
Oxford a week later. But I could not hold outside circumstances indefinitely at bay, for in late July I was due to report to the Personnel
Department of the Foreign Office and take my first steps into the mysterious world of British diplomacy.

I drove up to London with half my mind on our domestic miracle and half on the strange world of work that lay ahead. Two years earlier I had taken the Foreign Office examination, and the interviewers had asked my ignorant opinion of things like the consequences of the fall of Dien Bien Phu and the end of French rule in Indo-China. Successful then, I was promised a place in the Foreign Service once I had served the Queen in two years of national service. So now I was serving out my last months as a minor cog in the machinery of military intelligence.

In my quiet, scarcely soldierly corner of the British Army our job was to produce technical drawings of Soviet military equipment. Our raw material was photographs of tanks and guns and trucks loaded with rockets, all of them snatched by licensed British Army snoopers with the Soviet forces in East Germany or by military attachés watching parades in Red Square or anywhere that served the same kind of purpose in any of the Eastern European satellite capitals. From them, mathematically-minded colleagues of mine produced scale drawings that we hoped were more or less accurate. When, after Suez, the Israelis slipped us some pieces of Soviet equipment they had taken from the Egyptians, my former colleagues established that their drawings had captured the dimensions of the equipment (and hence essential information about their capabilities) to within four per cent of material reality.

My day job in that strange little unit was that of the salesman, hawking our products round interested departments of the War Office in London, but in my spare time my boss enrolled me to support activities of his own. He was a brilliant maverick, a major of the South Wales Borderers, universally known as 'the mad major'. He wanted to convince his superiors of the need for a new approach, something he christened 'instantaneous graphic intelligence'. Instead of despatching reconnaissance aircraft on dangerous photographic missions, awaiting their return, developing their aerial photographs and laboriously interpreting their significance, we would get our intelligence in what half a century later we all tediously call 'real time'. We would, for example, leave television cameras behind us beside the roads as we retreated, each of them recording the direction and strength of the enemy's onslaught. Ideas which are commonplace or long since overtaken today, then seemed by turns brilliantly innovative or madly impracticable. But in those distant days each was undoubtedly novel.

So the mad major, with modest help from me, wrote a book about it. The next problem was to sell his ideas to the military intelligence hierarchy. Senior officers, said the major, had short attention spans and shorter fuses. We had to find a way to attract their attention and keep it. Generals were notoriously averse to books. We could not expect them to turn the page too often, so we dispensed with pages. Instead we assembled our *magnum opus* into a scroll, sheet attached to sheet with strips off a sticky roll of brown paper, until we had a Roman volume, and with it we set off to Whitehall, Tacitus and his scroll-bearer on the way to beard Agricola. God knows what the Caesars who presided over our little world made of us, but they were always impeccably polite.

As I drove up to London, however, my mind was on the world of diplomacy that lay ahead of me, not my years as a temporary soldier. I turned into Carlton House Terrace, left my car by the kerb, as you could leave cars by central London kerbs in those postwar years, gave in my name at the door and asked for Personnel Department. Before long I was in the presence of two live British diplomats.

'We're starting you off in Levant Department,' they told me.

Levant, I wondered.

'One of the Middle East departments,' they interpreted. 'When will you be free to start work?'

My colonel had said I could slip away from my duties in mid-August, I told them. 'I hope he hasn't changed his mind,' they said, and smiled.

Why should he have, I wondered, with a pretence of understanding.

'In any event, Levant Department will keep you busy.' they said, with an insider's gleam in the eye.

Why, I wondered, still pretending that I knew what they were talking about.

'Let Michael Rose know the date you can start,' they said, 'He'll put you to work'; and again they smiled, almost laughed, knowingly.

What was all that about, I asked myself as the porter showed me out.

He had seen my kind before. 'Where are they putting you, sir?' he asked.

'Levant Department,' I told him.

'That should keep you busy, sir,' he told me, 'seven days a week they'll be working in Levant Department.'

I turned for enlightenment to the nearest *Evening Standard*. Nasser had seized the Suez Canal, it told me. Britain's jugular was threatened. The great crisis of 1956 had arrived, and taken me cruelly by surprise.

Within days of the nationalisation of the Suez Canal, the British armed forces went to action stations. Leave was curtailed, and national servicemen found their release dates called in question. Even my quiet backwater was stirred into activity as the photo-reconnaissance Canberras quartered the Middle Eastern skies. But my colonel remained as good as his word and I hung up my uniform for good. In mid-August I reported to Levant Department as planned.

To a newcomer, it was a mysterious organism, embedded in the much bigger organism of the Foreign Office. There were twelve of us in the department, from its head, who seemed to my awestruck eye to combine grandeur and charm, through his assistant and five first secretaries, all high-powered characters in their thirties, to me and a roomful of secretaries – known always, in those distant days, as the 'departmental ladies'. We were responsible for dealings with Israel, Jordan, Lebanon, Syria and Iraq, as well as a few general Middle Eastern subjects like oil, arms supplies and the Arab boycott of Israel. We occupied half a dozen shabby rooms on the second floor overlooking Downing Street, and on the floor above was a team of filing clerks who constituted 'Levant Division', our backup archivists.

My new colleagues' telephones rang incessantly, mine only when someone dialled a wrong number. Five or six times a day a box arrived with copies of the latest take of telegrams from embassies around the world. Thrice daily a pouchful of new papers was delivered to us from the division upstairs. Mysterious papers came and went in red boxes, grey boxes, beige boxes; and I gathered by osmosis that these concerned matters that were none of my tyro business. Emissaries from other departments – African Department, Eastern Department, even a mysterious Permanent Under Secretary's Department – appeared, exchanged quick yet laid-back words with the men around me who were capable of answering them sensibly, and went about their business. People came from News Department, and were told what they might and might not tell the press. Meanwhile I did as I was told and studied the Foreign Office telephone directory. It would give me an idea, a hurried mentor told me, of the structure of this strange new machine in whose cogs I was entangled.

I spent those early weeks getting uselessly in the way of the men around me and the work they were doing. At any time a Foreign Office department is an impressive part of an impressive machine. At times of crisis it goes into overdrive. When I joined it, Levant Department's job was to help make sense of the fast-moving Middle Eastern crisis which preoccupied the world. Eventually I was given a job. 'Walk this draft round the Office', one of my colleagues asked me. I did as I was told, hawking our draft telegram from African Department to Eastern Department and Northern Department and down stairs to News Department and indeed to any department whose name was inscribed in the margin of the draft. My job was to nobble somebody, preferably the right body, in each department and get his agreement to whatever instructions we wanted to send to Tel Aviv or Washington, Khartoum or Baghdad. Once I had accumulated their approving initials the draft would go up the ladder to higher authority. When it went out over the ether it carried the collective weight of the Foreign Office, for however lowly the subject matter it went with the authority of the Secretary of State himself, signed 'Lloyd'. It sounds like the most Fred Karno of procedures; in fact it could work like something approaching lightning.

We worked long hours. Across the corridor, African Department, with direct responsibility for Egypt and the Suez Canal, really was hard at it seven days a week. I used to get some faint idea of what was going on when we met for a cup of tea and a quick talk every afternoon. Michael Rose would tell us what was going on in the upper reaches of the Foreign Office. Peter Laurence, our Israel desk officer, came back from Joint Intelligence Committee meetings to talk about speculation there on Israeli intentions. Our man on Jordan was wrestling with the status of the Arab Legion, for if the Israelis attacked Jordan, we were treaty-bound to fight them. The constant backdrop to all this activity was negotiation with every nation with an interest in the canal. The aim was to build a coalition to force Nasser to disgorge the precious property he had nationalised, the Suez Canal Company and all its assets in Egypt. Above all we wanted to involve the Americans, for only the United States could really put the frighteners on Colonel Nasser.

I had no idea of what was really going on and over our daily cups of tea it gradually dawned on me that no one in Levant Department had either. They knew that Nasser was within his international legal rights in nationalising the canal, but they half-accepted the view which ministers asserted that with the canal in his hands Nasser had us by the windpipe. They acknowledged that it might be right to use the threat of force to get Nasser to disgorge what he had seized, but the rights and wrongs of an actual attack on Egypt were quite another matter. So much for conventional analysis by people who were paid to know the Middle East and the world in which the crisis was being played out.

It was clear, however, that the Prime Minister, Anthony Eden, who had taken direct charge of the crisis, was running ahead of obscure civil servants in Levant Department and African Department. In public he compared Nasser with the dictators of the 1930s and talked of the lesson that Munich had taught him, that appeasing an aggressor never pays. In public he refused to rule out the use of force, and the word around the Office was that in private he was eager for it. It was whispered too that at times the mood on the other side of Downing Street was close to hysteria. Our Secretary of State, Selwyn Lloyd, was a weak minister, and was dancing to Eden's tune. It gradually became apparent that Levant Department's daily work might be one thing but that ministers' real policy was something else. Quite what it was remained elusive, even mysterious, but here and there my colleagues in Levant Department picked up hints that ministers, and a handful of senior officials, were mysteriously engaged in talks with France and even with Israel. But none of them, not even the head of the department, was prepared for what actually happened in October-November 1956.

In every decade of the half century that separates us from 1956, events have drawn my mind back to the story of that extraordinary year. The first occurred two years later, in the summer of 1958, when I was seeing out my time in Levant Department. By now my masters felt that I could be trusted with slightly more serious matters, and I had become the desk officer for Lebanon. So I saw the telegrams that flashed around the world when army officers contrived revolution in Iraq and the Baghdad mob tore apart the country's King and its Prime Minister, Britain's special Middle East friend, Nuri es-Said. A new Middle East crisis was upon us and the United States decided that something must be done to stop the rot spreading. I played a tremulous bit-part in a meeting that turned the Mediterranean Fleet eastwards towards the Levant, while United States Marines were despatched to storm the beaches of Beirut, to meet nothing more formidable than Lebanon's famous bathing beauties and ask them: 'Where is the war?' Britain, back in step with the Americans and eager as ever to demonstrate that its relationship with Washington was a special one, sent parachutists flying into Jordan. It was all heady stuff, if ultimately pointless; but to all those people in Britain who had supported the Suez adventure two years earlier, the events of the summer of 1958 came as proof that they had been right all along.

That same summer was marked also by the judicial murder of Imre Nagy. It aroused a storm of futile indignation everywhere outside the Soviet camp. At about the same time Personnel Department told me that my time in Levant Department was up. They were sending me to Budapest, and when he heard my news a friend remarked that I sounded admirably calm for a man preparing to live in a graveyard. We set off across Europe, with two small children by now, and one hot day in July we crossed the Iron Curtain for the first time. For the next two years the story of the Hungarian uprising remained a present reality, as I spent my time logging rumours of arrests, secret trials and executions of freedom fighters who had fought the Russians in 1956.

So 1956 was not a year that one could easily put behind one. After Budapest the Queen had need of my services in Tokyo, and then once again in the Foreign Office in London. But by 1967 I was back on a Middle East desk, a solemn and responsible First Secretary now, entrusted with the affairs of Egypt. In June of that year Israeli forces once again stormed across Sinai and in six days they destroyed the Egyptian army. President Nasser announced his resignation, and at a fraught Foreign Office meeting I told the Foreign Secretary, George Brown, that I believed he meant it. Brown, infinitely wilier than I, was more sceptical, and in forty-eight hours Nasser was back, his resignation rejected by a packed and disciplined parliament. But movement through the canal was blocked as it had been in 1956, and again you could argue – and it was argued – that the events of 1967 demonstrated that Anthony Eden had been right after all. Yet in that same year Britain announced that its old, once-imperial role 'East of Suez' was over. In doing so the nation signalled that the canal was no longer the life-and-death matter it once had thought it.

The following year brought a different reminder of the events of 1956. In the spring of 1968 Czechoslovakia's Dubcek set his country on course for democracy and those of us who remembered him talked of the legacy of Imre Nagy. Moscow rattled its sabres and anyone who knew anything about Eastern Europe offered their opinions. The Russians would not attack Czechoslovakia, I opined; the events of 1956 in Hungary had done too much damage to their global reputation for them to behave that bloodily again. A friend of mine drew on different experience – he had spent years in Moscow engaged in reading the Kremlin's mind – to reach the same conclusion. But our collective wisdom did not stop the Soviet tanks advancing into Czechoslovakia, and the only difference between 1968 and 1956 was that the Czechs were too wise or too craven to go for broke as the Hungarians had done.

By the early 1970s there was talk of a Hungarian reform movement. Hungary, the press told us, was now the happiest barracks in the Soviet bloc. The Hungarians were choosing not Marx and Engels but Marks and Spencer. So when, in the early 1980s, I went back to Budapest, now as ambassador, I expected to find the place unrecognisably changed. Physically it was all too familiar, almost as shabby and down-at-heel as the place I remembered from the 1950s. But psychologically it was changed, the terror and hysteria gone, their place taken by a gloomy caution and tenuous hope. Margaret Thatcher came to Budapest, intent on reawakening Hungarians' capitalist instincts. Princess Margaret came to support the Royal Ballet. The Hungarian security policemen who took such good care of them turned out, when I chatted them up, to be as agreeable people as the visitors' British personal detectives. Yet these were the successors, perhaps even the sons, of the security men who had dealt so ruthlessly with the Hungarian revolutionaries in 1956.

In 1989, just three years after I completed that second tour of duty in Budapest, came central Europe's year of miracles. In June I returned to Hungary to see the ceremonial reburial and political rehabilitation of Imre Nagy. The ceremony, lasting the length of a long summer's day, moved thousands of us to tears. At the end of it, Hungary's course was set for freedom and democracy. I believed that day that at last the world was burying the last memories of 1956. Others that year felt quite as exalted as I, and everywhere you looked the world – and even the Middle East – seemed fresh, renewed. Someone even wrote that we were experiencing the end of history.

He was wrong, of course, and in every year since 1989, the year of miracles, we have seen the played out the same kind of issues as consumed the world in 1956. We saw wars fought just over Hungary's southern border, the Balkans given over to mayhem, the long and agonising war of attrition between Israel and Palestine and two great Western expeditions into the Middle East. Each was designed, just like the Allies' attack on Egypt in 1956, to put that troubled area to rights. One half-succeeded, one is more than halfway to failure. Today, fifty years afterwards, we see that the things that troubled the world in 1956 are with us still.

2
The World in the Fifties

By the mid 1950s memories of the Second World War were fading and its hardships were slowly giving way to better things. But the lessons and legacies of war remained immediate, and they shaped reactions to events which stemmed from quite different origins. 'Never again,' said men and women everywhere, but in the 1950s there was no escaping the war. Britain still treasured its wartime finest hour, while France strove to exorcise the ghosts of its defeat. The losers – Germany, Italy, Japan – were temporarily silenced, their slow return to influence and respectability scarcely begun. Across the sea, the United States sat complacently on the power and prosperity which war had brought it, while the Soviet Union nursed its wounds and asserted the rights its struggles had won. In Poland men and women grieved in strictest privacy the fact that a war begun to save them from one tyranny had ended up selling them to another; and the other peoples of Eastern Europe in their differing degrees similarly bewailed the fate which the outcome of the year had inflicted on them. Meanwhile nationalists in the colonies cherished one wartime lesson above all – the hollowness of the European imperialists' pretensions.

The consequences of the war sat equally heavily on society. In every Western country the men who had come home from war were clear about what they had fought for. They wanted peace, something like equality, educational opportunity, prosperity, social security. Their political leaders were older men, who had fought the war from desks in Washington or Whitehall, and deference to age, wisdom and authority persisted. But respect for class, money and position had been eroded; the Western world was more equal in the 1950s than in the 1930s, and in most respects than it is a half-century later. Yet with few exceptions it remained an easygoing kind of equality. Younger people, the war's schoolchildren, on the whole respected the world their immediate seniors had fought for. In Britain we were, said David Lodge the novelist, 'cautious, unassertive, grateful for small mercies and modest in our ambition'.[1] For most of us, our ambition was merely to mimic our seniors, not replace them, and it was the 1960s before youth began to throw its weight about. So I took without embarrassment to wearing that bowler hat my friend had given me on my twenty-first birthday, and my wife and her young friends took the middle-aged Duchess of Kent as their model of feminine elegance. In the 1950s the Western world enjoyed a sense of cohesion across the age groups as well as between the classes which it has not recovered since.

The picture was different in what Moscow called the Socialist camp, but it too was coloured by the consequences of war. Socialism, said the mantra, had defeated fascism and set the people free. It would put the working class in the saddle, purge the masses of nationalism and religion, and in time lead them to Communism. Central to all this was the Soviet Union, the first Socialist nation. The rest of the world could draw on its strength in resisting reactionary forces and on its example in finding the way to Socialism. Some in the Socialist camp accepted this picture of the 1950s world, more were silenced by the authoritarianism under which they lived. Outside the camp, and particularly in the Third World, millions believed that the Soviet Union (or perhaps China) could lead them to a Socialist nirvana.

Others in the Third World feared this Socialist internationalist zeal as a threat to their hopes of achieving nationhood, but most were more concerned with throwing off an older kind of colonialism. Much of the world, and Africa in particular, was still coloured British Empire red upon the map. Many other parts were painted French imperial blue or Belgian brown. The colonialists must go, as much from Africa and the Middle East as from south Asia. The countries which had already found their freedom – India, Pakistan, Burma, Ceylon, Indonesia – still remembered the heavy hand of their old colonial masters. They set themselves, like the slowly-emerging colonies, to build an identity free of Washington, the Western European capitals and even Moscow, and to put proud nations of their own in place of colonial rule.

The war had cost untold millions of lives and the atomic bomb that had ended it threatened millions more if the world ever went to war again. So 'Never again' remained the war's most powerful lesson, but the best strategic brains argued that the price of avoiding war was to prepare for it. So the United States and the Soviet Union piled their nuclear armouries high, each convinced that the other would exploit even passing weakness. Everyone remembered that in 1938 the Munich agreement had not saved the world from war but merely paved the way towards it. There must never be another sell-out like it. The doctrine reached out beyond direct East-West competition, and as they struggled to hold their empires together or prepare their colonies for eventual independence, the Western European powers professed to see the hand of Moscow behind every challenge to their authority. There was real fear of war in the 1950s.

Yet at the same time idealism was at work, spreading hopes to balance fears. Optimism found most fertile ground in the United States, to which victory had brought power and prosperity as well as peace. The 1950s were the years in which the suburbanisation of America found wings, and every four-square suburban house meant the fulfilment of an American dream. The returning veterans had flooded into the universities, and what they learned bolstered the old American belief in unlimited possibilities. Things were harder in Britain, but free health care, wider education, social security and full employment brought real satisfactions to British families. For France things were harder still, but the French, like the Germans, the Dutch and all the other Western Europeans, began to build their better world. In the Third World freedom was thought to promise prosperity as well, and happiness for the masses as much as for their leaders. The promises of Socialism were still grander, even if in the Soviet Union, China and the East European satellites few found them credible; and when Stalin died in 1953 it was possible to believe that the worst of the pains of transformation were over and the future held promise of better things.

The events of 1956 brought into sharp focus all these tendencies, inchoate as they seem to us today and scarcely recognised as they were half a century ago. The Suez and Hungarian crises of the autumn brought shooting war to Central Europe and the Middle East, and fear of a wider war, perhaps even a nuclear war, to the whole world. Suez marked the extinction of British and French power in the Middle East, and drove another nail into the coffins of their empires. Demonstrating that Britain and France, even if they acted together, were too weak to play a leading role in world affairs, it advanced still further the primacy of the United States. When it came to the choice, Washington showed that it valued the United Nations, international law and the futile pursuit of the goodwill of the Third World over loyalty to its erring allies.

The experience taught Britain and France different lessons, which set them on divergent courses. Britain resolved never to separate itself again from American power, while France sought national reassertion by building its own atomic bomb and taking the lead in creating a European community. For the Soviet Union, the crisis demonstrated that it could go it alone in its own sphere in a way that Britain and France could not, yet it cost Moscow most of its last remaining sympathisers in Western Europe and damaged its reputation in the rest of the world. Egypt successfully faced down the imperialist aggressors and so mightily advanced its pretensions in the Third World. Israel, which had proved itself startlingly effective in military terms and yet remained vulnerable to the antipathy of its neighbours, asserted itself as it had never done before. As for Hungary, it learned the hard way that there was no escape from the Soviet commonwealth.

The world's nerves were tense in 1956 and statesmen reacted then in ways which in fifty years of retrospect may seem exaggerated, even hysterical. But just eleven years after the war, the world was not really sure of peace. The lessons of the war were in the forefront of everyone's mind, and therefore recited too literally. So Britain and France saw Nasser as a new Hitler, or at the very least a Mussolini. They were determined not to give him a new Munich. To the Tory Right, Arab nationalists and freedom fighters seeking independence seemed to threaten Britain's very survival. Paris likewise saw a pan-Arab conspiracy behind every attack upon its power in North Africa. Moscow was haunted by different daemons, and claimed (perhaps even believed) that in November 1956 new fascists stalked the streets of Budapest. The United Nations, too, was only ten years old, still fragile, on its mettle. It would be years yet before its new members tipped the balance of the organisation away from a united West, but when the West was disunited, as over Suez, their opinions were taken seriously. Israel was as young, its nights haunted by the Holocaust, its days consumed by cares for its very survival. Even the United States, serenely powerful, feared the Soviet challenge with its growing appeal to Third World leaders and to colonial peoples clamouring to be free.

This background said different things to the men who played starring roles in the Suez and Hungarian crises. There were ten of them, each with his own outlook on the world. Nine of them led nations, one an international organisation. The lives of each of them, as of millions of others, were altered by the double-headed crisis. Yet as they made their

New Year's resolutions at the end of 1955, none of them had any real notion of the drama which the immediate future had in store. Like statesmen at any time and place, they were distracted by the multitude of different preoccupations that pressed upon them. It was only gradually in the course of the year that these preoccupations came together to create the twin crises of October-November 1956.

In December 1955 Dwight Eisenhower's attention was directed far from Central Europe or the Middle East. Middle America basked in postwar well-being, only gradually becoming aware of the domestic divisions, particularly about race, that would rack it for the next fifty years. 'Ike', war hero and much-loved peacetime leader, presided Buddha-like over this sense of well-being which his benign grin celebrated. By the end of 1955 he was recovering well from a heart attack that had struck him in September. He felt himself well enough to continue as President, and in the last weeks of the year his mind was focused on the election that he faced in the following November. He knew the sweep of world events, but he left the details of America's dealings with the world beyond its borders to his Secretary of State, John Foster Dulles. The two men rejoiced that for the time being the United States was all but all-powerful, though they saw its pre-eminence threatened by the advance of the Soviet Union. The Communists might be held in check in Europe, but they remained restive, hungry. They were building a hydrogen bomb, and the appeal of the Communism which they preached was growing among the newly emergent nations of the Third World.

In Moscow, Nikita Khrushchev was enjoying himself. When Stalin died in March 1953 an uneasy collective leadership had taken his place, and by December 1955 Khrushchev had emerged as its brightest star. As First Secretary of the Communist party, he outshone his partner, the Prime Minister Nikolai Bulganin. In the course of 1955 and early 1956 Khrushchev and Bulganin brought the Warsaw Pact into being, conferred at the summit in Geneva with Western leaders, paid an argumentative visit to Britain and started to repair the Soviet Union's relations with Yugoslavia. Day by day Moscow seemed to be filling out its claims to full equality with the United States and becoming a second global superpower.

France, by contrast, was harried and on the run. In the early 1950s one weak prime minister after another had shown himself unable to hold ramshackle governments together. More often than not what brought them down was unrest and revolt in Vietnam and in France's North African territories. By 1955 France had extricated itself from Vietnam and had hopes of disposing of Morocco and Tunisia too; but Algeria was in turmoil, and French politics were split down the middle over policy towards it. In December Guy Mollet, schoolteacher turned politician, a quiet pragmatist who reserved his political enthusiasms for the building of a European community, was hoping to take his turn at governing the ungovernable French. He faced a general election in the first week of the New Year. In it the coalition to which Mollet's Socialist Party belonged was victorious. To general surprise, the President chose Mollet to be Prime Minister. He had had six months at the top when the Suez crisis erupted.

In 1955 Britain believed itself a vastly more significant power than France, but shared many of its problems. It had fought unconquered from the first day of the war to the last and still thought itself one of the world's 'Big Three'. Yet its wartime expenditure had transformed it from the world's biggest creditor to its biggest debtor. The balance of its economy had been overthrown, and it was now quite inadequate to carry the weight of a global foreign policy, in which its history and its continuing pretensions held it entangled. Anthony Eden, who had succeeded Winston Churchill as Prime Minister in April 1955 after frustrating years as the Conservatives' heir apparent, personified the dilemma which Britain faced. For twenty years he had been the golden boy of Western diplomacy and he knew the great international issues better than any other professional politician. Now, as Prime Minister, he was confronted with the task of disentangling the country from its imperial commitments, while still involving it as America's closest ally in fighting the threat of Communism which the West detected, lurking behind the surge towards freedom for the Third World. Domestic affairs were his Achilles heel. He knew little of Britain's economic and social problems, nor of the fatal limitations they imposed on any British government's freedom of action in foreign affairs. And already his closest colleagues were muttering about his ill-health and his shaky emotional equilibrium.

In the eyes of the leaders of the United States, the Soviet Union, France and Britain the other actors in the drama of 1956 were far lesser men than they, yet each had a unique part to play in it. One of them, Gamal Abdel Nasser of Egypt, was to provoke the Suez crisis pretty well single-handed, just as Imre Nagy, by his heroic stubbornness, was to ensure that the Hungarian revolution would not be extinguished unhonoured by the world.

Nasser had come to power in April 1954 at the end of a tussle for supremacy among the Army officers who had overthrown the monarchy a year earlier. He wanted to win his country's full independence, give it back its dignity, make himself a hero among the Arabs and make Cairo the undisputed capital of the Arab world. In October 1954 he had concluded an agreement for the withdrawal by the summer of 1956 of British troops from the Canal Zone. By December 1955 he had survived an attempted assassination by Moslem extremists, engaged in a guerrilla war by proxy with Israel, bought arms from the Soviet bloc, joined Britain in granting Sudan its independence and opened negotiations with the United States and the World Bank to finance the building of a dam on the Nile at Aswan. At the end of the year he could look back on an unbroken run of success, and forward to hopes of more in 1956.

By the end of 1955 Nagy on the other hand had seen high hopes dashed and apparently destroyed. The world had first heard his name two and a half years earlier, when the Soviet leadership had plucked him from obscurity, made him prime minister of Hungary and set him to work to de-Stalinise Communism there. He started strongly, and in the course of 1954 leached the worst of hysteria and arbitrary excess from Hungarian politics. But in early 1955 the balance of forces in the Communist world started to turn against him. In April he was dismissed from the post of prime minister and expelled from the Politburo and the Central Committee. A month later he was stripped of every other distinction, and even his membership of the Communist Party which he had served for thirty years. By December, reduced to arguing his case in a series of essays which he circulated secretly to the few who still dared to support him, he seemed on course for a frustrated and ignominious old age.

While Nagy wrote his essays, Wladyslaw Gomulka was living under house arrest. Like Nagy, his reformist policies had got him into trouble with hard-eyed critics in the Kremlin and in the Polish Communist Party. Restored to power he would be very cautious about the way he used it. But his return to Polish politics would help to purge Poland of the worst excesses of Stalinism and set it on a course which combined decently humane Communist policies with respect for its national independence. In December 1955 there seemed little prospect of all that. Like Nagy he seemed to face a future of continuing obscurity.

Josef Broz Tito in contrast had had a good year in 1955 and as it ended looked forward to more good times to come. In 1948 he had broken with Moscow and his excommunication from the church of international Communism followed. He made good use of his time in the wilderness. Intense Soviet pressure helped him to hold Yugoslavia together, for his countrymen knew that if they did not hang together they would surely hang separately. His independence made him a world figure, and in the summer of 1955 he was one of the leaders who dominated the Bandung Conference of the non-aligned movement. In that same summer the Soviet leaders came warily to Tito's Canossa. Khrushchev conceded that there could be many roads to Socialism, and in June 1955 he and Tito signed a treaty normalising relations between their two countries. Now Tito could have both the penny and the bun, restored on the one hand to Moscow's suspicious affections and on the other happily at work building Yugoslavia's reputation as a nation sworn neither to Moscow nor to Washington.

The position of each of these men was special, but that of David Ben-Gurion stood out as most special of all. A Zionist stalwart for half a century, he carried now the burden of leading and protecting Israel. He had surrounded himself with young, hard, decisive men, among whom he sometimes seemed an impractical visionary. After seven years of precarious existence, Israel still felt itself surrounded by its enemies, sustained only by what influence world Jewry could bring to bear on Western governments. To have survived those seven years was success in itself; to keep Israel safe was Ben-Gurion's mission. At the end of 1955 he could tell himself that he had carried his country through another year of danger. But Nasser's increasing prominence in the Arab world heralded an increasing threat to Israel. For the old man, 1955 had been a dangerous year. The signs were that 1956 would be worse.

Last of the ten comes Dag Hammarskjöld, a man carrying the problems not of one country but of the world upon his shoulders. He had been elected Secretary-General of the United Nations in 1953. He brought to the job a penchant for philosophy which disconcerted and sometimes mystified those with whom he worked, deep commitment to the principles on which the United Nations was based, low cunning in getting his own way, and a phenomenal capacity for hard work. He had seen the United Nations' mission in Korea completed, South Africa walk out on its critics in the General Assembly, and Greek demands for Cypriot autonomy rejected. But he had turned his hand above all to holding in check the border clashes between Jews and Arabs in the Holy Land. They had shown no diminution in 1955, promised none in the year that lay ahead, and could all too easily lead to a general conflagration in the Middle East.

So these were the countries and these were the leaders seeing in the New Year on the night of 31 December 1955. And these were some of the issues they were to face in 1956.

3
Stars, Scribblers and Simpler Souls

So far this has been a book about statesmen and diplomats, soldiers and sailors and freedom fighters. What they said and did in 1956 will fill most of the rest of it, and their memoirs have gone a long way to shape our impressions of that distant world. But 1956 was no more the exclusive business of such people than any other year in history. Ordinary people disported themselves on that year's summer beaches. Writers wrote, actors acted, brides married their sweethearts. Pundits produced absurd opinions and serious men and women pondered grave matters such as the law's treatment of homosexuals and prostitutes. Home Secretaries ruled on hanging and Chancellors of the Exchequer scandalised the clergy with the introduction of Premium Bonds. This chapter takes a few snapshots of such matters, before we get back to the serious business of politics, war and the breaking of empires.

19 APRIL: GRACE KELLY WEDS HER PRINCE

On 19 April 1200 guests gathered in Monaco Cathedral to see Grace Kelly, the American film actress, marry Prince Rainier of Monaco. They represented the monarchies and aristocracies of Europe, the wealth of the United States and the nabobs of Hollywood. Anyone who in those early days could get at a set watched the event on television, fascinated to see screen fame and princely distinction brought together and broadcast round the globe. The wedding seemed the fulfilment of a fairy tale. Only rare insiders knew that it was also a marriage in which calculation played as large a part as romance. Ordinary people, fans of Hollywood or of royalty, were content to be carried away on an emotional surfboard on a wave of glamour vicariously enjoyed.

When she became engaged to Rainier in January 1956, Grace Kelly was a rising Hollywood star. She came from a background of wealth, created by the efforts of her Irish Catholic father, John Brendan Kelly, who had made his very considerable pile in the building industry. Money had bought him his place in Philadelphia society, but he added more distinction, as an Olympic gold-medallist oarsman. He wanted the best for his daughter.

Besides wealth, Grace Kelly was blessed with a translucent, melting beauty. She put it to work, family disapproving, first as a model and then in Hollywood. She won her first part in 1951 at the age of twenty-two, and a bigger, though still minor role, in *High Noon* in the following year. From then on her film successes came quickly, in *Mogambo*, a romantic film in an African jungle setting; in the sultry film interpretation of a sultry novel, *From Here to Eternity*; and then in three of Alfred Hitchcock's classics: *Dial M for Murder*, *Rear Window* and *To Catch a Thief*. And in 1955 she won her first Academy Award, for Best Actress in *The Country Girl*.

The studio image-makers projected Kelly as a chaste Roman Catholic girl, different from and a cut above your average Hollywood star. In reality there was something distinctly unchaste about her, and she involved herself with several gods of the silver screen like Clark Gable, Bing Crosby, Ray Milland and William Holden. Before he declared himself, Rainier made discreet inquiries about her. 'Grace is the best lay in Hollywood', he is supposed to have been told; and then, when his informant took in the expression on Rainier's face, 'Gracie Fields, of course'.

So in her short Hollywood career Grace Kelly cut quite a dash, though a carefully hidden dash, and when she met Rainier she was not at all the spotless angel whom film and society magazines portrayed. But the world's cinema-goers innocently worshipped their angel's image.

Rainier too had a past, and for six years he had pursued an affair with the French actress Gisèle Pascal. But he needed to settle down and he had a very particular dynastic need for children, which Pascal seemed unable to give him. He had to secure the future of his family, a family that combined a faintly comic opera character with dynastic and historical distinction.

Grimaldis had ruled in Monaco since 1297. They had had to accept first Spanish and then French protection, and during the French Revolution the family were for a time imprisoned (and one of Rainier's forebears guillotined). But at the Treaty of Paris in 1814, when Napoleon was despatched to a little principality of his own in Elba, the Grimaldis got back their principality of Monaco. A year later the Kingdom of Sardinia became the protecting power, but in 1861 France resumed that role, which – the years of wartime occupation apart – it has exercised ever since.

There was an extra twist to Rainier's need for an heir. The problem was that an old-established agreement with France provided that in the absence of an heir the principality would revert to France. It would be a sad end for the Grimaldis and sad too for the interests, some of them shady, which made the most of Monaco's special status as somewhere linked with but not part of France. Grace Kelly offered an escape from that fate for prince and people. She would bring Rainier and Monaco beauty, glamour, wealth and fame, and every prospect of children to continue the Grimaldi line.

So all eyes were turned on Monaco Cathedral that April day as Grace Kelly knelt, a virginal figure in white, beside her prince in all his antique decorations. The ceremony passed off smoothly to general delight, and by the summer it was announced that Her Serene Highness was pregnant. In January 1957 she gave birth to a child to continue the Grimaldi line. The baby was a girl, but a boy and a second girl followed. Each of the three grew up in the fullness of time to lead lives as rackety in their own ways as their mother's had begun.

But respectability reigned along with Prince Rainier and Princess Grace and for nearly thirty years they presided together over the little principality. They turned Monte Carlo into a home and resort for the very rich, its casino a haunt for glamorous high-rollers, and gave Monaco financial as well as dynastic security. Grace died in 1982, the victim of a road accident on the corniche above Monte Carlo, but their marriage had done what it had to do, and it had carried into the middle of the twentieth century the 100-year-old tradition that beautiful young American heiresses should ride to the rescue of dynastically distinguished but needy scions of the European aristocracy and minor European royalty. It was the single most glamorous event any of us saw in 1956.

8 MAY: AN ANGRY BRITISH AUTHOR...

On 8 May the Royal Court Theatre in London presented a new play to its audience. The theatre itself had only just opened as a self-consciously different kind of place from the showcases of the West End. The play was the first from an unknown young author. It could have sunk without trace, and at first the critics were unkind. But something

about *Look Back in Anger* bewitched its audiences. In that summer of
1956 the educated and liberal-minded younger middle classes in Britain
thought they were ready to enter a new era. For them, John Osborne's
Look Back in Anger was a symbol. It dispatched the postwar years of
deference and painful respectability and put in their place self against
society. It was full of anger, destructiveness and self-pity and many were
repelled by it. You loved it or loathed it. Kenneth Tynan, the most brilliant theatre critic of the era, spoke for the kind of audience who loved
it, saying 'I don't think I could love anybody who didn't love *Look
Back in Anger.*' Tony Richardson, the director of that first production,
let luvviedom run away with his tongue. Osborne was, he said, 'unique
and alone in his ability to put on the stage the quick of himself, his pain,
his squalor, his nobility – terrifyingly alone'.

So what was it about the play and the year which so spectacularly
worked upon one another? In his autobiography Osborne described the
making of the Britain of the Fifties, against which his hero Jimmy
Porter railed:

> The country was tired, not merely from the sacrifice of two back-
> breaking wars but from the defeat and misery between them. The
> bits of red on the map came down and the names we knew on
> mixed packets of postage stamps were erased. Like so much else,
> it all happened without people being very aware of it. The leaping
> hare of the Victorian imagination had begun to imitate the
> tortoise even before 1914, but in that summer of 1955, it was still
> easy enough to identify what we regarded as a permanent Estab-
> lishment.[1]

Osborne conceived his play as an attack on that Establishment. To
mount it he put before his audience characters of a kind not previously
seen on the English stage. Jimmy Porter became a symbol of a new kind
of man with new kinds of attitudes. He came from a working-class,
back-streets type of family. Free university education had torn him
from his roots yet left him defiantly identifying with them. In advancing
him as it had, a postwar Britain that thought it valued equality and
social justice had done well by Jimmy Porter. But Jimmy used his education to dissect the failings of that complacent world, the mediocrity of
the people and things he saw around him, and to rail at his own empty
prospects.

Looking back over fifty years it is hard to see why so many of us took

Jimmy Porter's rage so tragically. At the time the critics called him 'a young pup', 'rotten with self-pity'. He took out on country, society, best friend – and above all on his emotionally captive wife – the anger he felt against himself. He is, examined quizzically, a silly, destructive nay-sayer. His rage even lacks consistency: he tortures his wife into leaving him to return to her middle-class parents' home, and then sets up house with a woman who stands for everything he hates.

Yet in that season of 1956 *Look Back in Anger* and Jimmy Porter in particular took a certain kind of theatregoer by storm. Young men, even conformist young men beginning a career in the Foreign Office, identified with Jimmy's anger. Osborne himself was labelled, perhaps by a press officer with a gift for a soundbite, an 'angry young man'. Other writers became angry young men in his image: John Arden and Arnold Wesker in the theatre, Kingsley Amis, John Braine and Alan Sillitoe on the printed page. For a time their popularity put more conventional authors to rout.

Between them Jimmy Porter and John Osborne helped to condition popular attitudes to the public events that consumed the autumn of 1956. People who in the summer were moved by their diatribes against established society became natural rebels when, in the autumn, their leaders went to undeclared war with Egypt. London crowds took possession of Trafalgar Square, fighting running battles with the police the length of Whitehall. Throughout the country demonstrators bawled their anti-government slogans as few British crowds ever had before. The same kind of people took to the streets to demonstrate an equal anger at the Soviet Union's attack on Hungary.

A year after his triumph with *Look Back in Anger*, John Osborne brought another play to the London stage. *The Entertainer* provides a kind of epilogue to the Suez adventure. It tells the story of an ageing comedian (played at first by Laurence Olivier) who has lost his grip on his material, his audience and his hopes. He tries every trick in the book to reassert his old authority. None succeeds. Archie Rice is a tragic, broken figure, and in his tragedy ridiculous. Audiences which shared Osborne's bitterness against Britain's Establishment saw Rice as a symbol of its folly and weakness. His collapse into irrelevance was the collapse of Britain's last imperial pretensions. To many of us the weary tricks with which he tried to recapture attention were to the life the tricks of Harold Macmillan who in January 1957 had replaced

Anthony Eden in Downing Street. *Look Back in Anger* stands as a metaphor for the change that came over British attitudes towards the past and towards authority in 1956. *The Entertainer* consigns to history the men who led it then.

...AND A FRENCH ONE

In the same year a different kind of writer took France by storm. At thirty-six, Jean Dutourd was already an established writer, and in time he was to become a member of the French Academy. Taken prisoner in 1940 after a fortnight in uniform, then released, he had spent the war identifying with the Resistance and the Communist Party. In the autumn of 1956 he published a volume of essays about the condition of France. It was even more perverse than *Look Back in Anger*, and had the same kind of impact.

Dutourd called his book *Les Taxis de la Marne*. The title recalled what Dutourd, as addicted as Osborne to hyperbole, called 'the most glorious and least miraculous feat of the twentieth century'.[2] In 1914, with the victorious German armies only thirty miles from Paris, the commander of the city's garrison, General Galliéni, had bundled his troops into commandeered Paris taxis, five men to a taxi, and sent them trundling out of the city to join France's field army on the Marne. Together garrison troops and field army launched the counterattack which drove the Germans back from the gates of the capital. Paris was saved, the groundwork for eventual victory laid.

That, said Dutourd, was a supreme moment in France's history, but he found other twentieth-century moments to look back upon with nostalgia. For him, even so unfashionable a time as the 1930s had been glorious by contrast with the France of 1956. He recalled a prewar France 'with her institutions, her Cabinet ministers, her soldiers, her severe courts of justice, her sparkling navy, her strict prefects, her pacific empire, her cruel colons and her State patriotism'. Then had come the war and, after the shame of defeat in 1940, the gallantry of the Resistance. 'Here at last', wrote Dutourd, 'was the patriotism of the people, not the patriotism of the rich.'

France in 1956, by contrast, had lost all sense of patriotism. It was 'a weak and divided country ... bleeding from a thousand wounds', 'a dying carcass on which her maggot-ministers prosper'. So whereas John Osborne looked back in anger, Dutourd looked back with a strange nostalgia to times most of his contemporaries dismissed as bad ones, and turned his fire against the France in which he wrote. He railed against the political and social divisions which were tearing modern France apart. He attacked what he called a glorification of failure and condemned a pauper France which postured in the tattered fineries of the past. This pauper had lost all sense of France's innate greatness. It was being 'kicked out of Africa and Asia – spat on in the face by the guttersnipes of Cairo'. It dared to reject Dutourd's hero, de Gaulle, a man who 'wanted to lead his people on to new heights'. In short Dutourd damned the Fourth Republic as extravagantly as Osborne damned Britain's Establishment. He was as angry as Osborne, and as incoherent.

SMALL DELIGHTS

For all Jimmy Porter's dyspepsia and for all their leaders' anxiety about the economy and the Suez Canal, ordinary Englishmen and women found much to please them in the summer of 1956. Later, in the autumn and winter, things aroused their anger, first about Suez and then about Hungary. But it is worth pausing here to make a note of some of the things that made them happy that summer half a century ago.

The British, like most of the old world, had lived under the shadow of war long after it ended in 1945. But now it was receding into the past, and some of its austerities were vanishing. After a period of postwar restrictions even more intense than those of the war years themselves, food rationing had gradually been phased out. Clothes were cheap and attractive, cars available and increasingly affordable. To dashing young men and women the new coffee bars, an idea imported from Italy, seemed extraordinarily sophisticated. So did the new scooters, and some girls rode sidesaddle on the pillion, skirts billowing seductively, reminding the passer-by of the new wave of Italian films and hinting at the delights of a Mediterranean summer. Getting to France and Italy was again a possibility, precious to the middle classes, even if they had to smuggle out the odd five pound note to supplement their annual allowance of foreign currency (£50 a head some of the time and £75 at others, depending on the ups and downs of the national economy). For working men and women the pleasures of the new holiday camps were a real advance on the doubtful joys of the seaside bed and breakfast. So, in spades, were the new delights of the Costa Brava.

In those distant days the nation, and even the young, took pride in the monarchy. The Queen, crowned in 1953, had returned from a triumphant tour of the Commonwealth and still seemed to personify what phrase-makers had taken to calling the New Elizabethan Age. There was a lingering pride in Britain's wartime record, and in the empire. There was pride too in its technical achievements like radar, the jet engine and penicillin. People felt that things were getting better and, even if Suez had never happened, 1956 would probably have gone down in history as the year in which the country put the postwar period behind it for good. Looking back, the era seems remarkable for its naïveté – but perhaps the past always seem naïve to the present, that 'enormous condescension of posterity'.

There was something of a new feel about politics too. The postwar Labour government had laid the foundations of a new Britain, but by 1956 the Tories were securely back in the power they felt was rightfully theirs. In April 1955 Winston Churchill had resigned at last. All Britain felt for him when he finally surrendered No 10 Downing Street, standing gallantly on the pavement in full evening dress, knee breeches, silk stockings, Garter ribbon and Order of Merit, as the Queen left the last dinner party that he would ever give in the house that had been his home. But there was a general feeling that he had clung far too long to office and when Anthony Eden succeeded him he seemed to bring a younger touch, and even style and a certain sparkle, to the government and the Conservative Party. There was hope in the air that Eden and this younger team could perhaps work their way out of the corner in which circumstances, and Britain's economic straits above all, confined it.

So the summer season opened in its usual style. In June 1956 the Queen invested Eden and Clement Attlee, now removed to the Lords, with the Order of the Garter. All London flocked to the Royal Academy to admire Annigoni's portrait of her, depicted in all her girlish dignity. Nothing stopped the traditional events like Ascot and the Buckingham Palace garden parties, not even the weather. Yet the weather in 1956 was remarkably bad, the worst since the war: after a cold winter and spring, June was cool and unsettled, July cold, dull and wet, with one of the most violent summer storms the English Channel had ever seen, August the coldest the country had experienced since 1912. But even bad weather could be turned to advantage as an inexhaustible topic of conversation.

Innovation was in the air in this new Elizabethan age, and the new year of 1956 brought some splendidly dotty pronouncements about it. The idea of space travel was bilge, pronounced the Astronomer Royal. Comprehensive schools were a real threat to education, said the Head Master of Eton. Eleven years after the end of the war a Home Guard unit in Bath refused to disband, saying that they would soldier on in mufti. At the end of 1955 Macmillan moved from the Foreign Office to the Treasury, and in his first budget he introduced Premium Bonds, assuring the House of Commons that 'this is not a pool or a lottery'; but it was, said the opposition, 'a squalid raffle'. The first prototypes of Routemaster double-deckers appeared on the streets of London, the forerunners of a fleet of buses that became at first familiars, then old friends and eventually, when the Mayor of London and his acolytes removed them at last from service, objects of both fond nostalgia and no-holds-barred dispute. Self-service shops too made their first appearance in Britain and at once became matters of controversy, with their critics saying they would encourage pilfering, remove the personal touch, threaten the livelihood of small shopkeepers and lure women into overspending. And in August, as the British government geared itself up to deal with the existential challenge which Nasser of Egypt, the new Mussolini, had cast down before it, came plans for a new corps of traffic wardens to monitor parking meters and relieve the police of some of their traffic duties.

29 JUNE: THE GODDESS OF ENGLEFIELD GREEN

On 29 June Marilyn Monroe and Arthur Miller were married, he for the second time, she for the third. They settled down in England for an extraordinary kind of honeymoon. She was to join Laurence Olivier in filming *The Prince and the Showgirl*, while Miller watched over her and, while he was about it, saw Peter Brook's maiden London production of his play, *A View from the Bridge*. Shut away in the labyrinthine twists and turns of Miller's memoir, *Timebends*, is an account of their time in England. In it Miller, that most American of literary giants, provides a picture of an England that is long lost and in some part never existed outside his imagination, but glimpses too of an England that is with us still fifty years afterwards.[3]

Miller had grown accustomed in the United States to the impact on every man she met of Marilyn's confused and timid yet raw sexuality. He had seen her assailed by the demands of the Hollywood studios, watched heads turn and jaws drop on the streets of Manhattan as she passed. Miller was watching her at a press conference in New York where Olivier was dominating the proceedings. Suddenly one of Marilyn's exiguous shoulder straps slipped. Instantly, she had stolen the limelight from Olivier and turned it on herself. Miller felt it was her way of dealing with the barbarities of the press. He was the more sensitive to these things because he was himself still being pursued by the House Un-American Activities Committee. He saw his new wife as the victim of very different but equally menacing persecutors. Where he was confident that he could use his wits to defend himself, he recognised that Marilyn had only her sexuality.

Monroe and Miller brought with them to England an American team of minders, totally dedicated to guiding and guarding, some would say manipulating and bullying, their precious asset, the divine Marilyn. Meanwhile Olivier had assembled his production team, equally devoted to him as the reigning king of the English theatre. Thrown together, the two teams made an explosive mixture.

We have a second report of their encounter to put beside Miller's. At the bottom of Olivier's hierarchy of helpers was a young but well-connected Englishman whose parents were friends of his and of his wife Vivien Leigh. This was Colin Clark, son of a father whose skill at presenting art criticism to a television audience earned him the title Lord Clark of Civilisation, and younger brother of the ineffable Alan, whose snobbish, lecherous, self-pitying and brilliantly observant diaries won him posthumous fame as Bounder Clark. In the next few weeks, while Miller was discovering the English, Colin Clark was discovering Marilyn. Nearly half a century later he recorded the episode in a memoir which is as slight as *Timebends* is vast. He called it *My Week with Marilyn*.[4]

The first thing that Miller discovered about the English was their vulnerability to Marilyn's magic. Clark had used his family connections to find them a house to rent in Englefield Green, in a favoured corner of Surrey, twenty miles from London. The owner, a viscount no less, has come round to show it to them. He is coolly English, snobbish to the point of caricature, but he can't take his eyes off Marilyn. He was not the only one. Miller claims that on their first night under the viscount's rented roof they are awoken from their slumbers and find a choir of a hundred young men and boys gathered on the lawn to serenade her, their voices 'rising to a pitch of divine glorification' before they disperse in 'totally silent deference ... vanishing into the night'. Later the fan mail for Marilyn pours in by the mailbag. And Olivier himself, so different a theatrical deity, comes to call. Like all the others he is 'clearly enchanted with Marilyn'.

Miller prevails on a reluctant Olivier to take him to see *Look Back in Anger*. To Olivier it is 'just a travesty of England, a lot of bitter rattling on about conditions'. But like so many other people that summer, Miller falls under its spell. It 'gave me my first look at an England of outsiders like myself who ironed their own shirts and knew about the great only from newspapers.' In the interval they go to meet the author, John Osborne, and Miller witnesses the first edgy encounter between Olivier and Osborne. 'D'you suppose you could write something for me?' Olivier asks. The result, a year later, is *The Entertainer*.

Miller sees also a less attractive face of England. The British press has penetrated the carapace that is supposed to protect Marilyn from intrusive curiosity. The Hungarian couple who have been employed to run the viscount's house for her and Miller have clearly been taking Fleet Street's shilling. The retired Scotland Yard policeman who has been hired as Marilyn's bodyguard arrives to bully them. If there are any more leaks they will be on the next plane back to Budapest, he tells them. They wilt, subservient. The policeman turns politely to Miller: 'I don't think there will be any further trouble with these people.' Miller is appalled: 'The instantaneous transformation of the security man from such ferocity to the most sensitive British politeness stunned me.' Then the wisdom of bright-eyed American innocence intervenes: 'You need a long-lived empire to create such characters to police it' is Miller's conclusion.

Meanwhile, Colin Clark was getting drawn into the dramas which engulfed anyone who got close to Marilyn. She is unsure of herself, afraid, awed by Olivier and his godlike reputation, unhealthily dependent on her team of minders. Clark, still wet behind the ears, presents no threat and she draws him into the magic circle of her beauty. Miller goes away on business. Marilyn and Clark embark on a day of magical flirtation. He takes her to Windsor Park where they paddle in a stream. He takes her to Windsor Castle where his godfather just happens to be the librarian and a senior courtier. The old man and his books and pictures overwhelm the all-American girl from the wrong side of the tracks. On the way out she strikes a pose for tourists, all bosom and fanny: they applaud. He takes her to his old school, Eton, across the

river and they have lunch in the High Street. He takes her skinny-
dipping in the Thames. Their day of freedom is over and then – for
reasons too complicated to explain here: read Clark's book if you really
want to get to the bottom of the story – he spends the night with Marilyn. In the strictly literal meaning of the term he sleeps, all innocence,
with America's goddess of the silver screen.

Some of the details in *My Week with Marilyn*, like some aspects of
Timebends, leave me a shade doubtful of their absolute veracity. But
there can be no doubt that the collision of two worlds generated real
drama in Englefield Green in that summer of 1956.

HUNTLEYS & PALMERS

Throughout 1956 a committee laboured in Room 101 of the Home
Office. It had been set up in 1954 to consider the state of the law on
homosexuality and on prostitution. A number of high-profile trials on
charges of homosexuality had aroused public revulsion, some of it
against homosexuals and homosexual practices, some of it against the
harshness with which the law dealt with offenders. There was similar
concern about the extent to which prostitutes soliciting for business
seemed to have taken over the streets of the West End of London. Both
issues were held to have become a matter of public concern and perhaps
of public scandal.

The committee was chaired by John Wolfenden, a former public
school headmaster and now the Vice Chancellor of Reading University.
Fourteen men and women joined him: they included a consultant
psychiatrist, a High Court judge and a magistrate, a Presbyterian minister and a professor of moral theology, a Foreign Office minister and the
MP for Putney, and the Vice-President of the City of Glasgow Girl
Guides. Over the next three years they met on sixty-two days, more
than half of which were devoted to hearing evidence from witnesses.
The meetings were held under the auspices of the Home Office, whose
officials were so concerned about the impact of some of the material on
the sensitivities of gently-bred shorthand typists that they borrowed
from the biscuit business and dubbed homosexuals Huntleys and prostitutes Palmers.

The evidence put before the committee reflected the very different
attitude of society to the two categories of offence. The Churches
might take a different view, but most people saw female prostitution

as a fact of life that no amount of moral fervour or police activity could eliminate. Prostitutes were arrested, had up before the beak and relieved of some part of their immoral earnings. They then went straight back on the streets. This was the way it always had been and always would be, an aspect of informal private enterprise. Feminism in its modern form was as yet scarcely more than a gleam in the eye, and the very real problems of the street women themselves attracted little high-octane attention. The case for formalising this ancient business and making it safer for prostitute and client was little argued; it was enough to assert that Britain had nothing to learn from countries that legally acknowledged the seedy business of the brothel. If there was a problem about prostitution it was the public scandal caused by street soliciting (plus the problem of containing venereal disease), nothing more serious than that.

Homosexuality by contrast aroused real passions. In a way almost unimaginable today, many saw homosexuality as the unnatural vice that dared not speak its name. By the early 1950s the figures suggested that the police had embarked on a campaign against homosexual behaviour, with the number of cases brought before the courts eight times greater than in 1938. The steadily increasing numbers of arrests, prosecutions and sentences inevitably attracted attention. The press gave some of the cases, and particularly those that involved prominent defendants, massive publicity. Prurience drew the reader, and so did class resentment, for the cases the press chose to cover made it look as if homosexuality was the particular vice of bearers of well-known, double-barrelled names (and one glorious triple-barrelled name, the property of Edward John Barrington Douglas-Scott-Montagu) given to buggering merchant seamen and guardsmen, or interfering with boy scouts.

The other side of the argument got a hearing too. Some of the owners of double-barrelled names fought back and one of them, Rupert Croft-Cooke, wrote a book about his experiences in court and in prison.[5] They also took the opportunity to put their side of the matter to the Wolfenden Committee. One of them, Patrick Trevor-Roper, made a particular impact on its members. He was a Harley Street eye specialist, well-connected through his patients and through his brother Hugh, at the time a rising history star at Christ Church, Oxford. He put to the committee a story of a pattern of interest and behaviour that was exclusively homosexual and of a social life spent entirely in the company of men of a similar disposition. He succeeded in bringing out the sheer normality of a way of life that most of society at that time still considered an aberration.

The Wolfenden Committee pondered these issues throughout 1956 and they saw their efforts recognised when their chairman was honoured with a knighthood. But Wolfenden's own position was delicate. By the standards of the time his son was a somewhat flamboyant homosexual, and when in October he went up to Magdalen College, Oxford, his father suggested that he should go easy with the make-up and that for the time being it might be better if father and son kept out of each other's way.

A year later, in September 1957, Wolfenden's committee published their report.[6] The recommendations on the law and policing of prostitution became law, and dramatically reduced the extent of solicitation on street corners. Discreet labels on door bells, red lamp shades in windows and blizzards of postcards in telephone kiosks took its place.

Homosexual offences were a more controversial issue. On this the majority of Wolfenden's committee recommended that contact between consenting adults in private should cease to be a criminal offence, and that the age of consent should be 21. By December, the egregious Frank Pakenham, later Lord Longford (whom *Private Eye* later christened 'Lord Porn' when he took himself off to Copenhagen to study Danish pornography at first hand), had initiated a debate in the House of Lords and was arguing for legal changes. Opinion there remained sharply divided, however. Speaking for the government in the House of Commons the Home Secretary said he doubted whether the general population would support the changes that Wolfenden recommended. All the same, with the Wolfenden Committee the nation set out on the long march that would shift public opinion from mindless condemnation of 'queers' to an equally mindless celebration of the superior virtues of 'gays'.

THREE COOKS AND A HUSBAND TO DO THE WASHING-UP

In the 1950s the English were just beginning to discover the pleasures of foreign food and sophisticated cooking. Three women cooks marked the route and made themselves famous in the process.

Before the Second World War cooking was still something which the middle classes paid someone else to undertake. The war largely put an end to that, as cooks and kitchen maids vanished into the women's services or the arms factories. For the first time middle-class wives and mothers found themselves wrestling with problems more severe than how to time a four-and-a-half minute egg.

Margaret Patten stepped into the breach, setting herself to teach her readers and listeners about food and cooking. She had first to teach adaptability, as Britons grappled with the problem of stretching limited rations and bringing unfamiliar foods and above all unrationed food into the culinary equation. She taught simple cooking and practical common sense, and more than half a century later she is still with us, and still doing so.

Fanny Cradock was a far more flamboyant character. There was more showmanship than kitchen skills in her makeup, but she had the confidence to lay down the law to a television audience that was willing to be told what to do. By way of foil she had a much put-upon husband, an old buffer who did her washing up but who, some whispered, knew more about food than Fanny did. She had the inestimable skill of the populariser, and through her television broadcasts and as a popular lecturer she made cooking fashionable and she made it fun.

Elizabeth David was a more substantial person, whose views on food and cooking have never been allowed to go out of print. Above all, she introduced the British to other countries' ways of doing things, and showed them the delights of funny foreign food. Before her time, wrote Jane Grigson in a preface to a collection of her recipes, 'Basil was then no more than the name of bachelor uncles, courgette was printed in italics as an alien word, and few of us knew how to eat spaghetti or pick a globe artichoke to pieces.' In 1950 David published *Mediterranean Food*. A year later her *French Country Cooking* appeared. Her *Summer Cooking* came out in 1955 and then, in 1960, her best and best-loved book, *French Provincial Cooking*.

In her private life Elizabeth David had her quirks and quiddities, as who among us does not; but she convinced her readers that cooking was both a serious matter and a pleasure. 'Good food is always a trouble,' she wrote in *French Country Cooking*, 'and its preparation should be regarded as a labour of love.' Her book was intended, she went on, 'for those who actively and positively enjoy the labour involved in entertaining their friends and providing their families with first-class food'. The country had moved on from the long era of cook-generals and kitchen maids. Elizabeth David's work in broadening the British mind and stimulating the British palate built a reputation which, like her books, still endures.

23 OCTOBER : TOWARDS THE END OF THE ROPE

On a cold day in January 1956 Britain's most famous publican, Albert Pierrepoint, went to Strangeways Prison in pursuit of his occasional employment as the country's principal hangman. When he got there he found that the condemned man, one Thomas Bancroft, had been reprieved. The Under Sheriff of Lancashire offered Pierrepoint not his regular fee of £15 but a derisory £1 note for his out-of-pocket expenses. He appealed, and the Under Sheriff sent him £4 in full and final settlement of his claim.

Pierrepoint was incensed. To the man who had hanged William Joyce for treason and despatched thirteen Nazi war criminals in a day the offer was an insult to his self-esteem. He resigned his appointment, and some put it about that at long last his conscience was troubling him. The affair was nothing more than a nine-day-wonder, but it made a strange counterpoint to the persistent campaign for abolition of the death penalty which was waged throughout the postwar years and reached a denouement of a kind in October 1956.

Capital punishment had a long and disquieting history in Britain, and enjoyed – as it may just still enjoy – the support of a majority of the electorate. Labour's postwar victory brought a number of critics of the death penalty into Parliament and in 1948 the House of Commons caused general astonishment when it voted by 245 votes to 222 for an experimental suspension of capital punishment. The House of Lords soon reversed that decision, but the issue remained active. In 1953 there was disquiet over the execution of Derek Bentley, a petty burglar whose companion shot and killed a policeman. The companion was too young to hang but Bentley was not.

The hanging of Ruth Ellis for the murder of her lover aroused even more concern. Her youth and her sex attracted sympathy, and so did her behaviour at her trial, where she showed herself totally indifferent to what might become of her, quietly thanking the judge when he sentenced her to death. A campaign was mounted to save her, led by the Labour MP Sydney Silverman and the Left-wing publisher Victor Gollancz. The Home Secretary of the day, Gwilym Lloyd-George, was a conscientious and careful man and it was widely assumed that he would grant a reprieve, but for reasons that still remain a mystery he refused. She was hanged at Holloway in July 1955 while a crowd gathered to rage and pray at the prison gates.

The campaign for abolition continued through the winter of 1955–6 and it was a temporary suspension of executions which saved Thomas Bancroft's life. Then, in June 1956, the issue was put to a free vote of the House of Commons. They gave a bill bringing in abolition a third reading, but again the Lords blocked the measure. Now feelings generally ran high, angered as much at the role of the House of Lords as over the issue itself. On what was generally believed to be an issue of conscience opinions were dividing on party and even class lines.

The matter badly needed to be defused, and on Tuesday, 23 October, as the students in Budapest marched towards revolution and British ministers joined France in conspiracy with Israel to attack Egypt, Anthony Eden announced that a bill would be introduced to curtail, but not yet abolish, capital punishment. It was nursed through the House of Commons and the House of Lords as the political storm over Suez raged. It became eventually the Homicide Act of 1957, which greatly restricted the kinds of murder to which the death penalty would still apply. It was a major step towards outright abolition, but it was another eight years before that destination was reached at last.

4
The Middle East Cauldron

On New Year's Day of 1956, two flags were ceremonially lowered over Khartoum. The British and Egyptian flags came down and a blue, yellow and green flag went up. The Anglo-Egyptian Condominium of the Sudan was ended and the new Republic of the Sudan took its place. It was the largest country in Africa and the first, after Egypt, Ethiopia, Liberia and South Africa, to achieve its independence.

Britain and Egypt, the two countries in whose name the Sudan had been governed for over half a century, had been involved in its history for even longer. To Egypt, what mattered about it was not the desert stretching from the Red Sea to Central Africa; it was the Nile itself, Egypt's lifeblood. Whoever ruled Egypt had to dominate the upper Nile beyond the Second Cataract, and to impose his will on the peoples who lived along its banks. The British were similarly concerned with the Sudan in the main for its impact on their own interests in Egypt. Having been content to see the area governed haphazardly by whoever ruled Egypt, the British first focussed their attention seriously on the Sudan in 1884, with the despatch of General 'Chinese' Gordon to Khartoum. A new force had emerged out of the Sudanese deserts, the religiously inspired, half-crazed movement of the Mahdi. His men threatened to overwhelm and annihilate the little Egyptian garrison of the Sudan; Gordon's job was to secure its evacuation.

Gordon had spent a rackety lifetime about Britain's imperial business. He was as religiously inspired and some said almost as crazed as the Mahdi. To the new school of British imperialism he was also a national hero. Arrived in Khartoum, Gordon redefined for himself the mission he had been given and determined not to evacuate the Sudan but to stay on and rule it. But within months the Mahdi occupied the city and on 26 January 1885 his men killed Gordon. George William Joy painted a famous picture of the incident, showing Gordon facing his attackers, standing alone and unarmed on the steps of his house.

Between them the Mahdi, Gordon and Joy had brought the Sudan firmly into the forefront of British politics.

Gladstone was abused for having abandoned Gordon to his fate but he refused to avenge him. It was another thirteen years before a government of another colour despatched another colonial warrior, Kitchener, to dispose of the Mahdi for good. At the Battle of Omdurman in September 1898 a youthful Winston Churchill rode in a wild and rather impractical cavalry charge against the Dervish army, and British machine-guns did the more down-to-earth business of cutting the Dervishes to pieces. They lost 11,000 dead; the British 48.

The British still faced a threat to their interests on the upper Nile. The French, in empire-building mode, had despatched an impertinent expedition across Central Africa. Two months before Omdurman it reached the Nile at the little town of Fashoda. To the British, the expedition seemed to threaten their position in Egypt. Once they had disposed of the Dervishes they were quite clear that the French would have to go back where they came from. But Paris's emotions were as aroused as London's. For a time there was wild talk of cross-Channel war. In the end the French backed down. A few years later came the Entente Cordiale to turn the old enemies into uneasy and wary friends.

With the Mahdi gone and the French sent packing, the British saw their way clear to impose civilised rule in the Sudan. Egypt's historical claims to overlordship complicated the situation. It was decided that the Sudan would become not a British colony but an Anglo-Egyptian Condominium. In practice, the tone of the Condominium was set from first to last by British administrators, railway engineers, hydrologists and soldiers, and above all by the *corps d'élite* at the top of the administrative structure, the Sudan Political Service. The Service was minute, never more than 200 men to preside over the affairs of a country four times the size of France. Its officers were recruited through personal contacts at the best universities, who put a higher value on personal qualities and sportsmanship than on intellectual gifts: 'Blues ruling blacks and browns' was the catch phrase, in those days before the very idea of ethnic sensitivity was dreamed of. Even when I was at Oxford in the early 1950s there were still undergraduates who imagined that they might make a career of administering the Sudan – surely the most short-sighted career choice which the second half of the twentieth century had to offer.

The men of the Political Service came to the job with a strange mixture of arrogance and devotion. They were expected to work hard, in the harshest of environments, but they enjoyed godlike status and authority. Many of them brought to the work a simple but profound religious faith, inspired at first by the memory of Gordon's messianic enthusiasm and nurtured by the remains of Victorian Anglicanism. Circumstances in Sudan seemed to conspire to keep them simpler and more straightforward than the men who ruled India. Those who joined the Sudan Political Service after serving in the First World War came in a rather more worldly and disillusioned spirit, but selfless well-doing remained the characteristic among their colleagues that they most admired.

The British in the Sudan, like their equivalents elsewhere in the Middle East, had an admiration for the harsh simplicity of Arab life, and tended to look to the leaders of Sudanese society as gentlemen like themselves. One of the few of them who made a public name for himself was Wilfrid Thesiger, that lover of hard living in wild places, who administered the wilds of Darfur in western Sudan. They were expected to get on good terms with key Sudanese personalities, and a good command of Arabic was a prerequisite for promotion. Most of them took a different, more patronising view of the naked tribesmen of the south. They too had British administrators who would give their lives to their service, but these men were not thought of as quite the same class as the officers of the Political Service in the north: 'bog barons' they were called, with kindly condescension. To the administration both of north and south the British brought exalted ideas of service to the benighted natives. Such ideas were in some part self-serving and self-deceiving; but they were also real. They helped build real links between the British and the Sudanese.

In the early years of the Condominium, Egyptian officials played some role in running the Sudan, if always a relatively minor one. With the spread in the 1920s of Egyptian nationalism, relationships between individual Britons and Egyptians deteriorated, in the Sudan as much as in Egypt. In 1924 the British governor-general of the Sudan was assassinated while on a visit to Cairo. In the crisis which followed, Britain ordered all Egyptian troops out of the Sudan. From then on, Egyptian influence was more or less excluded from the country. But Egypt still had an existential interest in the Upper Nile which could not be gainsaid. Frictions over the future of the Sudan fed into steadily increasing friction over the British presence in Egypt itself and, above all, over the Suez Canal.

Between the wars British officials in the Sudan slowly began to recognise that the status quo there could not continue indefinitely, and after 1945 the new Labour government pressed forward measures to prepare the country for eventual self-government. In 1946 agreement was reached on a gradual build-up in the number of senior administrative posts in the Political Service to be held by Sudanese, with a twenty per cent target by 1952 and over fifty per cent ten years later.

In Britain, however, plans to withdraw from the Sudan, over however protracted a timescale, aroused tribal emotions. Churchill, out of office after 1945, led the opposition to the abandonment of imperial responsibilities. But when he scraped back into power in 1951 even he was brought up against the postwar economic and overseas realities that any British administration had to face. In 1953 he accepted the signature of an agreement with Egypt which heralded the end of the Condominium and the grant of self-government to the Sudan. The agreement left open the question whether the Sudan would eventually go its own way or be linked politically and constitutionally to Egypt.

Churchill's instinctive reluctance to see imperial possessions surrendered lingered among many members of the Conservative party. In the House of Commons they rallied around a notorious Captain Charles Waterhouse, the darling of the Tory irreconcilables, and Julian Amery. In the words of Anthony Nutting, a junior Foreign Office minister of the day, they were 'a hotch-potch collection of embittered ex-Ministers and young newly elected back-benchers anxious to cut a figure in Parliament by attacking the Government for selling out British imperial responsibilities'.[1] Talking darkly of 'scuttle', they opposed independence for the Sudan as vociferously as withdrawal from the Suez Canal bases. They were to exercise a malign influence from beginning to end of the Suez crisis.

By now the Egyptian monarchy was dying, with the forced abdication of King Farouk in July 1952 and the deposition of his infant son a year later. The army officers who came to power were more purposeful in their opposition to British rule than the monarchy had been, and in the Sudan they pressed for a quicker end to British administration. In November 1953 a first general election in Sudan gave a majority to a pro-Egyptian party, the National Unionists. In January 1954 a first

Prime Minister was elected, while the Sudan still remained under ulti-mate British and Egyptian authority. A year later, Britain and Egypt signed an agreement granting Sudanese independence, and that inde-pendence became a reality on New Year's Day, 1956.

Independence meant an end to British authority in the Sudan, an authority which had been gradually run down as Sudanese politicians and administrators took the administrative reins. Some British officers remained to help a sovereign independent Sudan settle down; others moved to British colonies, to the Colonial Office, to ICI, to Chel-tenham, to retirement. In 1956 the Sudanese started to rule themselves.

The euphoria which followed did not last long. 'Independence today, trouble tomorrow, civil war the day after,' one sceptic observed; and the Sudan almost at once began a descent into political conflict that before long became disorder. Regional clashes between Moslem north and Christian south had been a fact of life even before independence; now they proliferated. In 1958 a military coup overthrew the civil adminis-tration in Khartoum. In 1964 civil government was restored but again overthrown five years later. Political parties were abolished, a 'Revolu-tionary Command Council' led by colonels established. The country was renamed the Democratic Republic of the Sudan. There was talk of federal union with Egypt, which proved as elusive as any other political goal in a troubled Middle East. Within Sudan the ethnic and religious divide between north and south proved unbridgeable. Gradually the country lost itself in ethnic conflict, campaigns against provincial rebels and ever-present dangers of fragmentation. Today's troubles in Sudan can be traced back pretty well without a break to independence in 1956. It has turned out to be too big, too disparate a country to have been prepared for self-government by even the most enlightened and athletically distinguished administrators from Oxbridge and the British public schools.

1 FEBRUARY: EDEN VISITS EISENHOWER

In the 1950s the British Government, and most Britons who thought about these things, believed that the Middle East was vital to their country's well-being. Its oil came from the Gulf, its imperial communi-cations – which then seemed more vital than they do in retrospect – went through the Suez Canal. They felt that their interests there were threatened by the assertive rise of Arab nationalism, by the feud between Israel and its neighbours, and by the trouble the Soviet Union was intent on making in the area. The British saw themselves as the leading outside power in the region, but they knew how fragile was their economic position. In the Middle East as elsewhere they needed to lock the United States into full-hearted cooperation. Yet in their eyes the Americans were skittish, non-committal, preoccupied with commercial advantage, standing self-righteously aloof from anything they perceived as colonialism.

As Prime Minister from 1951 to April 1955, Winston Churchill had clung to his wartime faith in the special relationship with the United States as the guarantor of Britain's safety and its pretensions as a world power. Eden's confidence in the American cousins was less unalloyed, but like Churchill he recognised how little Britain, economically crippled as it was in those postwar years, could do without American support. These considerations came together in his determination to pay a visit to Dwight Eisenhower early in 1956.

He and his Foreign Secretary, Selwyn Lloyd, sailed to the United States in the *Queen Elizabeth*, accompanied by a strong team of advisers. The agenda for the talks was wide-ranging, but for the British the Middle East came first. They wanted American support for the Baghdad Pact, of which Britain was a member and for which the Americans were expressing tepid, strictly arm's length support. They wanted to agree a joint approach to the problems presented by Arab nationalism in general and by Nasser in particular. The Soviet Union seemed intent on exploiting these problems by selling weapons to Egypt and Syria, and could be deterred, if at all, only by a coordinated Western response. These arms sales heightened Israel's fears of its Arab neighbours, and the anxieties of both sides constantly threatened to explode into violence. The British wanted to settle a running quarrel with the Americans over Saudi and Gulf State claims to the Buraimi oasis, one side backed by Britain, the other by the United States. And they saw that central to all of this was agreement with the Americans on the right approach to Nasser.

Eden had had long experience as Foreign Secretary and had been seen for more than a decade as Churchill's natural heir. When he became Prime Minister the nation saw him as a brave defender of security and democracy, who would bring new vigour and youthfulness to Downing Street. It knew nothing of something rather different that lay behind Eden's glamorous persona. There was about him an anxious personal fragility, a nervousness and irritability that had only been increased by Churchill's wilful procrastination in handing him the keys to No.10. This fragility was to help shape the Suez crisis. It was already manifest to those around him. Rab Butler was the most waspish: 'Anthony's father was a mad baronet and his mother a very beautiful woman. That's Anthony – half mad baronet, half beautiful woman.'[2] Clement Attlee, laconic as ever, best anatomised Eden's inheritance: 'Yep, it's the heavy roller, you know. Doesn't let the grass grow under it.'[3] As for Winston Churchill, he confided as he left office for the last time, 'I'm not sure Anthony can do it.'[4]

Now, closeted with him in the *Queen Elizabeth*, Eden's staff saw him at his worst: nervous, histrionic, with an unattractive but at times almost touching self-regard. Selwyn Lloyd complained to Evelyn Shuckburgh, the Middle East expert on the British team, that Eden suspected him of disloyalty. The suspicion was absurd: 'I am a contented animal; I know I have been over-promoted; there can be no question of my disloyalty.'[5] Shuckburgh, who had served as his private secretary when Eden was at the Foreign Office, recorded a tantrum about the programme for the visit. He thought that Eden seemed 'thin, nervy and in a curious way frivolous. I don't think he is at all well or at all happy.'[6] The omens for personal rapport with the Americans seemed unpromising.

In the event, at the personal level things went relatively well, above all because Eisenhower and Dulles were manifestly more at ease with themselves than either Eden or Lloyd. To the surprise of the British, who in the 1950s still had a high idea of themselves as statesmen and diplomats, both performed well. In private the men around Eden were instinctively inclined to patronise the President as a simple soldier. In the war they had seen him presiding over, not leading the war in Europe: a 'château general' more than a fighting soldier. Now he had become, in Alex Danchev's words, 'lo and behold, the château President'.[7] As for Dulles, Eden and his advisers thought him simultaneously pietistic and devious, the soul of unreliability.

In Washington, however, the visitors liked what they saw of both men. Eisenhower was still recovering from the heart attack of the previous year, but to Shuckburgh he seemed 'in extraordinarily good form and health. He had an obvious grasp of the subjects – better than our man.'[8] By now Shuckburgh was well and truly disillusioned with his old master and he found the contrast between Eden and the Americans dispiriting: 'I think he is greatly deteriorated: seems to be thinking only of himself. I envy the Americans having Ike and Dulles to deal with over their foreign affairs. It seems to me that these two have continuity of policy, serious ideas and courage, and that our team by comparison is frivolous.'[9] Yet the President himself said afterwards that he had never known so harmonious a meeting of this kind.

In the retrospect of what happened to British-American relations later in that most traumatic of years, however, the Washington meeting is noteworthy not for positive vibes and mutual esteem but for what it failed to achieve. There was no clear-cut agreement on any of the main issues. The Americans still hung back from committing themselves to membership of the Baghdad Pact. Neither side could see a way to reconcile the tangle of issues which bedevilled Arab-Israeli relations. They were agreed that the Russians must be stopped, but had few instruments for doing so. They blew hot and cold over the key question of how to handle Nasser. Should they confront him, smother him with gifts and Western affection, seek clandestinely to overthrow him? The proposed Nile dam at Aswan, which the enthusiasts believed might lift the Egyptian poor out of their poverty and simultaneously bind Nasser to the West, had long been on the table, but the Americans, who would have had to foot most of the bill, remained hesitant, never more so than when Nasser seemed to flirt with the Russians, or, even worse, with the Red Chinese: why reward a nationalist who seemed prepared to invite America's enemies into the Middle East?

And for all their bonhomie the Americans still entertained dark suspicions that Britain had not put her imperial past behind her. When the British pressed for cooperation in defending joint Western interests in the Middle East some Americans saw a trap, a British plan to make the United States pay for the protection of their empire. Some of them entertained naïve hopes of getting alongside the leaders of the emerging countries, arguing that as an ex-colony America shared their suspicions of imperialism. Why risk Arab understanding to prop up allies who could no longer sustain their imperial positions for themselves? For their part, the British still feared that the Americans wanted to leave the heavy lifting in the Middle East to them, reluctant to recognise just how close to collapse the burdens of the Second World War had brought the British economy.

So in Washington in early February 1956 Eisenhower and Eden

missed perhaps a last opportunity to head off the disaster which threatened them, which in October and November would set them at bitter
odds, and which in one form or another has been a spectre at Anglo-
American love feasts ever since.

Eisenhower's calm confidence and Eden's nervousness personified in a
way the societies they represented. When Eden and Selwyn Lloyd
visited Washington it was clear that they were in a country far less troubled than their own. The British economy, near to bankruptcy ever
since the war, teetered on the edge of catastrophe, and Harold Macmillan, the Chancellor since the end of 1955, was fighting a private battle
to convince Prime Minister and Cabinet how small was the margin of
error within which he operated. The country still took a rather anxious
pride in its empire and world position, but its determination to stand
in the breach beside the United States, while hanging on to imperial
possessions until the day they were ready for independence, was eating
away the nation's political, moral and financial capital. In their bones
ministers knew that they could not sustain the country's world position
indefinitely, but the nation still demanded grandeur of its leaders, and
few were prepared to countenance a more modest world role. Hence
the policy tangles in which ministers embroiled themselves. Hence too
the influence of the Right in the Conservative party, men who, without
responsibility themselves, refused to respect the constraints within
which ministers were operating
    The scene in Washington was very different. Eisenhower had won
election in 1952 easily. Among his assets was that life-enhancing grin. It
told ordinary Americans that he was as happy as most of his fellow citizens, basking in peace, prosperity and a superpower's unparalleled
security. This sense of happiness infiltrated even the dustier corners of
policy-making, and sustained the imperturbability in White House and
State Department which so struck the British visitors. If America's leaders decided that a policy was necessary and right they had the resources
to carry it through to success. Of course they might face stiff battles in
Congress, with special interest groups, with businessmen who found
taxes morally repugnant and who had a big influence over this Republican administration. In 1954 America had seen off a particularly
malign threat to its sense of well-being, with the Senate's condemnation
of Senator Joe McCarthy and his vicious campaign to destroy others'
reputations for his own political advantage. With half the world's gross

national product at its disposal the United States had the material underpinnings for happiness. It could afford to be generous, to its people and to its friends.

Several things challenged this contentment. One of them was race. Since the United States' foundation, the political and social condition of America's blacks had been a silent witness to the injustice at the heart of the American dream. Now the blacks were beginning to find their voice. So in Alabama they demanded access to public colleges and in the end, in March 1956, the Supreme Court upheld a ban, grudgingly imposed by the state's courts, on segregation. The transport company in Montgomery, Alabama, consigned blacks to the back of the buses. In 1955 Rosa Parks refused to give up her seat to a white man. She was arrested. An unknown young clergyman, Martin Luther King, organised a boycott of the company. He too was arraigned and convicted for so disturbing Montgomery's deep southern peace. He told the press that he would use passive resistance and 'the weapon of love' to end segregation, and a month later saw blacks riding proudly in the front seats. Yet in April white extremists dragged Nat King Cole, the black singer, off the stage in Birmingham, Alabama, as he presumed to entertain a white audience, and the Klu Klux Klan still ruled the back roads of Mississippi.

In the spring of 1956 the campaign to end segregation still had far to go. A strong southern bloc in Congress challenged Supreme Court rulings. The Federal Government said it wanted to see justice done to the blacks, but even a man as benevolent as the President instinctively felt that they should be patient in their desire for change, and when crises came positioned himself midway between the leaders of the black movement and the white rabble-rousers in the southern states. Things were changing, but with a dangerous slowness.

Another concern was the United States' security. From Pearl Harbor to the Twin Towers, Americans have found any threat to their domestic invulnerability an offence against nature. It was the same in the 1950s. In the summer of 1955 the Administration held a major exercise to test the nation's readiness to face catastrophe. 'Operation Alert' envisaged that in a nuclear attack on the United States' fifty-three major cities had been destroyed or badly damaged, that their populations were fleeing and that order was threatened. The nation was shocked by these hypotheses, and Eisenhower took the exercise with deadly seriousness. He assumed emergency powers and did what he had to do to master the situation, but the emotions the exercise released showed how intense were the nation's fears of sudden attack by the Soviet Union. They tied Eisenhower's hands. In 1955 he had gone to the Geneva summit hoping to find agreement with the Soviet Union's new leaders, Bulganin and Khrushchev. But he had reached no meeting of minds; and his service advisers and the right wing of his own party were suspicious of his search for agreement with the Russians.

The nation's third concern was the President's health. In September 1955, while on holiday in Colorado, Eisenhower suffered a major heart attack. He recovered well and after six weeks in hospital he flew back to Washington and to work. Never a man for the small print of government, he was careful now to undertake only the duties that seemed to him essential. The key question was whether he would be fit to stand for the Presidency in November. Eventually, in February, he announced that he would stand again, but he was determined to hold aloof from the punishment of the campaign trail. Then, in June, he was struck down again, this time by a serious intestinal inflammation. There were those who muttered 'cancer'. He needed surgery, and underwent a serious, two-hour operation.

Again Eisenhower emerged safely from hospital. Now his mind was focused even more sharply on his own mortality, writing in a note about his own future: 'As I embark on the last of life's adventures'. He wanted to use his energies to tackle long-term threats to the United States' wellbeing, not immerse himself in day-to-day business. Aged sixty-five, always a delegator, now more than ever he was a President who wanted to be chairman of the board rather than chief executive.

So there were worms in America's apple, but the general mood was one of contentment and good times. The spread of American suburbia continued, and with it the advance of ordinary Americans' living standards. *My Fair Lady* opened on Broadway and a successful test of the hydrogen bomb, far away on Bikini Atoll in the Pacific, reassured Americans once again that they really were the most powerful people on earth. Meanwhile, the political expression of American contentment was getting into gear. The presidential election was due in the first week of November. The campaign would start in the late summer, and the jockeying for position was beginning. So in April Richard Nixon announced that he would again seek the vice-presidential nomination. Adlai Stevenson and John Kennedy would be the Democratic candidates, but as the nation embarked on its summer holidays, Eisenhower's personal position seemed unchallengeable. His smile signalled that all was well with him, and in the summer of 1956 everything, or almost everything, seemed well with America.

On 1 January 1956, as Sudan celebrated its independence, the Third Republic held France's umpteenth postwar election. It was called to resolve fundamental differences about the future of Algeria. By 5 February, after complex manoeuvring between the parties, the French had a new government, which claimed it could resolve this most intractable of colonial problems. On the following day the new Prime Minister flew to Algiers.

The man who had surprisingly emerged to lead the new government was Guy Mollet. He was a teacher of English from Arras, a strict disciplinarian who had turned himself into a formidable party functionary. He had a good wartime record in the resistance and had been close to the Communists after it. Now he was a figure of democratic socialist orthodoxy, with something of the down-to-earth aura of Clement Attlee, Britain's postwar Labour leader. He lacked the glamour of one rival, Mendès-France, the ruthless drive of another, Maurice Bourgès Maunoury, and the human warmth of the man who had brought him into the Socialist party, Léon Blum. But in 1956 he had a vital qualification for office. He claimed to have the solution to the problem of Algeria.

In 1956 the story of French politics since the Second World War seemed an inglorious one to most Frenchmen and women, and to almost all Anglo-Saxon observers. At the election the picture seemed as muddled and obscure as it had been ever since the war. The Communists came first among seven main political groups, with a quarter of the votes. Their polar opposites, the men around the Le Pen of the day, Pierre Poujade, spokesman of the small shopkeeper and the politically malcontent, won eleven per cent. The Gaullists, who within two years would destroy the Fourth Republic, attracted less than a million votes. In their different ways, these three groups placed themselves outside the pale of conventional politics. That left four centre-Left and centre-Right groups, and within the limits imposed by electoral arithmetic Mollet somehow conjured up a majority. His government was to rule France for fourteen months, longer than any government since the war, and to ride out all the storms of 1956.

If one gave France closer attention than the average Englishman then lavished upon it, one could discern signs that things were looking up. By 1956 France seemed to be putting some of its postwar troubles behind it. Society and economy had recovered some semblance of equilibrium. Agreement to German rearmament had somehow been wrung out of France's politicians. Disengagement from Indo-China was complete, and future tragedies there would consume the youth not of France but of Vietnam, Laos, Cambodia and the United States. The problem of Algeria continued to divide France, however. A bitter Moslem insurgency was stretching the French garrison to the limit and enraging the settlers. Mollet owed his office to his promise to resolve the problem. Impetuously, he flew to Algiers the day after his new government was complete.

The excursion was a disaster. The Prime Minister was protected by lines of troops and by Republican Guards flown in from France for the purpose. He travelled safely into the city from the airport, through silently hostile Arab crowds. In the centre things were different. Mollet found himself confronted by an angry European mob. As he went to lay a wreath at the war memorial the security forces lost control. He was pelted with tomatoes, rotten eggs, and abuse. 'To the gallows, Mollet,' the demonstrators shouted.

'Yesterday's events', reported the Paris correspondent of *The Times*, magisterially even-handed as ever, were 'disgraceful outrages or understandable demonstrations of patriotism, according to the standpoint of the commentator', but there could be no disputing their violence.[10] There was a real danger to Mollet's life. He was badly shaken, above all by the fact that the people baying for his blood were working-class French men and women, the sort of people whom, back in France, he would have wanted to make his own. The poor whites, the 'pieds noirs', were determined to hold on to their modestly privileged position against the unenfranchised Arab majority. Jean-Marie Le Pen, still rabble-rousing with us today but described by the *Times* correspondent in 1956 as 'M. Le Pen, the youthful Poujadist,' mounted an hours-long filibuster in the National Assembly. And a Poujadist newspaper twisted the knife between Mollet's ribs with its answer to its own rhetorical question, were the soldiers who had guarded him there to protect him against Arab attack? 'No; merely against the booing of honest Frenchmen who were unwilling to see the destiny of Algeria handed over to a professional liquidator.'[11]

Mollet had hoped to win over the Algerians by political and social concessions and so get their backing for a settlement that would keep Algeria within the French Union. Now he abandoned the man who he had hoped could deliver that miracle, the septuagenarian General Georges Catroux. In his place as Governor General he put Robert Lacoste, a no-nonsense political pro. Faced with the settlers' anger, Mollet and Lacoste abandoned the policy on which they had come to power. They turned to crushing the Arab insurgents and appeasing the settlers. 'We can have our differences about the solutions ...,' Lacoste told the National Assembly, 'but there is not a French person who would accept the spectacle of France driven from a land which she settled by the indisputable power of armed force but which she conquered by the indisputable right of a civilising mission marked with generosity.'[12] France could not abandon the colonists, Mollet said, 'she will never abandon Algeria, she cannot abandon Algeria'.[13] France's Socialist government was showing itself far more intransigent in its defence of empire that the Conservative government in Britain.

Mollet could argue, however, that Algeria was a special case. The hand had been played differently in the other countries that had for a century made up French North Africa. Morocco and Tunisia also had their French settlers and administrators, but they packed less political punch than the French business interests and settlers in Algeria. Negotiations with the Sultan of Morocco and with Tunisian national-ist leaders had been handled with finesse and were well advanced. Now, under Mollet, they were clinched. The Sultan was brought home from exile in Madagascar, and in March 1956 France recognised Moroccan independence. Three months later Tunisia got a similar settlement. Actual independence, if still 'l'indépendance dans l'inter-dépendance', as the French glossed it, came to both countries within a year.

The Algerian cancer remained, and gradually it was to consume not just Algeria but most of the energy of the French state, and eventually the Fourth Republic itself. Mollet enormously reinforced the troops in Algeria, and by the summer of 1956 400,000 soldiers were patrolling the streets of Algiers, guarding outposts and outlying settlements, and trying to hunt down the Algerian freedom fighters. The elite parachute regiments were particularly ruthless, and soon turned to torture. Arab casualties mounted at a rate ten times those of the soldiers and settlers. It was the archetypal 'dirty war', fought viciously by both sides.

Inevitably, the Arab world was loud in support of the fight for independence, with Cairo Radio in the lead. Wider opinion came to the nationalists' support too. In July three totemic figures of that new international entity, the Third World, met in a Yugoslav hideaway on an Adriatic island. There, in Brioni, Nehru and Nasser were happy to join Tito in condemning France. The French detected a Communist conspiracy against them, but much of the world found itself agreeing with Tito and his guests. Algeria was placed on the agenda of the General Assembly that would meet in November in New York. And Washington convinced itself that if it was seen supporting French colonial policy in Algeria it would lose its race against its Soviet rivals for the prize of Third World sympathy. Bitterly criticised, France was bitter in return, talking of the rights of the settlers, of the crimes of the rebels, of the dangers of Arab nationalism, and of France's civilising mission in North Africa.

When, in July, Nasser nationalised the Suez Canal, it was the Algerian tragedy more than any other single factor which shaped French reaction. Nasser had shown himself France's enemy over Algeria. Now he was seizing an asset which French enterprise had created. In doing so he was giving France an opportunity to strike back. 'One French division in Egypt', said Lacoste laconically, 'is worth four French divisions in Algeria.'[14] French people of every political persuasion knew what he meant, and most of them applauded.

I MARCH: THE KING SACKS THE GENERAL

Less than a month after Mollet fled for his life from enraged French settlers in Algeria, a more personal conflict was taking shape in the desert kingdom of Jordan. In late February, its young King Hussein made up his mind to get rid of Sir John Glubb, the British officer who commanded the Arab Legion, Jordan's army. He kept his own counsel, and on 29 February received Glubb for what the general described as 'a particularly pleasant and congenial interview'. On the following day, however, he ordered his Prime Minister, Samir Rifai, to inform Glubb of his dismissal.

Samir Rifai summoned his colleagues to discuss the King's order. He called in the British ambassador, who urged him to persuade the King to change his mind. But the Prime Minister could see no escape from his instructions. He invited Glubb to his office and told him of the

King's decision. He tried to temper the blow: 'Perhaps in a few days we'll all be welcoming you back. I've been Prime Minister several times, then I have been dismissed, and now I'm back again.' 'That may apply to politicians', was the reply, 'but I don't think it can apply to me.'[15] Early next morning, the Glubbs left for the airport with their adopted Jordanian children. Only the Defence Minister, the head of the royal divan and the ambassador saw them off. They flew away, he forlornly clutching a signed photograph of the King handed to him at the airport. Glubb Pasha never returned to Jordan.

His departure marked a signal victory for the forces of Arab nationalism in the Middle East. It marked also the end of an era in which British advisers, soldiers, academics and travellers had explored, organised, loved, governed and exploited the Arab world. Glubb was the last of a series of remarkable men and women such as T. E. Lawrence, Gertrude Bell, St John Philby and Freya Stark, who like the administrators of the Sudan had immersed themselves in things Arab, and particularly things Bedouin. They felt an affection for desert Arabs, soldierly Arabs, if not for the Arabs of the towns. As James Morris put it: 'With his patrician style and his picturesque appearance, his great flocks of goats and camels, his taste for coffee and beautiful boys, his blend of arrogance and hospitality, his love of pedigree, his fighting ability and what would later be called *machismo*, the Bedouin was every Englishman's idea of nature's gentleman.'[16]

Glubb and his like served British interests in the Middle East while convincing themselves that they were simultaneously serving its peoples. Glubb himself had spent thirty-five years in the Arab world. He had gone to Mesopotamia at the end of the First World War, where he travelled among the tribes, telling their leaders with astonishing honesty that he was drawing maps for the use of Royal Air Force aircraft that would be sent to bomb them if they rebelled. He went out into the desert to organise Iraq's defences against tribal raiders, so that a local paper wrote of him that he 'lives on dry barley bread and the water of the rain pools and rests neither day nor night'.[17]

In the 1930s he did the same for Transjordan, threatened first by raiders from Saudi Arabia and later by the effects of the Arab revolt in Palestine. In the Second World War he led Jordanian troops beside the British in attacks on the pro-German authorities in Iraq and on the Vichy French in Syria. The war won, he built up Jordan's capacity to defend itself, against Saudi raiders and against the Israeli army. In the only Arab victory of the Arab-Israeli war of 1948 he led the Arab Legion to the capture of Jerusalem. The Arab Legion grew into a division-sized army, remarkable in the region for its efficiency. Over the years Glubb built an almost mystical rapport with the Bedouin of the desert, to the point where he felt more at home in their black tents than in the palaces and embassies of Amman. He was a little man, but his presence and reputation loomed over everything in Jordan. 'For the peasant and the tribesman in Jordan', a British visitor recorded, 'Glubb Pasha is still more than the government.'[18]

King Hussein, the man who dismissed him, was less than half Glubb's age, short like Glubb, a wisp of a man in his twenties. Like Glubb, Hussein was a man of two worlds. As a child he had been at his grandfather's side when the old man was assassinated in Jerusalem. He was a schoolboy at Harrow when he succeeded his father. He went from Harrow to Sandhurst, and from Sandhurst made the usual privileged young man's forays into the fleshpots of London and Paris. He knew that his little kingdom depended on British subsidy and in the last analysis on British protection. But he remained a Hashemite king of a Hashemite kingdom, a prince of the Arab aristocracy. In the Arab Legion, these worlds met: 'Arab princelings in the desert used to send their sons to serve in Glubb's Bedouin desert patrol of the Arab Legion, as potentates might have sent their sons in the European Middle Ages to do a stint as a page to the neighbouring potentate because it would be part of their education'.[19] In this feudal world Hussein was clear that the Legion was his, not Glubb's.

Several things came together in Hussein's decision to get rid of Glubb. Many who knew him, British as well as Jordanian, had begun to feel that Glubb was living in the past and losing touch with a changing Arab world. He might know the Bedouin, but not other Arabs: one of his British colleagues remarked that 'he remained absolutely ignorant and indeed careless of the mood, humour and indeed character of the cultivated Arab.'[20] There were many Jordanians who resented this foreigner's influence over their country. His Arab officers bridled when he asserted that it was too soon to promote them to senior commands. Some Jordanians perceived that his loyalties were divided and believed that, despite his victory in Jerusalem in 1948, he would be unwilling to lead the Legion against the Israelis again. So when he deployed Jordan's limited military strength well back from the Israeli border to avoid defeat in detail, some suspected treachery. When Glubb explained his caution, the young King denounced it: 'I will never surrender one hand's breadth of my country. The army will defend the demarcation line. Then we shall attack. I will sanction no withdrawal.'[21]

The Egyptian propaganda machine worked hard to feed suspicions of Glubb's disloyalty: Cairo Radio inveighed against him, and so did the Egyptian military attaché in Amman. Over the years Glubb's position had grown anachronistic, suspect not just to Arabs but to American critics of British colonialism, and to the British Left. A British journalist wrote of him: 'General John Bagot Glubb is in fact the most unpopular man in Jordan. . . the fault is not his own. The fault is with the policy which London now orders him to carry out. This policy comes dangerously near to one of outright military dictatorship.'[22]

Right or wrong, this was how many now saw British policy towards Jordan. And London stretched tensions still tighter when it urged Hussein and his government to join Iraq, Turkey and Pakistan in the British-backed Baghdad Pact. To its advocates, the pact's purpose was to protect Arabs from Soviet influence. To its critics it was an assault on Arab nationalism, neo-colonialist, anti-Egyptian, covertly pro-Israeli. The British insisted on pressing the merits of membership on the Jordanians, and in November 1955 the Chief of the Imperial General Staff himself, Field Marshal Sir Gerald Templer, descended on Amman to clinch the argument. It was a disastrous visit. Templer was a peppery soldier, 'a bundle of nerves', according to Harold Macmillan;[23] 'shouting and punching the table', said a Jordanian participant in the talks, 'making the tea cups and the coffee cups on it dance', he urged the Jordanians to commit themselves to the pact.[24]

At first King Hussein seemed willing, but the Prime Minister prevaricated. He feared public opinion, played on by Egyptian propaganda. Templer went on his way disgruntled, leaving rioting in Amman behind him. When the Legion put it down with a heavy hand, Glubb's critics found further ammunition. After that it was only a matter of time before the King would decide that Glubb, long Jordan's protector, had become an insupportable liability instead.

For the British government, pure coincidence made the shock of Hussein's decision worse. In late February the Foreign Secretary had embarked on a tour of the Middle East. On the evening of Glubb's fall Lloyd was dining in Cairo with Nasser himself. News of Hussein's action reached Nasser before the dinner, Lloyd only after it. The talk over the dining table had seemed to go well but when Lloyd heard the news on the way back to the embassy he was consumed by angry embarrassment. He spent the night telephoning Eden, and there was talk, fortunately not pursued, of his flying to Amman to confront the young King in person. After a very short night Lloyd went back next morning for a farewell meeting with Nasser. Nasser proceeded to rub salt into his wounds. He 'congratulated me on having arranged for Glubb's dismissal in order to improve relations between Egypt and Britain... This pretence seemed to me to be outrageous and I showed and said what I thought of it.'[25] From Cairo, Lloyd flew on to Bahrain, where stone-throwing demonstrators added to his chagrin.

When he got back to London Lloyd found the Prime Minister incandescent. Eden took Hussein's action as a personal insult, and as a deliberate attack on Britain's strategic position in the Middle East. Yet for months the Foreign Office had been persuaded that Glubb was overplaying his hand, his days in Jordan numbered. When he returned to London Glubb himself urged Eden to make allowances for King Hussein's youth. But Eden's mind was made up. For him, this was Egypt's doing; and he was convinced (wrongly, as it turned out) that Hussein had told Nasser in advance what he was about. From Glubb's expulsion dates Eden's obsessive distrust of Nasser: 'I want him destroyed,' he said to Anthony Nutting, then a junior minister at the Foreign Office: 'And I don't give a damn if there's anarchy and chaos in Egypt.'[26]

British domestic politics stoked Eden's anger. The Conservative Right was still incensed at what it saw as Eden's weakness over the Sudan, and agitating against his plans, now well advanced, to withdraw from the Suez bases. Now it saw in Glubb's dismissal the consequences of appeasing the Arabs. The trouble came to a head when the Prime Minister reported to Parliament, and disastrously mishandled the occasion. His speech was, Eden recalled, 'one of the worst in my career'.[27] He lost his temper, shouting 'Really, the House *must* listen to the Prime Minister.'[28] 'The events in Jordan have shattered A,' his wife wrote in her diary. 'He is fighting very bad fatigue which is sapping his thought. Tonight's winding up of the debate was a shambles.'[29] At the end of a long week of anxiety and anger in Downing Street, Evelyn Shuckburgh, whom we have seen accompanying Eden to Washington, recorded in his diary: 'He seems to be completely disintegrated – petulant, irrelevant, provocative at the same time as being weak. Poor

England, we are in total disarray.' On the following day he noted 'Today both we and the Americans really gave up hope of Nasser and began to look around for means of destroying him.' Four days later he recorded the Prime Minister's own words on Nasser: 'It is either him or us, don't forget that.'[30]

9 MARCH: ARCHBISHOP INTO EXILE

In the 1950s Britain had its hands full with colonial wars. Friends of mine fought against the Communist insurgency in Malaya, and one of them produced a book about it, the first by an Oxford contemporary to make its way into print. A school friend did his national service with the King's African Rifles in Kenya, and in letters home told me more about the sexual feistiness of grass widows in Happy Valley than about operations against Mau Mau. Things were getting difficult in Cyprus too, where Greek demands for independence or for union with Greece encountered British colonial stubbornness and a Turkish backlash. Events threatened to turn an old-fashioned campaign against the colonial power into a vicious little civil war, with much the same bitterness on all sides as had consumed the Palestine Mandate a few years earlier.

Cypriot unrest started to gather force in the summer of 1955. Greek Cypriot attacks on the garrison provoked British army raids on the nationalists' political headquarters. Riots followed, then stiff prison sentences for possession of explosives, and an invitation to the Turkish and Greek Governments to discuss the crisis in London. The talks achieved nothing and the British Governor outlawed EOKA, the Cypriot group campaigning for union with Greece. The Greek Cypriots called a general strike and a mob sacked and looted public buildings, reducing London's popular press to frenzy when they burned portraits of the Queen. By November the Governor had called a state of emergency and in December British residents in the island were busy forming Home Guard units to look to their own defence.

1956 opened with the murder of a Turkish policeman, and Turkish threats to kill five Greeks for every Turk. Britain despatched men of the Parachute Regiment to the island and sent them fruitlessly hunting Greek terrorists in the Troodos mountains. But EOKA's bombing campaign continued and the Cabinet decided to give the soft hand of diplomacy another trial. In February the Colonial Secretary, Alan Lennox-Boyd, flew to Cyprus for talks with the Greek Cypriots' leader,

Archbishop Makarios. They talked about self-determination, but with constitutional recognition of the rights of the Turkish minority. Makarios, devious politician as well as moral leader, would not or could not settle.

Once again, British policy was reversed. In the first week of March, the week in which it was absorbing the fact that a client king, Hussein of Jordan, had sent a British general packing, the British Government determined to get tough. On 9 March Makarios was arrested on his way to Nicosia airport to catch a flight to Athens. He was put instead on a Royal Air Force plane that whisked him away into exile. His journey was typical of the strengths and weaknesses of what was left of postwar empire. Makarios was flown first to Aden, then a British coaling station and strong point at the mouth of the Red Sea. From there a ship of the Royal Navy took him to Mombasa. Here a cloak-and-dagger transfer to another ship had been planned, but Fleet Street's finest hired an aircraft and monitored the archbishop's every movement. Away the ship sailed to the Seychelles, where Makarios was installed in the Governor's country residence, a dignified victim of British high-handedness.

What happened next followed a familiar late-colonial sequence. Two years earlier the Kenyan leader, Jomo Kenyatta, had been sent into exile and given a seven-year gaol sentence. He was released in the early 1960s. A few years later I once set myself to weed the Foreign Office 'line to take' telegrams about him. It was laughable to see how they evolved over that period. They started by calling him the leader of a Mau Mau movement which committed unspeakable evil, acts not fit to be described even in a confidential telegram lest ladies might be involved in the deciphering. They contained, of course, no mention of the comparable atrocities which Britain was inflicting on blacks in Kenya. They explained his deportation as a necessary measure to decapitate the uprising. As it continued to flourish the telegrams' emphasis gradually shifted. With all his faults Kenyatta, they conceded, had authority over ordinary Kenyans. Perhaps, they began to hint, he could help solve the problem he had created. He had, after all, his personal merits. In the end, five years on, they were welcoming Kenyatta's return to public life as a reliable friend of Britain and the father of his people.

Makarios's case followed the same parabola, though on a shorter timescale. His exile angered Greeks from ordinary Cypriots to the King himself. A bomb was planted in the British governor's residence, which failed to explode. Britain started jamming Greek broadcasts to the island; Turks rioted and looted Greek shops; the first British civilian was murdered; and British troops went on fruitlessly combing the mountains in search of killers. It was a wearyingly familiar story. But violence produced a search for settlement, as it nearly always does, proclamations that civilised society can never yield to terrorism notwithstanding. By the end of 1959 Makarios was back in Cyprus, the elected President of the new and independent republic there, talking solemnly of the need for Greeks and Turks to work together with sincerity and mutual respect. Today, the leaders of the two communities produce the same sentiments, perhaps with the same qualified sincerity as may have burned in Makarios's breast almost half a century ago.

5 APRIL: ISRAEL IN THE FIFTIES

A friend and I were talking about the way the Israelis throw their weight around nowadays in the occupied territories of Palestine. He is an emotional and sometimes idiosyncratic character whom I take with a pinch of salt, but every now and then he stops me in my tracks.

'These Likudniki can't last,' he said.

I asked him what he meant.

'Coming in with their Uzis from the Bronx,' he said, and I presumed he meant American Jewish fundamentalists clinging to illegal settlements.

They showed every sign of lasting, I replied.

They couldn't, he said. 'Look at the Kingdom of Jerusalem.'

Did he mean the Frankish Kingdom of Jerusalem?

He did, he said.

Wasn't comparing Israeli settlers with the crusaders who captured Jerusalem in 1099 stretching analogy further than it would go?

Not at all, he said – twelfth and twenty-first centuries are all one to him.

All the same, I said, parallels between those crusader princes and his 'Likudniki' seemed a bit far-fetched .

He didn't agree. Whether they carried swords or sub-machine guns, he told me, Westerners trying to colonise the Arab world were doomed to eviction sooner or later.

'Even when they've got nuclear weapons and American backing?' I asked.

All irrelevant, he suggested. The 'Likudniki' were doomed, their moral authority undermined by the wickedness of their occupation of Arab lands: 'Look at them watering their lawns with water stolen from the Arabs.'

'The kingdom of Jerusalem lasted a hundred years,' he reminded me. 'Israel has had getting on for sixty already.'

People did not talk like that in the 1950s. Israel had then been in existence for less than ten years. It was a small, fragile state, surrounded by its enemies, and in liberal circles in the West Israel and the Israelis enjoyed enormous good will. The young people my friend and I once had been saw the Israelis as people who had escaped the Holocaust, created a new state and successfully resisted aggression by all their neighbours. Now they were making the desert bloom, bringing democracy to the Middle East and giving the world an example of a new kind of Jew building a new kind of society. To the enthusiastic, Israel looked like a shining beacon for the world. It was the toast of enlightened London, and young men from the Foreign Office who presumed to suggest that the Arabs too had their story got a frosty reception at liberal dinner parties.

Others in the West saw things differently. Some traditional anti-Semitism had survived the Holocaust. Ordinary British people remembered Zionist terrorism: the Stern Gang, Irgun Zwei Leumi, the terrorist attack on the King David Hotel in Jerusalem, and above all the hanging of captured British soldiers, which aroused the same kind of indignation then as the beheading of Western hostages in Iraq did the day before yesterday. Zionists in the West and the diplomats of independent Israel alike seemed shrill and demanding, almost wilfully determined to make themselves unlovable. But still Westerners insisted on loving Israel.

The Israelis knew of this Western sympathy and made the most of it. Yet experience had taught them that, even more than the rest of us, Jews must in the end look to their own security. Despite their victory in the Arab-Israeli wars, they were ever-conscious of their new state's vulnerability. Hemmed in between the Mediterranean and the hills of Judaea, they told anyone who would listen that an enemy who took Israel by surprise could cut across its narrow waist in a day. Their concern grew all the shriller when, in 1955, it became apparent that the Soviet Union planned to supply arms to Egypt and Syria, using Czechoslovakia as a go-between.

Right-minded liberals knew the answer to that one too. The West should arm the Israelis with the weapons that would give them superiority when next it came to war. Statesmen and their foreign ministries were not so sure. Arab interests had to be accommodated if a negotiated peace were ever to be achieved. A Middle East arms race between Western and Soviet suppliers would only increase the risk of conflagration. And even if general war could be averted, without peace Israelis and Arabs would be doomed to the edgy existence we see them living today, fifty years later.

Meanwhile, clashes between Arabs and Israelis continued, and things like Sharon's bloody onslaught on the Arab village of Qibya in 1953 reminded dispassionate observers that the Arabs were by no means always the aggressors. Israel should always talk of peace but never make it, a shrewd but indiscreet Israeli diplomat once said. Israeli hands were not as clean as Zionism would have us believe. In any case, the Western powers had interests of their own to protect in the Middle East. Britain's economy depended on oil from Iran coming through the Suez Canal. Britain was pledged to defend Jordan against attack. In the Baghdad Pact it was trying to create a bloc of friendly Middle Eastern powers which would stand between the area and Soviet expansion. Even the United States, friend of Israel as it was, hoped also to be a friend of the Arabs: it had big oil interests in Saudi Arabia. The West's cars, a banality of the period recalled, did not run on Jaffa orange juice.

So when the Israelis and their Zionist supporters demanded that the West should take steps to make Israel militarily safe their friends in London drawing rooms applauded, but Western statesmen responded very cautiously. In May 1950 the United States, Britain and France had signed a Tripartite Declaration, which bound them to cooperate on Middle Eastern issues and in particular to consult one another to keep arms supplies to the region properly balanced. Now, as relations between Arabs and Israelis grew more tense, they clung to its terms, empty of solid content as they were, as if it were a lifebelt in a stormy sea.

In the early months of 1956 friction between Israelis and Arabs began to take more violent form. Arab guerrillas stepped up their incursions into Israel. Israel's retaliatory raids became more bloody. The Gaza strip, then held by Egypt, had always been a potential flashpoint. In 1956 Egyptian military intelligence began to provide increased backing for Arab guerrilla raids across the border there. The Israeli response was stepped up. What had initially been nothing more serious than firefights between patrols escalated into larger engagements between regular forces.

There followed the usual fruitless attempts to establish which side was the more to blame. United Nations observers in Gaza believed that while the guerrilla raids might have started the trouble the Israelis were seeking to exploit them. Their patrols were taking to showing themselves provocatively right up to the border wire, so that when Egyptian artillery fired on them Israeli guns could engage them in return. Then, on 5 April 1956, the escalation reached a new level. On that day the Israelis fired their mortars at a shopping street in the middle of Gaza city. Shocked United Nations observers reported that they had killed fifty-six civilians and wounded more than a hundred.

Dag Hammarskjöld had been hoping for some time to engage Egyptians and Israelis in defusing the situation by putting an end both to guerrilla raids and to heavy-handed retaliation. The killings in Gaza added urgency to his efforts. They were to keep him occupied throughout the late spring of 1956 with occasional forays into what later generations called shuttle diplomacy and which might, in a different world, have continued indefinitely. But with the nationalisation of the Suez Canal in July the Middle East found a different focus of political, diplomatic and military attention to capture the Secretary-General's attention.

The politicians and diplomats with whom Hammarskjöld and Western statesmen had to deal in those early years of Israel's existence were formidable people, and none more so than David Ben-Gurion. In 1956 he turned seventy, after a working lifetime dedicated to the Zionist cause. He came to Palestine from Poland at the age of twenty. There he devoted his early manhood to farming, agitation and political organisation. When in 1917 Balfour promised the Zionists a national home in Palestine Ben-Gurion joined the British Army's Jewish Legion. When in 1939 the British restricted Jewish immigration he called for action against them, if necessary armed. By 1942 he was calling for a Jewish commonwealth in Palestine, and from then until independence he led the struggle against the British administration of the mandate. Throughout he maintained at least an appearance of keeping at a reasonable distance from the men of violence. When war with the Arabs came he stood back from the terror which set so many Palestine Arabs in flight; but he did nothing effective to prevent it. Once Israel was established he reined in the extremist Jewish groups and created a unified administration, a unified defence force and a unified State of Israel.

He built it on the ruins of a long-established Arab community in Palestine, part Moslem, part Christian. Ben-Gurion saw the dismal fate of that community as a historical necessity. For him, new-born Israel was the direct descendant of the Biblical Jewish state, re-established after a 2,000-year hiatus. With good reason, he saw himself as its personification, a man with an eye both to today's realities and to his place in history. He could see the perils of Israel's position in the Middle East, but he had confidence in its strengths, and a passionate belief in its enduring destiny. Among his many qualities was the ability to inspire an equal faith in those around him, and in particular among the young soldiers and civilians who formed his close-knit court. In 1956 the speed and decisiveness of their response to the challenge which their country faced were to astonish the world.

13 JUNE: THE BRITISH LEAVE THE CANAL

At fifteen minutes past midnight on 13 June 1956, the last British troops left their bases beside the Suez Canal on their way to Cyprus or home. For the first time in seventy-four years there remained no garrison, no army of occupation, no Eighth Army, no British military bases in Egypt.

Almost two years earlier, in October 1954, Britain and Egypt had signed an agreement which stipulated that British troops should leave Egypt in June 1956. Now they were going, five days ahead of schedule. The handover itself was a sadly subdued affair. A British brigadier shook hands with an Egyptian colonel at Navy House in Port Said and stepped aboard the ship that was to take him to Cyprus. The most the British could say of the leave-taking was that it was conducted 'quietly and with dignity', but there was about it nothing of the warmth and sentimentality that accompanied the transfer of power as floodlit Union flags came down the flagpoles in so many newly independent former colonies in those postwar decades. The story of British-Egyptian relations did not lend itself to that kind of sentiment.

In 1956 the canal was almost a century old. It had been built in the mid-nineteenth century by a combination of the vision and willpower of one Frenchman, Ferdinand de Lesseps; by French capital; and by Egyptian forced labour. At first the British Government stood ostentatiously aside from the venture, just as they did with the Common Market one hundred years later, claiming that it would prove to be a commercial failure and was, in any case, driven by France's hostility to Britain. The canal went ahead, nevertheless, and was completed in 1869. Six years later Benjamin Disraeli saw an opportunity to snap up the 44 per cent of the Canal shares that were held by the ruler of Egypt. He famously borrowed £4,000,000 from the Rothschilds and told Queen Victoria that Britain's possession of the Canal was vital to her authority and power.

Yet the Suez Canal Company remained Paris-based and French-managed, with Britons occupying only three seats on the board of directors. It was only in 1882 that events altered the balance of power between France and Britain in Egypt. In that year a mob in Alexandria rioted and killed fifty Europeans. The Royal Navy was sent to bombard the place and a British military expedition was despatched to seize control of Egypt. From then on, until after the Second World War, British officials and businessmen controlled the levers of power, paying no more than lip-service to the rights of Turkey, which was until the First World War the nominal sovereign power in Egypt, and thereafter to the rights and interests of the Egyptian king, government and people.

The international status of the canal was in principle governed by the Constantinople Convention of 1888. It provided for the free use of the canal by the ships of all nations, even in time of war. But the British delegates secured exceptions to these principles, by stressing Britain's duty to protect Egypt against attack. British troops were stationed in Egypt to protect both the canal and the safety of the European colonies in Cairo and Alexandria. In the First World War they were actively employed in repelling the overland Turkish threat to the canal. But when such threats vanished there was no talk of removing the army of occupation.

Thus British imperialism clothed the empire's needs in hypocritical concern for the king and people of Egypt, and between the wars more and more educated Egyptians came to resent it. Egyptian ministers found themselves caught between British requirements and the fevered demands of Egyptian nationalists. Matters came to a head in the Second World War. The British in Egypt looked defeat in the face, as Rommel's tanks advanced through Libya towards Alexandria. Nationalists saw their chance to be rid of the British for good. In the end, in 1942, the British sent tanks to King Farouk's palace to back up their demand that he should dismiss a prime minister they did not trust. Farouk's public humiliation fed still further the grievances of Egyptian nationalists, among them the young army officers who were to emerge ten years later as the leaders of Egypt's demands for sovereignty and dignity.

The end of the war brought new hopes of colonial freedom all over the world and new expectations that the imperial powers must soon move, willingly or at gunpoint, to the exit door of history. But in the eyes of the British, Egypt and the canal presented very particular difficulties. Britain's lifeblood, they said, flowed through the canal. It was an essential route to the British empire in Asia and, once India and Pakistan had their independence, a vital expression of the intimacy of the Commonwealth relationship. Through the canal came the Iranian oil on which British industry depended. Egypt faced a potential threat of subversion from the expanding Soviet empire; and in 1955, with the first rumours that the Soviet Union was sending arms to Egypt, that threat became actual. Britain's prosperity and life itself, ministers persuaded themselves, depended on the canal.

In Egyptian eyes it all looked very different. British garrisons in Egypt were a standing affront to patriotic sentiment. British squaddies treated Egyptians with the same brutal contempt they brought to their dealings with natives anywhere, and their attitude added a thirst for revenge to the average Egyptian's vaguely patriotic sentiments. Time after time through the long years of occupation, British negotiators prevaricated, procrastinated, postponed the date of eventual departure. None of this made for good relations, for mutual respect between Britain and Egypt.

Once King Farouk was gone and Egypt's revolutionary army officers were in control, hostility to the British presence became more outspoken. Egyptian crowds regularly rioted and Egyptian workers, on the canal and elsewhere, as regularly went on strike. Mobs killed foreigners and burned their property; British troops fired back, and sometimes first; there were clashes between British troops and Egyptian police, in which the Egyptians showed themselves anything but the craven creatures British jingoists thought them. Freedom fighters stole copper cable and stretched it across the road beside the canal to decapitate jeep-borne British patrols; and when he caught them at it at least one decorated British officer threw them from a fast-moving jeep to their deaths. The insurgency was going the way of all insurgencies, and the occupation the way of all occupations.

By 1950 the British Labour Government had become convinced that it must bring occupation of the Canal Zone to an end. But the opposition felt differently: it was easy and popular to accuse the government of scuttling. The Right-wing Conservative MPs who had opposed independence for Sudan also opposed withdrawal from Egypt, and when Winston Churchill came back to power in 1951 they imagined that their views had prevailed. But even he was forced to recognise that the Suez base was poisoning Britain's relations with the Arab world, costing Britain resources it could no longer afford, and no longer serving any convincing military purpose. Grudgingly he went along with Eden's negotiations with the Egyptians. Hence in the end the agreement of October 1954 to end the occupation of the Suez Canal bases; hence too that sad little ceremony at the quayside on 13 June 1956.

5
Showdown with Nasser

19 JULY: A DEAL DENIED

At 4 pm on 19 July, the American Secretary of State, John Foster Dulles, told the Egyptian ambassador in Washington, Ahmed Hussein, that the United States would not back a World Bank loan to build the Aswan High Dam. In doing so he drew a line under a prolonged saga of diplomatic comings and goings, and took the world a decisive step down the road to the Suez crisis of 1956.

The physics, engineering and economics of the Aswan High Dam project were straightforward. From time immemorial, Egypt had depended on the Nile for its survival. The project involved damming the Nile, creating a vast lake on the Egyptian-Sudanese border, and using the controlled flow of water for irrigation and power generation. At a stroke it would ease the weight of the fellaheen's labour and bring modernity and industry to Egypt. It was just the kind of project that appealed to ambitious young leaders throughout the developing world, and it had a very particular attraction to the officers around Nasser. It appealed also to the World Bank's scientists, engineers and economists.

The capital costs of this, the world's largest civil engineering project, would be high. The World Bank had been established to finance such projects, drawing on the strength of the industrialised countries to provide loans for Third World development. The main financial burden would fall on the United States, which provided the World Bank's president and for all practical purposes controlled its policies. America's international do-gooders supported such projects, and the State Department saw in Aswan a way of binding Egypt's new rulers to the West. The United States Treasury looked at the project through beadier eyes. To George Humphrey, the Secretary of the Treasury, it would use American money to reward a dangerous nationalist who was playing footsie with Communists and, for good measure, help the imperialist British, forever at odds with Nasser as they were, out of a tight corner. In so far as the American public knew or cared about such matters, more would have agreed with Humphrey than with the State Department.

For months in 1955 discussions about the High Dam wound their tortuous ways through politicians' meetings, diplomats' telegrams and newspaper headlines. At first Harold Macmillan, Eden's Foreign Secretary until the end of the year, was enthusiastic about this way of binding Egypt to the West. But throughout these same months rumours of Soviet arms supplies to Egypt were making their equally tortuous ways. Was a positive decision to finance the dam a way of blocking the advance of Soviet influence? Would a refusal of finance deter Nasser, or at least deter other Third World leaders from following in his footsteps? The arguments shifted with the wind of events, not least with fears that an Egypt armed with Soviet weapons would pose a mortal threat to Israel. By the end of 1955 the weight of Western argument had turned against financing the dam, but opinions went on shifting.

Discussion of the project and of related issues like the arms deal, Egyptian-Israeli tension and Egypt's intentions in the wider Middle East, ran on into 1956. The British convinced themselves that Nasser had brought about Glubb's expulsion from Jordan; that seemed an argument for aborting the dam project. It was rumoured that Moscow was considering financing the dam if the World Bank withdrew; that seemed a reason to provide the finance and keep Russian influence out. Egypt recognised Red China; and to Washington that seemed a decisive reason for punishing Nasser. The West's thinking on the dam became entangled with the programme for Britain's final withdrawal from the canal. Throughout, Britain and the United States consulted, agreed, collaborated and disagreed; and not for the first or last time the British found the powerful men in Washington as impossible to live with as they were impossible to live without.

On 13 June the last British troops sailed away from Port Said. Three days of Egyptian celebration followed. The Soviet Foreign Minister, Dimitri Shepilov, was invited, and in the course of his discussions offered Nasser favourable terms for a Soviet loan to build the dam. No deal was clinched, and Ahmed Hussein, home on leave from Washington, argued against it, asking Nasser whether he really wanted to replace Egypt's British overlords with Russians. But accounts of Shepilov's offer shivered timbers in Washington and London. Nasser decided to play on these concerns and put the West's intentions to the test. So he sent Ahmed Hussein back to Washington with instructions to withdraw Egyptian conditions on the dam deal to which the Americans had hitherto objected. On 19 July Ahmed Hussein went to his meeting with Dulles convinced that this concession would clear the way for the World Bank to finance a dam that would feed Egypt and bind it to the West.

Instead Dulles gave him a lecture. The United States, he told him, would not back the World Bank offer, and without American support it was dead. With the agonising slowness which so irritated anyone who had dealings with him, Dulles took Ahmed Hussein through the United States' reasons for pulling out. He focused not on America's political grievances against Egypt but on the economic burden which repayment of the World Bank loan would impose. That, he said, would damage the esteem that ordinary Egyptians felt for the United States. To the Egyptian, all this smelt of condescension and hypocrisy, and afterwards even Eisenhower expressed concern at what he called the United States' 'abrupt' shift of position, and feared that Nasser might claim that the Americans had doublecrossed him.[1] As for the British, they complained at the short notice which the Americans had given them of the summons to Ahmed Hussein, but they did not disagree on substance; like the Americans, their patience with Nasser was exhausted.

But impatience, even great power impatience, exacts a price. As the British Treasury official dealing with the dam project noted: 'Nasser will undoubtedly be appalled by the apparent breach of faith by the two governments and will seek to revenge himself. There is not much he can do against the United States but a lot he can do against us. Obvious examples are renewed pressure on the Suez Canal Company or stirring up trouble in the Gulf.'[2]

26 JULY: MAJOR YOUNES STRIKES

On the evening of 26 July Major Mahmoud Younes of the Egyptian Army Corps of Engineers led a small squad of soldiers into the Ismailia office of the Suez Canal Company. At the same time other squads moved into its offices in Cairo and Port Said. They were there to take control of the company and seize its records.

Three days earlier Younes had received secret orders from Nasser. The President was preparing a speech to be made on 26 July in

Manshiya Square in Alexandria. It was to mark the fourth anniversary of the abdication of King Farouk, the event that had started Nasser on his rise to power. Now he must give his people something glorious to celebrate. He had made careful plans, and Younes had a central role in them. At a given signal, he was to strike and recover Egypt's patrimony. The signal would come when Nasser mentioned the name of Ferdinand de Lesseps, the man who had used French capital and Egyptian labour to drive a canal from Port Said to Suez. Complex, conspiratorial, plunging back into history in search of resonance and significance, the arrangement was typical of Nasser, and of his understanding of the people he wanted to lead to glory.

First, Nasser had to tell his Cabinet what he intended. They were not eager to be led to glory. 'Many of them were graduates of Western universities', recalls Mohamed Heikal, 'and this was not at all the sort of political game that they had expected to take part in.'[3] But Nasser had prepared his ground carefully, even sending under-cover officers to Cyprus to assess British readiness for military action. They brought him the reassurance that the British there had their hands full containing terrorist violence. So reassured, Nasser spoke with confidence to his colleagues. A bold stroke would succeed provided they could prove themselves capable of running the canal. He rallied his Cabinet. The way was clear for him to take Ferdinand de Lesseps's name in vain.

When Nasser spoke he faced a square packed with an excited crowd. He spoke at length, without a text, in man-of-the-people style. He rehearsed all Egypt's grievances against the West, from the fate of the labourers who had died to dig the canal, through the British bombardment of Alexandria in 1882, to the long oppression of Egyptians by a monarchy which danced to Britain's tune. And he reminded his audience of grievances they had experienced personally, talking about the arrogance of Egypt's British occupiers in the Second World War and the violence used to crush demonstrators against the Suez bases. He got the kind of response he wanted from the crowd, for they had imbibed these stories with their mothers' milk.

Nasser turned to Egypt's present grievances, and here the response was still clearer. The West had tried to force Egypt into making peace with Israel, refusing to sell it arms unless Cairo would recognise Israel's needs: 'Israel's requests must be granted, they said. Israel's frontiers exist. But when you ask: "What about the people of Palestine?" they say, "That is a subject which we shall talk about later."'[4] So Egypt had shown its mettle by turning to the Soviet Union for arms; and then there was 'a big hullabaloo'.

Nasser went on to a yet more recent grievance, the West's refusal to finance the Aswan Dam; and again he linked the story with nineteenth-century indignities. If the Egyptians had fallen in with the West's demand to commit their own resources to the project, before long they would have found themselves confronted with a choice: 'Stop halfway, after throwing $300 million down the drain, or accept our terms – the sending of someone to occupy the Finance Minister's seat, or another one to occupy the seat of the Minister of Trade and of yet another to occupy my post, while we sat in this country unable to move without their instructions and their orders.'[5] Once again, Nasser invoked the history of British oppression, and this time he named Lord Cromer, the Englishman who had dominated Egypt in the late-nineteenth century. If he and his colleagues had accepted the West's proposal they would have found themselves back in Cromer's days. Even worse, back in the days when the canal was being built: 'I started to look at Mr Black [the American President of the World Bank] ... and I saw him in my imagination as Ferdinand de Lesseps'[6] – and at de Lesseps's name Major Younes and his men went into action.

The canal had brought little benefit to Egypt, Nasser argued: 'Instead of the Canal being dug for Egypt, as de Lesseps had told the Khedive, Egypt became the property of the Canal.'[7] Today Egypt received $3 million a year from the company, out of gross canal revenues of $100 million. 'Why shouldn't we take it for ourselves? ... Today, O citizens, the Suez Canal Company has been nationalised.'[8] Out of its revenues Egypt would finance the building of the dam for itself. And at the end of his speech Nasser came back to Major Younes's coup. 'At this very moment, as I talk to you, some Egyptian brethren ... are starting to take over the Canal ... which is situated in Egyptian territory, which is part of Egypt and which is owned by Egypt.'[9] It was a triumphant moment, as Nasser brought to a conclusion a century-long story of national humiliation.

There was dancing in the streets of Cairo and Alexandria. The Egyptians had had enough of the indignities done to their country. So they cheered when Nasser said that if the imperialists did not like what he had done they could 'choke to death on their fury'. They thrilled with excitement when he promised them that he would build the Aswan Dam and industrialise Egypt. 'We are marching from strength to strength,' he assured them, and they believed him.

Nasser's speech played well in the Arab world. But it reached other less enthusiastic audiences, among them the Western statesmen with whom Nasser had dealt over arms, the dam and the canal itself. Their version of the story was less dramatic than his, but just as deserving of a hearing. Like Nasser, they had had their national interests to consider and a range of conflicting considerations to reconcile.

Ever since the birth of Israel the British, French and Americans had tried to check an arms race in the Middle East which could only feed Arab-Israeli enmity. So in 1950 they had bound themselves to restrict the flow of arms into the region. In doing so they looked (or at least told themselves that they looked) as much to the interests of the Arabs as of Israel. And they were prepared to make sacrifices to do right. So for better or worse, Britain had bound itself to a treaty relationship with Jordan, which the Jordanians could invoke if the Israelis attacked them. For better or worse, Eisenhower was prepared, even in an election year, to stand up to the Zionist lobby in the United States. And for better or worse the French, despite the grief which Arab nationalism was giving them in Algeria, were still sending the Israelis only a trickle of the arms which they demanded. The British, French and Americans were still trying (or at least they believed that they were trying) to play fair and support peace in a troubled Middle East.

But in the summer of 1955 Nasser had turned to the Communist bloc, buying Soviet arms on favourable terms. In doing so he was destroying the balance which the Western powers were trying to maintain and threatening the peace of the Middle East. The thought of Soviet bombers in Egypt's hands, perhaps flown by Soviet volunteers, terrified the Israelis; they clamoured for fighters to protect their cities. And the thought of the Soviet Union establishing a favoured position in Egypt terrified the West, for the Americans saw themselves locked in global existential rivalry with their Communist opponents while the British and French feared that if Communists controlled Egypt they would choke the canal through which Europe's economic lifeblood flowed. Yet still, in 1955 and in the first half of 1956, all three had tried to maintain an even-handedness in their approach to the Middle East.

They had gone on agonising also over how to deal with Nasser and Arab nationalism. 'There is the $64 question of Nasser,' Evelyn Shuckburgh had mused as he travelled with Eden to his meeting with Eisenhower in January, '– do we write him off or try to work with him?'[10] When they pulled out of the Aswan Dam deal, Eisenhower and Eden thought they had written him off, but now Nasser was briskly writing himself back into the argument. Eden and Ike had Nasser's answer, and Eden at least was convinced that the days of trying to work with him were over.

27 JULY: DRAMA IN DOWNING STREET

On the evening of 26 July the occupants of 10 Downing Street laid on a glittering diplomatic and social occasion. Anthony Eden was a Knight of the Garter of a month's standing, with a much younger wife, Clarissa. Their principal guests were young King Feisal of Iraq, his uncle the Crown Prince, and Iraq's perdurable Prime Minister, Nuri es-Said. These were Britain's key allies in the Arab world, and their country was the lynchpin of the Baghdad Pact. That pact in turn seemed to be the only effective shield against Soviet penetration of the Middle East. The Iraqis' visit to London was a major diplomatic event. It was the sort of occasion at which Eden shone. He knew the issues, the arguments, the personalities, and he brought to such occasions a sharp emotional intelligence and an all-conquering charm. His wife's air of diffidence hid an insider's confidence. She had known No.10 since her childhood, for Winston Churchill was her uncle.

The news of Nasser's speech and Major Younes's coup reached Downing Street at 10.15 pm. The first reaction, as word of what had happened spread, was resolute. Nuri was one of the Arab world's most experienced political operators: he knew how to deal with Nasser. 'Hit him, hit him hard, and hit him now' was his advice. Selwyn Lloyd talked confidently of an 'old-fashioned ultimatum'. And at this opening of a Middle East crisis which was to set opposition against government, Hugh Gaitskell, the leader of that opposition, advised the government to act quickly. If they did they would get popular support. But he also warned them to make sure to get the cooperation of the United States.

The news from Cairo posed an immediate challenge to Anthony Eden. At many points in the long crisis which lay ahead he allowed his nerves to lead him into histrionics, but now he was calm. The party dispersed, ministers present remaining. The service chiefs, the French ambassador and the American chargé d'affaires were summoned to join them. Eden dominated the proceedings. He was adamant that Nasser 'must not be allowed to get away with it' and could not be permitted 'to have his hand on our windpipe'.[11] He talked of the Foreign Office looking into legal remedies but demanded to know at once from the Chiefs of Staff what could be achieved by force. Long after the event, Mountbatten claimed that he proposed that a quick *coup de main* by the Navy and the Royal Marines could seize Port Said in a matter of days. But there is no contemporary evidence that he spoke as he claimed, and even if he had, no *coup de main* could have recovered the whole canal. To do that would require a major deployment of forces, and for that the British armed forces were not prepared. In the words of a waspish civilian observer it became clear that 'we could do nothing immediately ... Britain was armed to participate in a nuclear Armageddon with the Soviet Union or in small colonial wars ... but had no capacity for this kind of emergency.'[12]

When ministers saw the next morning's newspapers – the newspapers I had not bothered to look at before reporting to the Foreign Office that day – they found them full of Nasser's speech in Alexandria. They were united in condemning Nasser's action, as much for the way it had been executed as the deed itself. They spoke that day for the bulk of British opinion, for the professionally involved as for the man in the street. To Nigel Nicolson (who before the crisis was over was to throw away his political career by opposing Eden's policy) it looked like 'a highwayman's exploitation of the geographical accident that the isthmus of Suez lay in Egyptian territory'. Opinion in Britain, Nicolson went on, saw Nasser's move as 'an act of robbery which the British nation, and most of the Western allies, were not prepared to accept with a mere protest'.[13] There was, too, a patronising contempt for the Egyptians. 'An international waterway of this kind', wrote the London *Times*, 'cannot be worked by a nation of as low technical and managerial skills as the Egyptians.'[14] At that first stage the man and woman on the Clapham omnibus seem to have felt the same.

Feelings still ran high when, at 11 am, Eden made a brief statement in the House of Commons. He spoke calmly and moderately, but the mood of the House was indignant, almost exalted. For the moment MPs, press and nation seemed to be out ahead of the government. Statement over, Eden quickly left the chamber, but members lingered and discussion continued in the lobbies and corridors. Already there were comparisons with Hitler's acts of aggression and with Mussolini, and warnings of the danger of appeasement. 'If there were any voices raised in defence of the Egyptian action,' says Robert Rhodes James, who was there as a young parliamentary clerk, 'I did not hear them.'[15]

The almost unanimous vigour of the popular reaction in Britain to Nasser's coup is as odd as much else about that extraordinary summer and autumn of 1956. For all of us the past is another country, and Britain was another country in 1956. Few then found it easy to take people like the Egyptians entirely seriously. As for the British government, they were painfully conscious how hard they had tried, and had some of the bitterness of the rejected suitor. In 1954, after a half-century of procrastination, they had formally acknowledged Egypt's ultimate authority over the canal. Only a month ago they had withdrawn their last troops from the Canal Zone. When the British withdrew from a colony they liked to think they did so graciously, not at the whim of a dictator on the make. Now Nasser's seizure of the canal seemed to government and public alike as much of a doublecross as the West's refusal to fund the dam had seemed to the Egyptians.

If the British despised the Egyptians, they were uneasily aware of how far their own country had fallen since its wartime glory days. It was economically weak, politically overstretched. A closure of the canal, for whatever reason, might tip the British economy over the brink into disaster. Yet at first sight it looked as if the country lacked the political and military capacity to secure the canal against such a fate. The British instinctively kicked against that reality, but they could not change it. As they lacked sufficient power of their own they needed international support, and most of their efforts over the next two months were devoted to trying to secure it. If things came to war they would need allies, and only France seemed to offer unambiguous support. But would Britain and France be enough? Britain would need the blessing and support of its wartime partner, the United States, and that, as the crisis wound on through August and September into October, it was never to secure.

The Parliamentary statement out of the way, the full Cabinet came together to consider the problem. Eden was dominant again, and again calm. The Cabinet were determined that resolute action was necessary, and what they had seen that morning in Parliament showed that they would be supported. But they recognised that they would be on weak ground if they argued that Nasser had acted illegally, for it was an awkward but incontrovertible fact that he was as much within his rights in nationalising the canal as Britain's Labour government had been when they nationalised the railways and the mines. Britain's case must therefore be argued on wider international grounds: '...the Canal was an important international asset and facility, and ... Egypt could not be allowed to exploit it for a purely internal purpose.'[16] Yet they could not turn to the Security Council because the Soviet Union would be bound to veto action if they did. The inescapable fact was that they could not afford to rule out forceful action by air, land and sea. From day one the Cabinet were prepared to act militarily and if necessary alone. As the Cabinet minutes recorded:

> The fundamental question before the Cabinet, however, was whether they were prepared in the last resort to pursue their objective by the threat or even the use of force, and whether they were ready, in default of assistance from the United States and France, to take military action alone. The Cabinet agreed that... even if we had to act alone, we could not stop short of using force to protect our position if all other methods of protecting it proved unavailing.[17]

The Cabinet really did believe that they had their backs to the wall that day.

But the French ambassador and the American chargé d'affaires had been at the meeting in Downing Street on the previous evening. Their governments already knew how thinking in London was shaping. To act alone really would be a last resort. The French looked as eager for action as the British, but it was the United States that really mattered. So in the calm and pedestrian words of the minutes, the Cabinet 'invited the Prime Minister to send a personal message to the President of the United States asking him to send a representative to London to discuss the situation with the representatives of the Governments of the United Kingdom and France'.[18]

27 JULY: 'DEAR IKE'

Eden wrote to Eisenhower as the Cabinet had agreed. He wrote in terms which seemed to him measured and reasonable, but which Macmillan noted 'left no room for uncertainty or equivocation'.[19] The message at once set alarm bells ringing in Washington. From the very beginning of the Suez crisis, the old allies found themselves looking at the same issues from different starting points, through different spectacles. It is ironic how often we find the Americans dismissing British arguments in 1956 as emotional, exaggerated, even hysterical – exactly the criticism that twenty-first-century Britons so often lay at Washington's door. Nevertheless, Eden's letter of 27 July marked a gentlemanly start to a disagreement which was to gather intensity in August and September, lead both countries into acrimony in October, and culminate in open conflict in November, a conflict which reached a resolution only because one party was so manifestly the weaker and had no option but to comply with the wishes of the other.

Eden made six points, in a message which was numbered like any other British government document addressed to insiders in the Whitehall system or to people whom the British thought of as such. There was agreement in London that Nasser could not be allowed to seize the canal, that united action would attract the support of all the maritime nations and that if the West failed to take action its influence in the Middle East would be destroyed. Second, Western Europe's oil supplies were threatened; it might need American help to fill the gap. Third, Egypt could not be relied upon to run the canal or finance its future needs; its management needed to be put on a 'sound international footing'. Fourth, the West should not get drawn into legal technicalities – the very technicalities on which the British Cabinet knew they could not win the argument. Fifth, economic pressure alone would not achieve results; the threat of force, and perhaps even force itself, was needed. And as a first step, the United States, Britain and France must align their policies and 'concert together how we can best bring the maximum pressure to bear on the Egyptian Government'.[20]

When Eisenhower read this message he felt that it grossly exaggerated the urgency and seriousness of the problem. There was no reason to panic. The Western powers needed to talk the matter through. When the President focused on Eden's message, Dulles and his deputy, Herbert Hoover, were otherwise engaged. So it was the Deputy Under Secretary at the State Department, Robert Murphy, whom Eisenhower told to 'just go over there and hold the fort. See what it's all about.' He wanted Murphy to make certain 'that any sweeping action to be taken regarding Nasser and the Canal should not be an act of the "Big Three Club"'.[21] Instead, Murphy should propose as a first step a conference of interested nations. So from the very beginning, Eisenhower instinctively wanted to complicate a situation which Eden, equally instinctively, wanted to keep starkly simple.

By the time Murphy met Selwyn Lloyd in London on Sunday, 29 July, Pineau, the French Foreign Minister, was already with him. Feelings in France were running as high as in Britain, and Pineau talked them up further. According to Lloyd he 'said that the French were ready to go with us to the end in dealing with Nasser'.[22] They saw in the Suez crisis above all a chance to bring Nasser down and rid themselves of his malign influence in Algeria: 'one successful battle in Egypt would be worth ten in North Africa,' Pineau told Lloyd.[23]

Murphy therefore was joining a meeting in which the atmosphere was already heightened and Lloyd now opened the three-power discussion by asserting that Nasser's coup could not be allowed to stand. International control of the canal was necessary, supported by as many nations as possible, particularly neutrals. So far so good for Murphy. But Lloyd and Pineau were convinced that only the possibility of military intervention could bring Nasser to reason. It was manifest, if unstated, that only American participation could make such intervention real, but Murphy left them in no doubt that Washington did not yet see it as an option. The maritime nations needed to bring their case against Nasser before an impartial tribunal, he said, something like the International Court of Justice – naming just the sort of tribunal before which, the British Cabinet had already acknowledged to themselves, they would have no adequate legal case at all.

The three broke off for dinner: '...an excellent meal at the Carlton Club. Pineau, a good French Socialist, seemed quite at home,' Lloyd recalled long afterwards, with that laboured attempt at humour which his officials so rarely found even remotely amusing.[24] As the talks continued over dinner conversation, much of it indiscreet, blossomed. Pineau urged a blockade of Egypt and a boycott of the canal. It was an idea that attracted no support for it would have precipitated the oil crisis in Western Europe which all wanted to avoid. He also confessed that he had considered involving the Israelis but claimed to have thought better of the idea. Nevertheless, he talked openly about supplying more French fighter aircraft to Israel. Lloyd responded that he had that day consulted Nuri (who for the British was the nearest thing they had to an Arab oracle) who believed that whatever happened Israel must not be involved in any action to bring Nasser down.

On the following day Murphy lunched with Eden and dined with Macmillan. Both talked in bellicose terms. Macmillan in particular, presuming on wartime intimacy with Eisenhower, let himself go. 'Whatever conferences, arrangements, public postures and manoeuvres might be necessary,' he told Murphy, 'in the end the Government were determined to use force.'[25] He and Eden both discounted the danger of any effective Soviet intervention, but Eden said he assumed that, if there were pressure from Moscow, the Americans would 'take care of the Bear'. Both men were deluding themselves, convinced that the United States must see the problem as they did. For his part, Murphy gave no ground. He represented a government with a fundamentally different approach from Britain's. What the British saw as an existential threat to their own position, Murphy saw as a problem to be kept within the same kind of limits as all the other world problems in which the United States' megapower was involved.

Murphy reported all this sabre-rattling to Washington and with it the news that Eden was willing to convene the international conference that Eisenhower wanted. Two days later, on 31 July, the President gathered his advisers to discuss the American position, and fifty years afterwards the record of their conversation still shows just how wide the Atlantic had become. By then, he had received another message from Eden, in which he talked about early military action. The President could see no case for that. Even if he did, Congressional approval would be needed for United States support. It would not be forthcoming – and though Eisenhower does not say so, anything that looked like war would have played badly throughout America in election year. '...the British were out of date in thinking of this as a mode of action,' Eisenhower said; and if they took action 'the Middle East oil would undoubtedly dry up, and Western hemisphere oil would have to be diverted to Europe, thus requiring controls to be instituted in the United States' – something else that would have brought the President few votes in November.[26]

Admiral Burke, the Chief of Naval Operations, took a quite different tack. He was thinking in terms not of American elections but of geopolitics, and above all of the strategic stand-off with the Soviet Union. Like the British, the American Chiefs were convinced that Nasser's power in the Middle East must be broken and that, if it came to war, the United States should support the Europeans. But his was a lone voice that afternoon, and another participant saw the situation very differently. George Humphrey, the Treasury Secretary, espoused an American foreign policy that looked to the nation's financial interests in the narrowest terms. He had had his way on the Aswan Dam. That had led only ten days later to Nasser's seizure of the canal, but Humphrey was unrepentant. The canal was not America's problem; the British 'were simply trying to turn the clock back fifty years'. To us, looking back, it is unsurprising that when, much later in the crisis, the British really did try to turn the clock back by force, Humphrey was eager to use America's financial strength to ensure that they failed.

As a soldier Eisenhower might have been expected to see Burke's point as much as Humphrey's, but he was intent on winning re-election in November as a 'Peace President'. He seems to have agreed with Humphrey. To join with the British against Nasser, he said, perhaps picking up Burke's geopolitics, 'might well array the world from Dakar to the Philippine Islands against us'. And then, in an interpretation of recent history better suited to a golf club bar than the Oval Office, he added that 'the British went into World War I and World War II without the United States, on the calculation that we would be bound to come in again', and now they thought they could work that particular trick again.[27] It was Day 4 of the crisis, and already London and Washington were living in different worlds.

I AUGUST: DULLES TAKES CHARGE

An immediate consequence of the President's meeting on 29 July was the despatch of Dulles to London. He met Selwyn Lloyd and Pineau on 1 August.

Foster Dulles was not one of those Americans with whom British ministers felt a natural rapport. He was not like Eisenhower or Murphy or his own brother, Alan Dulles of the CIA – all of them men with whom they could draw on memories of wartime association. Eisenhower thought highly of him, but his temperament was very unlike his President's. He was a lawyer, and a pedantic lawyer at that. His mind seemed to move slowly, his tongue more agonisingly slowly still. He had a complicated, confusing, almost crablike way of approaching things. Many thought him devious. Yet though no one could have called Foster Dulles flashy, he had a certain conceit of himself. His successful legal career was one reason for it, his position as the closest adviser to the most powerful man in the world a second.

Once again Lloyd stressed the urgent need to settle Nasser's hash, with the usual comparisons with Hitler and Mussolini. Pineau spoke even more forcefully, asserting that even if the British and Americans sat on their hands France would take military action to bring Nasser down. In response Dulles agreed that the canal must be brought under international control, but the way to achieve that was through political and diplomatic pressure. In international law the provisions of the 1888 Constantinople Convention governed the Suez Canal. The right thing to do was to bring its signatories into play. So far so clear – and for Lloyd and Pineau so disheartening. But with his maddening way of complicating every situation, Dulles also said that 'a way had to be found to make Nasser disgorge' what he was attempting to swallow. With its implication that the United States might yet consider the use of force, the phrasing was music to British and French ears.

Dulles brought with him a letter from the President, dictated by him just before his Secretary of State left Washington. It urged a diplomatic solution, but to British eyes it seemed, like Dulles's word 'disgorge', to recognise the possibility that force might be required. There were nuances of difference between what Dulles said and Eisenhower had written. The British and French were delighted by some passages and sought to ignore others. An honest reading of Eisenhower's and Dulles's words showed that the United States saw no present need for war and would not endorse it. But Lloyd and Pineau persuaded themselves that the Americans, after a hesitant start, were coming round to their way of seeing things.

If the Americans insisted on starting with a search for a diplomatic solution, however, so be it. A conference of the Constantinople Convention powers was an obvious way to begin. Britain and France feared that it could easily lead to deadlock or at the very least delay, and even at this early stage they suspected that Dulles was primarily concerned to head them off from military action. But if they wanted American backing they had to accept a conference and, talk as they did, they were far from ready to forego the chances of American support. The solidarity of the Western Big Three was a prize of real importance to the British and the French.

So discussion turned to timing and length of the conference. Britain and France wanted it held quickly, and kept short. Dulles argued for a longer period of preparation – three weeks against Lloyd's preference for two. On length, the three settled on a week. But in all this there was once again room for suspicion. Dulles in London half-reassured Lloyd and Pineau when he said that he hoped the moral pressure which the gathering generated would induce Nasser to back down. But then, on his return to Washington, he told the press that 'some people' wanted immediate military action. That would be against the United Nations Charter. 'We do not want to meet violence with violence,' he said – and that statement, whether it was taken as applying to all three or to the United States alone, relieved Nasser of the worst of the fears which British and French military preparations were intended to inflame.

AUGUST: THE FORCES DEPLOY

While the politicians busied themselves with all this diplomacy, Britain and France were massing their forces for military action against Egypt. The public position was that force would be used only if diplomacy failed, and that meanwhile military preparations served the useful diplomatic purpose of reminding the Egyptians of the trouble in store if negotiation failed. In private, however, British and French ministers assumed that only the use of force would compel Nasser to disgorge the Canal, and most of them welcomed the prospect.

It was agreed from the start that British officers would be in overall command of the operation and that air, land and sea forces of both countries would be involved. Two aims were stated: to re-establish international control of the Canal and to restore peace and order in Egypt (which really meant the removal from power of Nasser and his regime).

On the face of it the soldiers' task did not seem particularly onerous. The United States apart, these were the armed forces of the two most powerful western nations, Europe's biggest contributors to NATO. Only eleven years ago Britain triumphantly and France with rather less good reason had celebrated the end of a victorious war against a powerful enemy. Almost ever since their armies had been at war in Palestine, Vietnam, Kenya, Malaya, Cyprus and Algeria. The record of these wars had been inglorious at times, but they had given the men engaged up-to-date experience of action. Britain had serious forces at its disposal. It had an armoured division in Libya, could send the redoubtable Canberra and the brand-new Valiant jet bomber against Egyptian airfields and could deploy five aircraft carriers in the Mediterranean. France had the famous Mystère jet fighter, an aircraft carrier and, above all, the renown of its parachute regiments.

The opposition to all these men-at-arms looked almost laughable. In Britain and France there flourished a cheerful assumption that Nasser was a windbag like Mussolini and that Egyptian soldiers were militarily contemptible, men who would sell their schoolgirl sisters for a pound. There was an old, much-cherished joke that the Egyptian Army 'had never won a battle since the second act of *Aïda*'.[28] In any case, faced with the threat of aerial attack the mobs of Cairo and Alexandria would see Nasser for the man who had brought them ruin and throw him out. Suez 1956 promised at first to be a jolly little colonial war to put beside Omdurman in the battle honours.

Closer examination revealed the difficulties that lay ahead. The British embassy in Tripoli was certain that the Libyans, allies and clients of Britain as they might be, would never agree to the use of the armoured division against Egypt. Cyprus was only 200 miles from Port Said, but its ports and airfields were inadequate for the sort of armadas that the planners were assembling. In any case, the Cyprus terrorists would make things hot for troops based in the island. So Malta with its Grand Harbour must be the main base, and Malta was 1,000 miles from Egypt.

There were problems too with equipment. France had no heavy bombers, few landing craft. Britain's new Valiant bombers still had their teething troubles. The Eighth Army's desert experience had been forgotten, and the Army's modern equipment was designed for operations in the north German plain, not in hot and sandy Egypt. Radio communications remained problems for the British and French armies and for the ships and aircraft that would support them in action.

Even manpower presented difficulties. Britain and France had large conscript armies which had been able, with leadership and stiffening from regulars, to support all those troublesome colonial campaigns. They must have enough men to conquer Egypt. But in peacetime far too many regulars were taken up with training conscripts, and too few conscripts were adequately trained for combat. So in the British Army in particular, reservists were recalled. Some came willingly, eager for a temporary change of occupation and a month away from the wife, others resentfully from the start. As action against Egypt was repeatedly postponed and as time frames stretched away first from August to September and eventually to the end of October and even early November, resentment grew. When action finally came most of the men went ashore in Egypt willingly, morale high, expecting quick victory. But the long occupation that would follow victory would have brought units with very different attitudes to Egypt, as garrisons for the Canal Zone, Cairo and Alexandria.

These were the difficulties that the planners started to encounter as they got down to work, first in London and then in Cyprus, where the Allied commander-in-chief, General Sir Charles Keightley, had his headquarters. On the surface Keightley exuded courtesy and calm, and two French observers rather charmingly called him 'God-the-Father-Sitting-on-a-Cloud'.[29] He did his best to make a reality of cooperation with his French deputy, Admiral Barjot, and his political adviser from the Foreign Office. The land force commander, Sir Hugh Stockwell, was a different kind of character. He was 'excitable, gesticulating, keeping no part of him still … sweeping objects off the table with a swish of his swagger cane', as an astonished French observer noted.[30] He was, in fact, the very antithesis of what one would expect a senior British officer to be, had we not already seen the Chief of the Imperial General Staff himself, Sir Gerald Templer, betraying the same kind of excitability when he visited Amman in November, 1955.[31] His French deputy, General Beaufre, found him hard to take.

The command structure over which Keightley presided was cumbersome, but it had the merit that at least in theory it concentrated in Keightley's hands, and in the hands of his French colleague, responsibility for dealing with their ministers. If that remained true it would keep the politicians off the backs of the other men leading the attack. When it failed, the muddling of political and military factors became the final complicating factor in an already complicated situation.

The problem which had brought all these men together and summoned up all this activity was the Egyptian seizure of the Suez canal. The natural way to reverse it was to grab the canal back. This must mean the seizure of Port Said at the northern end of the canal, and of Port Fuad on the other side of the waterway, followed by an advance along the canal to Suez at its southern end, the best part of 100 miles distant. But there were problems with this as with every other concept which the joint planners came up with that summer. First, you had to put the Egyptian Air Force out of action, and it had airfields spread across the country, some of them dangerously near civilian centres. Second, you needed to ensure that the Egyptians, faced with attack, did not at once block the canal to shipping; or, since that was clearly a tall order, you had to have equipment ready to clear obstructions as soon as the waterway was in your hands. The land war looked easier, but to get from Port Said to Suez called for a rapid thrust on a narrow front, essentially along a road beside the canal. It was an operation which brought tank generals unhappy memories of their attempt to get a division through to Arnhem in 1944, and airborne generals memories of what happened when that failed.

So the planners looked for a different plan of campaign. They conceived a landing around Alexandria and a quick advance towards Cairo. This would make all Egypt the objective. It would, they reasoned, draw the Egyptian Army into open battle, in which it could quickly be destroyed. That, surely, would bring Nasser down, and the allies could reoccupy Egypt and restore it to subservience, order and friendly relations with the international community. Fully considered, the long-term consequences of all this might be horrendous, particularly if Western troops got drawn into patrolling the streets of Cairo and Alexandria, but the services would have carried out the task the politicians had given them, and more completely than if they had only cleared the canal.

So the reasoning and the planning developed as D-day was repeatedly postponed. Eventually all concerned recognised the difficulties that a landing around Alexandria and an overland advance towards Cairo would entail. Planning then swung back to landings at Port Said and Port Fuad and a quick thrust to Suez. But here too the difficulties remained manifest, and nothing the planners could do would remove them. In the end it was fresh political thinking, not military planning, which changed, with the decision to bring in the Israelis to help crack the problem of Nasser, Egypt and the Suez canal. It was thinking which today would be praised as thinking outside the box, but it was to turn a crisis into a catastrophe.

3–9 SEPTEMBER: MENZIES MEETS NASSER

The three powers had agreed that London was the right place for the conference which would either solve the Suez crisis or give the British and French the excuse to invade Egypt. Anthony Eden issued the invitations, which went to twenty-four nations: the eight original signatories of the Constantinople Convention in their modern guises, the eight shipowning countries which made most use of the canal, and eight nations whose trade was particularly dependent on it. Twenty-two of the twenty-four accepted, and together they formed an imposing cross-section of the nations of the world. Greece declined, with a frivolity that has marked its foreign policy-making from that day to this, essentially because it was at odds with Britain over Cyprus.

Egypt declined too, but after more careful thought. Nasser was tempted by the idea of turning up to show his mettle to a world audience. But he knew that the Western powers would manipulate the conference. He would be up against an ultimatum, however politely formulated, and in a minority. Eden made matters worse in a broadcast to the British public, in which he prejudged Nasser's position by arguing that his record showed that he was not to be trusted. It was a remark that had even British observers muttering about the courtesy expected of a host. Once it had been made would have needed all Nasser's courage to show his face in such a gathering. He refused the invitation, but sent a close associate to London as an observer.

The conference opened on 16 August, with Selwyn Lloyd in the chair, and soon found itself considering two competing resolutions. One was put forward by the Indian delegate, Krishna Menon, a sharp-tongued intellectual with all the worst faults of the agile lawyer which his British education had made him, a man who in those years attracted more cordial hatred in Western countries than seems, fifty years afterwards, quite comprehensible. His resolution recognised Egypt's sovereign rights over the canal, called for a review of the Constantinople Convention, and proposed the creation of a body representing users' interests, to be associated with the Egyptian management of the canal. In retrospect there is a clear reasonableness to the proposal; but in all essentials it acquiesced in Nasser's coup, did nothing to assuage the Western powers' indignation at Nasser's action and glossed over their conviction that international management of the canal's operations remained essential.

Dulles put forward an alternative resolution. It called for a new convention to set up a Suez Canal Board which would run the waterway. Egypt would always have a seat on it; other members would be chosen to reflect their usage of the canal, their trade patterns and a representative geographical spread. The board would be responsible for development and enlargement of the canal, as well as daily operations and maintenance. Egypt would get a fair and rising income from the canal. Arbitration machinery was provided for as well as sanctions against abuse. The United Nations would be involved in any crisis over the canal that threatened to lead to the use of force. This met all essential British and French requirements. It would put the management of the canal back in international hands. If Nasser accepted it his position in the Arab world would be destroyed and if he did not they would have their *casus belli*. It was manifestly unpalatable to Nasser, and glossed over the reality that in international law the canal was Egypt's.

So, as is normal on such occasions, the opening speakers talked past one another. The Soviet delegate, Shepilov, savaged Dulles's proposal and supported Menon's, as did two delegates from the Bandung bloc of countries. They were in a small minority among the twenty-two, the rest of whom lined up behind Dulles's proposal. The vote demonstrated that as long as the Big Three held together they could still call the shots.

There remained the problem of how the majority view should be put to Nasser. The man he had sent to London had reported faithfully, but he could not take delivery of the conference's conclusions. Britain and France wanted Dulles himself to take the package to Cairo. They were in no doubt that Nasser would reject what was proposed, and wanted the United States to be directly involved when that happened. Dulles saw what they were after and swerved away. In the end the twenty-two chose a five-man delegation: the foreign ministers of Ethiopia, Iran and Sweden and a senior Middle East expert for the United States, with Robert Menzies, the Prime Minister of Australia and an old friend whom the British trusted, in the lead.

For the British and French there was no question of checking their military preparations while the delegation met Nasser. At the least, the build-up of the military threat would serve to concentrate Nasser's mind. More likely, he would turn the conference proposals down, leaving Britain and France with no alternative but to do what they wanted to do anyway, let loose their forces against him and destroy him. When they did that they still hoped at least for American understanding, and perhaps for American support.

So the delegation set off for Cairo, with Menzies billed in advance as a tough, no-nonsense Australian who would talk sense into Nasser. They met him on 3 September. On that date seventeen years earlier Britain and France had drawn a line under their long appeasement of Adolf

Hitler, the man with whom they had too often compared Nasser's rather different menace to the world. Menzies did his best to put across Dulles's proposal, but wrap things up as he might, his conviction that his real job was to tell Nasser what the world expected of him showed through. Nasser on the other hand was looking for a chance to pick away at the proposal on the table, perhaps reshape it, or, if that was never in prospect, to show his people just how resolute he could be in defence of Egypt's canal. He wanted to draw Menzies into negotiation. They talked, but there was never much chance of agreement unless Nasser's nerve cracked.

It did not. For several days the visitors and the Egyptians went round the houses of argument, but there was nothing on which they could have based a deal. The differences between them had been clear in London to anyone who compared Dulles's approach with Menon's. Now they had moved beyond diplomatic glosses. On 9 September the mission packed up to go home. They had a farewell meeting with Nasser but it brought no glimmer of agreement. When they had gone Nasser said to the American ambassador: 'The British and French are going to stay out there in the Mediterranean until they find a pretext to come in.'[32] He was right, for that was exactly what Eden and Mollet wanted.

12 SEPTEMBER: USERS' ASSOCIATION OR UNITED NATIONS?

It had taken Menzies a week to establish that Nasser was not to be moved by threats, soft words and ingenious diplomacy. Now, on 12 September, British MPs were coming back from their summer break and Eden had to tell them the bad news. It was a grim political and diplomatic prospect. Britain and France remained convinced that only force could solve the problem, the sooner the better. In Washington however the Americans went on making their doubts slyly public, and in doing so they lessened the already slim chance that Nasser could be browbeaten into submission. The British hoped that they might see sense when once their presidential election was out of the way, but that was still two months distant. Meanwhile, international pressure on Britain and France was increasing, and opinion in Britain – initially so robust – was fragmenting.

On 4 September, however, fresh back from his Labor Day holiday,

Dulles came up with a new proposal, the idea which became known first to diplomacy and then to history as SCUA – the Suez Canal Users' Association. He suggested that a body representative of users and of the international community should be formed. It would collect canal dues, just like the group proposed under the plan Menzies took to Cairo. But SCUA would do so alone, without Egyptian cooperation, and it would operate from ships stationed offshore, at both ends of the canal. The canal would go on operating but the financial benefits would flow not directly to Nasser but initially at least to SCUA.

It was a far-fetched proposal and opinions about it were divided. The French were confident that Dulles was not in earnest, but merely playing for time. A general reaction was that the scheme was operationally impracticable. In any case it would lead to dangerous friction with the Egyptians, who could easily sabotage it. It might lead to open conflict – a prospect which some saw as a fundamental drawback of the scheme and the British and French as its hidden advantage. Selwyn Lloyd thought SCUA could be made to work and exploited if it did not, and in a two-day meeting in Downing Street persuaded Mollet and Pineau that they should try it. But it must not look like an Anglo-French proposal: Dulles's name and reputation as its author must be firmly attached to it.

Should Britain and France also turn to the Security Council? Neither set much store on its value, and the French, now that they were converted to the attractions of SCUA, argued that to go to New York would undermine whatever hopes there were for the users' group. But as the Allies' military preparations and psychological pressure built up, they feared that if they made no move to involve the United Nations, Nasser would get there first with a complaint of his own. In any case, for the British an appeal to the Security Council had positive attractions: it would unite the nation behind Eden. Yet Dulles, with mysterious considerations of his own in his devious mind (some thought they included a proprietorial reluctance to encourage United Nations interest in the Panama Canal), stood out against involving the Security Council.

The British were faced therefore with a choice. They could go to the United Nations or stay with the Americans. Lloyd agonised and then, on the eve of Eden's statement to the House of Commons, told the Prime Minister that he was convinced they should turn to the Security Council. Eden too wrestled with the dilemma and then chose to stand with Dulles. He presented to the House of Commons not the reference to the United Nations which members were expecting but the Users' Association proposal.

Eden used precise language that had been agreed with the Americans and the French, but precision and agreement did not save him. At once, his critics turned on him, arguing that SCUA, with all its risk of a collision with the Egyptians, was a deliberate provocation. Some condemned it out of hand, others argued that it must at the very least be accompanied by reference to the United Nations. Eden was in trouble in Parliament, as he had not been since the debate about Glubb's expulsion from Jordan back in March.

Then Dulles, who had created Eden's dilemma, made matters worse. He went into a press conference in Washington straight from a meeting with the Egyptian ambassador. The ambassador had argued that the users' association would carry the risk of war. Not at all, Dulles told a journalist: 'We do not intend to shoot our way through. It may be we have the right to do it; but we don't intend to do it as far as the US is concerned.'[33] Even worse, Dulles presumed to speak for Eden: 'I did not get the impression that there was any undertaking given by him to shoot their way through the Canal.'[34] The agreed front between Britain, France and the United States fell apart at its first test. At the Foreign Office the Permanent Under Secretary, Ivone Kirkpatrick, tried to summarise the reasoning of that most devious of American Secretaries of State: 'Dulles, having rejected the idea of going to the Security Council, having decided that other economic pressure was not possible, having thought up SCUA, would very soon find out that SCUA did not work. The choice would then be force or surrender to Nasser.'[35]

Eden had to face the music in a deeply divided House of Commons. Even the Conservative Party was split: 'a good many Tories', Macmillan recorded, 'mostly young and mostly sons of "Munichites" ... began to rat ...'[36] The two-day debate was one of Eden's worst Parliamentary experiences. In the end 248 members voted against the government, only 319 in support. In private Eden recalled memories of Munich. The mood of embattled national unity with which most Britons had greeted the seizure of the canal in July was by now dissipated. The country was near to war, its military preparations deliberately flaunted before the world, and yet it was divided, split down the middle into hostile camps.

Three days later, on 15 September, most of the Suez Canal Company's non-Egyptian staff withdrew their services. In pulling them out the company acted by agreement with the British and French governments, but there was no trouble with the Egyptians, who promptly issued exit permits to all the departing foreign staff. The Greek pilots stayed on; twenty-two new foreign pilots were recruited, as well as thirty-six Egyptians.

This was the moment to demonstrate that the Egyptians could not run the canal. The British Ministry of Transport rather transparently contrived that an unprecedented number of ships should present themselves at Port Said and Suez to use the canal, calling the wheeze 'Operation Pile Up', and hoping that it would overwhelm the Egyptians. If they failed Britain and France would have an excuse to demand the right to sort things out, but the placid waters of the canal remained undisturbed: 'The Suez Canal started yesterday functioning without any help from foreign pilots', Nasser announced; and then, rubbing Britain's nose in the failure of its little conspiracy: 'Yesterday, for the first time in living memory, fifty ships arrived at Port Said and Suez wishing to transit.'[37]

The Egyptians had demonstrated that they could manage the canal unaided. They had also shown that in operational terms the users' association was superfluous. The neutrals, particularly the Scandinavians, began to back away from it. Dulles, still in the driver's seat, negotiated changes that steadily eroded SCUA's authority. 'Dulles pulled rug after rug from under us', wrote William Clark, Eden's press secretary, 'and watered down the Canal Users' Association till it was meaningless.'[38] SCUA went the way of many another piece of ingenuity wrung out of the cross-purposes of 1956, and sank into oblivion.

By now British and French suspicions of the Americans were running deep. British ministers could not bring themselves to see their wartime friend Eisenhower as an enemy, but they dismissed him as a lightweight, a man who, in election year, wanted to hear only news of peace. Dulles they thought malignant. He was no lightweight but he was secretive, devious, inconsistent, preoccupied with his own shifting policies. He talked of finding common ground with his allies but seemed impervious to their difficulties. Over SCUA as over much else he seemed to the allies then, as Eden commented long afterwards, 'as tortuous as a wounded snake, with much less excuse'.[39]

6

Communism Stirs

In mid-February, getting on for 2,000 delegates assembled in the Kremlin for the twentieth congress of the Soviet Communist Party. It was the first to be held since Stalin's death almost three years earlier. Most of those attending were from the Soviet Union, representing over seven million party members, but fifty-five foreign Communist parties were there too, with the Yugoslavs alone excluded. Most of the delegates were party middle managers; but among all the awestruck men and women enjoying a rare visit to the Kremlin palaces were several hundred movers and shakers of the Communist world and the Communist movement at large.

It was a leisurely congress, with its deliberations spaced out over ten full days, and precisely orchestrated. The outside world was given only an authorised version of the proceedings, but it learned of two major highlights, with Bulganin and Khrushchev sharing the glory between them. Bulganin, as Prime Minister, reported on the progress and prospects of the five-year plan; Khrushchev, as First Secretary, on the party's domestic and foreign policy. Their message, to the delegates and to any outsider who was interested, was that all was for the best in the best of all possible socialist worlds.

The congress was to end on 25 February, and the delegates were already packing for home when the Soviet representatives among them were summoned to an unscheduled final meeting. Its agenda and proceedings were to be strictly secret but the substance trickled out first to the foreign delegates, lingering curiously in their Moscow hotels, then over the next few months to ordinary Communists, to the people of the Soviet empire, and to the outside world

Khrushchev was the only speaker, and for four hours he mesmerised his audience with a sustained denunciation of a man, Joseph Stalin, whom they were accustomed, even required, to revere as a genius and a god. In a speech whose text takes up fifty-nine pages of his memoirs,

Khrushchev itemised in passionate language and painstaking detail the sins of the fallen leader.[1] He started modestly, like a speaker at a golf club's annual general meeting, complaining that thirty years ago as her husband lay dying Stalin had been unacceptably rude to Lenin's wife. He went on to document the dead dictator's steady accumulation of power into his own hands. Stalin had ordered the arrest of honest Communists, their examination under torture, their condemnation in travesties of trials, and their despatch to the executioner or to the labour camps. He had refused to face up to evidence that a German attack on the Soviet Union was on the way, and had collapsed when war came. His nerve recovered, Stalin had taken the management of the war into his own hands, but he sheltered himself from its realities, never visiting the front, scarcely leaving the Kremlin. From there he had presided over the Soviet Union's campaigns, careless of the human price of war, dismissing the arguments of his generals, taking personal credit for every military success. Thirty years' unchecked power had turned Stalin into a monster, instinctively arbitrary, paranoid and insatiably vain. Only his death had saved Russia from the consequences of his last months, as he convinced himself that even his doctors were bent on his destruction.

The observant had noted signs earlier in the congress that Stalin's posthumous star was on the wane. Nevertheless, none of the delegates was prepared for Khrushchev's attack on the old leader, and early in his speech he was interrupted more than once, not by anything as untoward as barracking, but by delegates instinctively rising to their feet in the old way to offer ritual applause at a mention of Stalin's name. But as Khrushchev continued, his passion apparent in every gesture and aside, even the most hidebound old Bolshevik began to grasp where the speech was leading. Over those four hours Khrushchev reversed the whole official account of the Soviet Union's history. As he did so it became clear that from now on a different system of belief would be expected of loyal Communists. This was the first major revolutionary event of 1956.

In his memoirs Khrushchev gives an account of the events which had led to the secret speech. It is as partial as anything else in that tendentious book, but it starts, inevitably, with Stalin's death in March 1953 and the struggle for power within the Kremlin which followed. The first step was to contain the powers of Stalin's security chief, Lavrenti Beria;

the second to arrest and execute him. Then, says Khrushchev, the Polit-buro put in train a review of the history of the last thirty years. A review of the trials had led not just to the doors of Stalin's satraps but of Stalin himself.

Next the Politburo had faced the question of how they, Stalin's heirs, should act on all this information, and here opinion was divided. Could they correct injustice and put the record straight without condemning themselves? They had, after all, been Stalin's intimates, working, dining and drinking with him, transfixed like rabbits caught in headlights by their leader's basilisk stare. Here Khrushchev's memoirs, like the speech itself, are markedly disingenuous. In the end, he says, 'the comrades' decided that they must tell the story to the Congress; and in the end they insisted, Khrushchev modestly dissenting, that he should be their spokesman. So much for the genesis of the most important speech Khrushchev ever made.

Its reception, Khrushchev claims, was entirely favourable. In saying this he does less than justice to his own courage. For inevitably the dele-gates were shocked, frightened, divided. In its early stages, recorded a KGB man in the audience, there was 'a deadly silence; you could hear a bug fly by'. Someone else felt 'anxious and joyous at the same time' and marvelled that Khrushchev 'could have brought himself to say such things before such an audience'. 'We didn't look each other in the eye,' recalled a third, ' ... whether from shame or shock or from the simple unexpectedness of it, I don't know.' Yet another remembered that as the delegates streamed out of the hall one heard everywhere a single word, endlessly repeated, 'yes'.[2]

Khrushchev stressed the sensitivity of what he had to say: 'We cannot let this matter get out of the party, especially not to the press. It is for this reason that we are considering it here in a closed Congress session. We should know the limits; we should not give ammunition to the enemy; we should not wash our dirty linen before their eyes.'[3] But it was inevitable that the speech would leak, and quickly; and Khrushchev intended that it should: 'I very much doubt that Father wanted to keep it secret...,' his son Sergei said long afterwards. 'His own words provide confirmation of the opposite – that he wanted to bring his report to the people. Otherwise all his efforts would have been meaningless. The secrecy of the sessions was only a formal concession on his part ...'[4]

After the speech Soviet spokesmen read the text slowly to Eastern European delegates at the Congress, giving them time to take notes. Within a month the Polish Communist Party distributed translations to every party cell in Poland, and from the party it leaked to the public at large. The Israelis got hold of a copy in Warsaw and passed it to the CIA. By the spring the Western newspapers were printing special supplements, giving Khrushchev's astonishing words to the world.

In one light the speech said nothing more about Soviet history than any open-minded observer of Soviet politics from outside the Communist world had known for many years. The liquidation of one Soviet politician after another, like the decimation of the officer corps in the 1930s, was a matter of horrifying record. The demands of wartime good fellowship had moved the West to play down accounts of the failure of Stalin's nerve in the early months of the German attack, and to go along with glorification of his wartime role; but it was clear to anyone with eyes to see that he was not the all-knowing god of war that Soviet hagiography had made him. And after the war, as West and East became enemies, Western critics were happy enough to play up Stalin's crimes. The secret speech provided welcome confirmation, out of the mouth of a Soviet leader himself. 'I told you so' was the Western response, usually accompanied by the wry observation that it was only Stalin's treatment of his party comrades which had provoked Khrushchev to such venomous indignation, not his greater crimes against the Soviet people at large and against the satellite nations.

Veljko Micunovic, the Yugoslav ambassador-designate to the Soviet Union, picked up this last point in his diary even before he left for Moscow. 'Not even in secret', he wrote, 'did Khrushchev mention the millions of completely innocent Soviet citizens whom the Soviet leaders sent to their deaths; he spoke mainly about a few outstanding individuals, high officials of the CPSU [Soviet Communist Party] who were executed for nothing.' Nor did he recognise that Moscow had imposed 'the very same system of executing innocent and decent people …on all the countries of Eastern Europe'.[5] And six weeks after the speech, when he called on Khrushchev for the first time, he noticed a portrait of Stalin, still on display with one of Lenin, in the outer office.

The Congress provided clues to the future development of Soviet policy. To William Hayter, the British ambassador in Moscow of the day, it was the Congress's doctrinal innovations which were important: 'They were in essence two. The first was the repudiation of Lenin's doctrine that war between the capitalist and the Communist countries was ultimately inevitable. The second was the announcement that Socialism or Communism could in certain circumstances be established in a bourgeois state constitutionally ... and that a violent revolution was not a necessary antecedent.'[6] For practical reasons, the Kremlin was trimming its ideology in its search for détente with its Western enemies, and that development of Soviet foreign policy was the ambassador's natural first concern.

But for the ordinary Russian citizen who got to hear of the secret speech, or for the citizen of any of the countries of the Soviet camp, it had a more immediate significance. If Khrushchev could condemn Stalin's crimes against Communists today, he might condemn his crimes against ordinary people tomorrow. And that might lead to some relaxation of Communism's iron grip upon society, some attention to the everyday concerns of ordinary people. Perhaps before too long the detainees would be coming home from the camps; perhaps their origins would not always mark down 'Kulaks' or other middling citizens as class enemies; perhaps at last ordinary people might get jam today to spread on the promise of a socialist New Jerusalem in their grandchildren's day. Perhaps, in short, they might see a reduction in the hysteria with which ordinary Russians had been governed for thirty years and ordinary East Europeans for a decade.

MARCH: NAGY CONSTRAINED

It did not take long for word of Khrushchev's speech to reach Imre Nagy. The man who for two years after Stalin's death had tried as Hungary's Prime Minister to give Communism a human face and set it on a more positive course, and who before 1956 was out was to lead his country in revolution against Stalinism and Soviet occupation, was now living in retirement, in semi-isolation and profound political disgrace. But he had not been a Communist for forty years for nothing. Comrades still whispered to him what was happening in the Central Committee, and at least hinted at what was said to have passed in the more secretive Political Committee. They told him something about Khrushchev's astonishing words.

Nagy's rival, Mátyás Rákosi, had drummed him out of office as Hungary's Prime Minister in April 1955. He also deprived him of all the usual trappings of a Communist leader: membership of Political and Central Committees, seat in Parliament, university chair, place in the Academy of Sciences. Rákosi, who called himself Stalin's best pupil, left Nagy only his pension and his house.

Nearly thirty years after Nagy's execution I visited that house, let by then to a Western diplomat. It is a retiring, rather cramped villa in Orso utca, a tree-lined road in Buda, with a very bourgeois parlour on the ground floor and a conservatory down one side. The first floor, where Nagy took his meals and spent a lot of his time in valetudinarian repose, is adequate but cramped. It is a middle-class, middle-brow sort of house, a suitable home for a middle-of-the-road man like Nagy. He lived there with his wife throughout 1955 and most of 1956. His daughter, son-in-law and two small grandchildren lived next door. The security police kept a close eye on him and few of his friends found the courage to visit him. He was not yet sixty, but he seemed doomed to an obscure old age. 'For all practical purposes', the British Legation reported to London in January 1956, 'Nagy must now be written off as a factor in the political situation of this country.'[7]

Yet Nagy had not written off his political career. He always brought an owlish, academic attitude to Communist politics, and here, in his enforced retirement, he turned to writing. In the course of a year he produced twenty-five essays[8] in which, in laboured prose, he set out his views on political, economic and social issues. He wrote them down to justify himself, and distinguish his position from the men who had driven him from power. Nagy took care to present his essays as contributions to the search for Marxist-Leninist orthodoxy. Only very occasionally did he embark on outright attack on his enemies. But in these essays he defended his own position on one topic after another, and if his arguments were doctrinally correct, as he was convinced they were, it followed that the positions of his party enemies were doctrinally flawed. This was a series of arguments about Marxism-Leninism, pursued with all the tenacity Nagy brought to his politics, with an academic commitment to clear thinking and the search for truth.

Nagy circulated these essays in typescript, cautiously and by hand, to party members whom he thought he could trust and who would at least give him a hearing. It was a dangerous game, and if Rákosi had ever felt able to bring him to trial the essays would have formed a central part of the indictment. Nagy knew that Rákosi was deterred by the knowledge that Moscow kept a careful eye on Communist party doings in each of its East European satellites. For whatever reason, some people in the Kremlin retained an interest in keeping Nagy alive and at liberty, if in the confined liberty of the house in Orso utca, and Nagy felt safe in pursuing the party argument through his coded words.

There is scarcely anyone left today who takes the dictates of Marxism-Leninism with the seriousness which Nagy brought to them. To the rest of us, most of his essays seem tedious, 'how many angels on the point of a needle?' examinations of the world of Marxist-Leninist theory, doctrine and semantics. But over the turn of the year 1955–6, he wrote two which retain a general interest even now, half a century afterwards. In both he threw caution to the winds.

He called the first essay 'Ethics and Morals in Hungarian Public Life' and in it he explored what had gone wrong with Communism since it had seized power in Hungary seven years earlier.[9] Hungary's new rulers, he wrote, 'completely forgot about living society, about man with his manifold, complicated, individual and social relations, at the crux of which are ethical and moral problems'. They had 'crushed the basis of Hungary's young democracy and liquidated our people's democratic forces and the democratic partnerships of socialism'. Sharpening his focus, Nagy turned to the destruction of fellow Communists, in particular László Rajk, Minister of the Interior in Communism's early years in power in Hungary, whom Rákosi had framed and executed in 1949. 'Whatever has become of Communist morality, human respect, and honour,' he asked, 'if there are Communist leaders according to whom the unjustly executed Comrade László Rajk was a coward because he admitted to false charges in order to deceive the party leaders, leaders who act as if it were not themselves who contrived the mendacious charges and the means of getting the confession?'

Nagy had written those criticisms of Rákosi in the winter. Now, in the spring, he learned that Khrushchev in his secret speech had attacked Stalin on just such grounds. It brought him sweet justification, and hope for better things.

Nagy called his second major essay 'The Five Basic Principles of International Relations and the Question of our Foreign Policy' and in it he looked not to past crimes but to future promise.[10] He took as his starting point the five principles of Bandung. The Bandung conference of the leaders of the non-aligned countries convened in the summer of 1955 made quite a splash in the world of the 1950s. It brought together the grand panjandrums of the emerging countries of the Third World, men like Nehru and Soekarno, Nasser and Tito. They saw Russia and China as potential allies, and those profoundly aligned countries were happily invited to a conference of the non-aligned. With equal contentment they joined in subscribing to Bandung's five principles: national independence, sovereignty, equality, self-determination and non-interference, principles which had been crafted to hold any lingering pretensions of the old colonial masters at bay. On these principles the men of Bandung thought they could build their position in the world.

But these principles were sharply at odds with the basis on which Communist internationalism was built, the principle of universal working-class solidarity. They clashed also with the Soviet Union's ingrained assumption that its allies must follow everywhere that Moscow led. When Yugoslavia's Tito refused, Moscow had done everything it could to break him. Now the Russians sat with him at the Bandung conference table, half-reconciled, and subscribed to principles which underwrote his independence. They were principles which if consistently applied would bring down the Soviet empire in Eastern Europe as decisively as what was left of Britain's and France's empires in Africa and Asia.

Thirty years after his execution I settled down to write a biography of Imre Nagy. I found it impossible to decide for certain whether, when he embraced the five principles of Bandung, he recognised how profoundly destructive of Moscow's pretensions in Eastern Europe they were. Was he naïve, or did he write with tongue in cheek? I am still not sure, but I suspect he did not really know what he was doing, nor the risks that he was taking. Nagy showed real heroism later in his career, when he faced execution and refused the recantation that might have saved him, but I think that when he wrote that particularly explosive essay he was confident that Moscow's signature on the principles of Bandung gave him sufficient endorsement and protection.

Yet just as the first of his essays, 'Ethics and Morals', laid a mine under Rákosi's Stalinist system in Hungary, so the arguments in the second, 'Five Basic Principles', laid a mine under Moscow's rule in Eastern Europe. When, in the middle of the 1956 revolution, Nagy based himself on the principles of independence, sovereignty, equality, self-determination and non-interference, Moscow rapidly put him right. There was no room in the Soviet world for principles like these, and

Soviet forces moved in to destroy Nagy's last illusions, and the Hungarian revolution.

APRIL: MR B AND MR K COME TO TOWN

In the middle of April Nikita Khrushchev and the Soviet President, Nikolai Bulganin, paid an official visit to London. It was their first expedition to a Western capital. For them it was a wary exploration of one of their capitalist enemies, for Anthony Eden a chance to meet and size up the Soviet leaders in more relaxed circumstances than the Four Power Summit in Geneva in the summer of the previous year. For anyone determined to look on the bright side, the visit was a further step along the path of détente that had seemed to open in the years that followed Stalin's death: first the Austrian State Treaty of May 1955, then Moscow's attempts to rebuild its bridges to Tito, then the Big Power summit meeting at Geneva, then Khrushchev's secret speech, now London, perhaps eventually Washington.

The visitors, and perhaps Khrushchev especially, suffered a bad attack of nerves, which produced bluster to conceal their insecurity. Sergei Khrushchev travelled with his father, and wrote afterwards: 'Father was nervous. He was particularly worried about making a fool of himself.'[11] MI5 bugged his room in Claridge's, gaining only a knowledge of his social insecurity: its listeners heard 'long monologues addressed to his valet on the subject of his attire'.[12] Years afterwards, in semi-disgraced retirement, Khrushchev himself recalled a conversation with Eden in which the chip on his shoulder is still manifest: 'The next day we had an appointment to visit Queen Elizabeth. We didn't have to wear any special sort of clothes. We had told Eden in advance that if the Queen didn't mind receiving us in our everyday business suits, it was fine. If she did object, that was just too bad ....we weren't going to go out of our way to get all dressed up in tails and top hats...'[13] All the same, Khrushchev went to Buckingham Palace in a brand new suit.

A different kind of insecurity seems to have dictated the Soviet leaders' decision to travel to Britain by sea. Malenkov, a Politburo member on his way down a snake in the Kremlin leadership's perilous board game, had been despatched to Britain to prepare the way for Khrushchev and Bulganin. He travelled by air, in the Soviet Union's new jet airliner, the TU 104. On his return to Moscow the aircraft failed to land on its first approach. 'My Air Attaché', recalls William Hayter, who was waiting on the tarmac, '...told me the aircraft could not have fuel for more than five minutes' flying time left... We kept our anxieties from Malenkov's wife and daughter ... and in due course the aircraft came round again and landed safely, its parachute brakes trailing.'[14]

Such risks were not for Soviet leaders at the top of the Politburo ladder, and Khrushchev and Bulganin sailed for Britain in a modern cruiser of the Red Fleet. In his memoirs Khrushchev of course admits to no fears of flying. He says that they chose this route because the train journey to London would give them a chance to see the British countryside, and records some naïve impressions of 'long stretches of the little red-brick houses' that they passed on the way, 'because they reminded me so much of houses I had seen during my boyhood in the Donbass'.[15] He also tells an elaborate story of the British naval attaché who travels in the cruiser with them. They fear that he will pry into its every secret corner, but they drink him under the table instead. It is a story that gathers resonance from later events in this first top-level Soviet visit to Britain.

Eden was conscious of the potential dangers of the Soviet leaders' visit. Khrushchev, in particular, was a mystery to him and his colleagues. 'How can this fat, vulgar man,' Harold Macmillan had asked himself in Geneva in the previous year, 'with his pig eyes and ceaseless flow of talk, really be the head – the aspirant Tsar – of all those millions of people and of this vast country?'[16] Khrushchev had used a recent visit to India and Burma to abuse the old imperial power; would he, Eden wondered, 'let himself go in extravagant hyperbole' as he had in Burma? But: 'The violence of Mr Khrushchev's speech showed the depth of his ignorance of our country and I did not think this a reason to deny him the chance of informing himself.'[17] Behind this leaden language lay Eden's determination to build on the progress that he believed he had made at Geneva in 1955.

And so to the talks themselves. They covered Anglo-Soviet relations; the European scene; the Middle East and the Far East; and that will o' the wisp of the postwar years, disarmament. They started in Downing Street, and Eden seems to have relished them: they were 'the longest international discussions between two powers in which I have ever taken part'. Khrushchev felt or professed to feel the strain of the discipline they demanded: 'See how well trained we are,' he said to Eden, 'we file in like horses into their stalls.'[18] Bulganin played the role of figurehead with some of the aplomb of a gentleman of the old school, but Khrushchev quickly took the leading role from him. Both impressed Eden: 'I found Marshal Bulganin and Mr Khrushchev perfectly capable of upholding their end of the discussion on any subject. They did this without briefs or detailed guidance from any of their advisers. I have spent my whole life conducting international affairs and I viewed this performance with respect'.[19] Khrushchev's recollection of the talks is more dismissive: 'Substantively our talks didn't add much to what had come out of our Geneva meeting ... The West were still trying to coax us into an accommodation on their terms.'[20] And a cold-eyed Foreign Office official recorded in his diary that the visitors told the British that 'they would make as much trouble for us in the Middle East as they possibly could. They were as good as their word.'[21]

Their hosts wanted to expose Khrushchev and Bulganin to a variety of experiences in Britain. So 'Bulge' and 'Crush', as the irreverent called them, went to Oxford, where to their mystification a large crowd sang 'Poor old Joe'. Crowds booed them and again mystified Khrushchev, but when he was told what the racket signified he started muttering 'boo' back. Selwyn Lloyd records a sharper incident, a happening which strains one's credulity and which security precautions would make quite unimaginable today. A woman spat at Khrushchev. Incredibly, Khrushchev took the insult calmly: 'I wonder why she did that; I have never done her any harm.'[22] The Queen had the visitors to tea, and congratulated them on their new airliner which had so nearly been the death of Malenkov: 'Yes,' Khrushchev told her, 'it was an excellent plane – very modern, undoubtedly the best in the world.' In his memoirs he praises the Queen too: 'She was completely unpretentious, completely without the haughtiness that you'd expect of royalty. She may be the Queen of England, but in our eyes she was first and foremost the wife of her husband and the mother of her children.'[23] Chequers, when Eden invited them there, did not much impress the visitors: long afterwards Khrushchev recalled nothing more than its placid countryside, like 'our own Orel and Kursk provinces'; and the sulphur generated by the house's anthracite-burning stoves, which covered everything with a sticky film and reminded him of the Donbass coalfields in which he had grown up. With something like shamefacedness he also recalled the brutality with which he had told Clarissa Eden that the Soviet Union had missiles that 'could easily reach your island and quite a bit further'.[24] But the experience that most took him aback was dinner in London with Hugh Gaitskell and other leaders of the Labour Party.

It had the inevitability of social disaster about it. The visitors could not bring themselves to see non-Communists as real Socialists. Their hosts were well aware of what Communists had done to Social Democrats in Eastern Europe. Khrushchev and George Brown had both drunk too much. Tempers flared, voices rose and the animosity consumed the whole party. Richard Crossman, himself no slouch at contempt for others, recorded in his diary: 'I will never forget his contemptuous attitude to us, his couldn't-care-less suggestion that we should join the Russians because, if not, they would swat us off the face of the earth like a dirty old black beetle.'[25] It all ended with Khrushchev leading his party out of the room in anger, and refusing to shake Brown's hand when he tried to make up on the following day.

The collision had involved two men of similar temperament, both self-righteous and thin-skinned. The incident went wider than a personal clash, however. It must have brought home to Hugh Gaitskell an exchange with a colleague earlier in the visit. Khrushchev, Gaitskell said, seemed to him rather like an 'agreeable pig'. 'Yes', was the reply, 'Animal Farm.'[26] In terms of Realpolitik the clash did no lasting harm, and may have given the Conservatives some innocent pleasure. But it illustrated how far East and West were from the meeting of hearts and minds which the visit was intended to bring about.

A second incident came to cloud the bonhomie and outweigh any goodwill the visit might have generated. While Khrushchev and Bulganin were still exchanging pleasantries and insults with their various hosts, the press got hold of an explosive story. A Royal Navy reserve officer, Commander 'Buster' Crabb, had gone missing while diving in Portsmouth Harbour. The Russians complained that they had spotted him near their ship. A succession of British admirals mishandled the inquiries that followed, and eventually – far too late – the story got to ministers. The Prime Minister had long since decreed that no attempt should be made to study the ship's secrets while she was in British waters, but the order had gone astray; officers far down the chain of command had blithely launched Commander Crabb on his ill-fated expedition.

A month afterwards, Crabb's headless and handless body was found floating in the murky waters of Portsmouth Harbour. The press went to work, and established that Crabb had spent a night in April in the Sallyport Hotel in Portsmouth. But the Chief Constable of Portsmouth had sent an emissary to remove the relevant page from the hotel register. Stonewall as the government might, it was quite obvious that some British agencies had been behind Crabb's fatal expedition. It seemed equally obvious that Russian frogmen had disposed of a troublesome snooper, but the Soviet Naval Attaché in London could stonewall with the best of them: 'Commander Crabb was an English frogman, not a Russian. Therefore we cannot say anything. It is a matter for your Admiralty'.[27]

For the British government the affair was a profound embarrassment. For the visitors it was further proof that, for all the Queen's openness and the Prime Minister's professional charm, the capitalist tiger could not shed his stripes. The First Sea Lord, Lord Mountbatten, tried to brush aside the diplomatic disaster his service had provoked: 'I'd go to Moscow tomorrow to meet Khrushchev,' he told a friend. 'I'd say "You want to be friends? Let's be friends!" I know they killed all my family but that mustn't stand in the way of getting on with them now.'[28] It would take more than Mountbatten's boyish charm and impassioned name-dropping about his royal connections to repair the harm that the whole daft episode had done to Eden's attempt – as it turned out, his last – to build better relations with the Soviet Union.

7 JUNE: IMRE NAGY ENTERTAINS

On 7 June Imre Nagy celebrated his sixtieth birthday. A 'round birthday' is a considerable occasion everywhere east of the Rhine, and many of his friends and acquaintances took their political courage in both hands and took tram or taxi or even official car to his house to celebrate with him and his wife, daughter and son-in-law.

All the same there was a lot of tension in the air in Orso utca that afternoon. Nagy, whom we last saw scribbling away in quiet retirement in March, was still in political disgrace. Since then the shock-waves of Khrushchev's denunciation of Stalin had spread through the East European satellites. Men who had been held as political prisoners since the late 1940s were coming home and describing bad food, foul conditions, torture and the ever-present threat of execution that had shaped their lives behind bars. The odd brave dissident was beginning to draw quiet attention to the parallels between Stalin's rule and Rákosi's. But Imre

Nagy's expulsion from the party and from every kind of public office still stood. Someone in Moscow was clearly protecting him, but the Russians seemed as far as ever from putting him back in power, in Rákosi's place.

Nagy had been slowly recreating his political profile in those first months of 1956. His essays had reminded his old comrades of his existence and of his views. It was more difficult for him to remind the general public of what he had stood for in his time in power from 1953 to the end of 1955. But a friend recalls him saying 'I am going out to draw attention to myself.'[29] By the early summer he had taken to showing himself in public, a benevolent, bourgeois figure in spats, stiff collar and bowler hat, who now occasionally took one of Budapest's thumping, belching buses from his suburban backwater into the heart of the city in Pest.

Stephen Vizinczey, at the time an unpublished and unknown Hungarian playwright for whom the notoriety earned by his book *In Praise of Older Women* lay a decade and a new language away in the future, met him on one of these expeditions: 'Or rather, I walked beside him for a while on Rákóczi Avenue in Budapest in the spring of 1956. I was among the first to recognise the portly gentleman with the farmer's moustache, strolling in the sunshine, and so I was able to stay quite near him on the sidewalk; those who came by a few minutes later could find room only on the road. Soon there were so many people trying to follow him that they filled the whole avenue. It was ... the Budapest version of a ticker-tape parade: silent cheers for a man in disgrace.'[30]

Sometimes Nagy took his grandchildren into town with him – a boy of five and a girl of four. He sat in a coffee shop with them, bought them ice creams, smiled in his grandfatherly way at anyone whose interest in the children caught his eye. It was a very unpolitical way of making a political point, and in Budapest, that most instinctively political of cities, word of his demonstration spread from mouth to mouth. Now, on his birthday, people came to see him. Some of his visitors were in disgrace as he was, others were comrades who had kept their party cards and were now taking a calculated risk in visiting him. As they arrived some of them defiantly turned (and many more of them subsequently claimed that they turned) to show their faces to the security policemen and their cameras. His guests filled Nagy's crowded living rooms and conservatory, spilled over into the garden. They drank a glass of wine with him, brought him a flower, a bottle of brandy or a book of poetry. It was a very conventional event, and yet political symbolism and some danger ran right through it. A bold minister of the government came to a happening which a Communist party hack was to describe long after Nagy was dead and buried as 'a demonstration against party policy and in favour of Imre Nagy'.[31] As political demonstrations go it was very low-key, but it served to remind party and country that Nagy was still available for political service.

27 JUNE: THE PETÖFI CIRCLE DEBATES THE PRESS

The mood in party and country had been changing in the few months since Nagy sat down in isolated disgrace to write his subversive essays. The party's confidence had been profoundly shaken by Khrushchev's denunciation of Stalin. Critics and dissenters now felt bolder. The ordinary people sensed that change was in the air. And by the early summer, about the time of Nagy's birthday party, that sense of unrest had begun to take concrete and effective form.

Young intellectuals, most of them still Communist party members, had begun to form discussion groups and invite their elders to address them. At first the party seemed to accept these meetings and try to take control of them; but soon they developed into unheard-of challenges to the party's authority. One group in particular emerged, the Petöfi Circle, named after the young revolutionary poet who was killed in the 1848 uprising against the Habsburgs and whose poetry still remained central a hundred years later to Hungarians' awareness of themselves and their nationhood. Through the spring and early summer of 1956 the Petöfi Circle held a series of debates, each with a different theme, each with different principal speakers. So its members heard passionate discussions of the economy, history, philosophy. Each occasion produced collision between party loyalists and the party's critics. One encounter between old party activists and younger people had people calling the leadership 'criminals'. Finally, on 27 June, just three weeks after Nagy's birthday party, the Petöfi Circle scheduled a debate about the press.

Earlier meetings had attracted two or three hundred people. This one was heard by an audience of 6,000, gathered in the meeting room itself, in overflow gatherings nearby, and on the street outside. It started at 7 pm and went on into the small hours. Speaker after speaker threw aside the old coded caution and attacked Rákosi by name. They condemned the way a small number of people at the heart of the party machine had assumed a mantle of infallibility. They talked about the persecution they themselves had experienced, and some of them about their experiences in Rákosi's gaols. When finally the meeting came to an end the audience dispersed in a mood of daring exultation.

Of course, Rákosi had his spies at the meeting, and he determined to stop the rot of criticism. He hoped at the same time to eliminate the growing threat presented by Imre Nagy, and if he had had his way there would have been mass arrests, show trials, prison sentences. The result might have been to provoke immediate revolution, a revolution that took place not in October but in July. But at this stage the Kremlin, anxiously watching developments in Hungary, took a hand. A Soviet *apparatchik* had already privately visited Nagy to sound out his intentions. Now, as matters came to crisis, Anastas Mikoyan, the Kremlin's most experienced troubleshooter, was despatched to Budapest. On 18 July he came as of right into a meeting of the Hungarian Communist Party's top leadership, the Political Committee. Rákosi was still arguing that the Petöfi Circle must be destroyed, and with it all opposition to the party. Taking their cue from Mikoyan, however, the members of the Political Committee one by one turned against their leader. Mikoyan offered him asylum in the Soviet Union. He was put on a plane to Moscow and seen no more in Hungary.

14 AUGUST: THE DEATH OF BRECHT AND THE ECLIPSE OF MARX

On 14 August Bertolt Brecht died of a heart attack in the Charité Hospital in East Berlin. Three days later he was buried in the Dorotheen Cemetery, in a zinc coffin to hold at bay the putrefaction whose prospect had haunted him. He had written that he wanted his gravestone to say 'He made suggestions, others carried them out', but this was a suggestion of his that others did not implement. In fact, his headstone carries the single word 'Brecht'. He lies close to his favourite philosopher, Hegel.

Brecht's life was of a piece with the unfolding tragedy of German history in the first half of the twentieth century. Born into a comfortable middle-class family in Augsburg, Brecht came to Berlin in 1924 at the age of twenty-six. He was full of radical passion, and in Berlin in the 1920s he created an entirely new kind of theatre. It was dry-eyed, sceptical and rational, an explicit challenge to Expressionism, which he saw as a product of the self-indulgence which had taken Germany into the First World War. As the threat of Hitler grew, Brecht's commitment to Marxism increased. He knew that he was becoming a marked man and on the day after the burning of the Reichstag in 1933 he fled from Germany with his family.

Brecht spent the next fifteen years in exile – first in Scandinavia and then in Los Angeles. In exile he wrote his masterpieces, most notably *Mother Courage and Her Children* and *The Life of Galileo*. But like any artist of the Left in postwar America, he got across the House Un-American Activities Committee. Smoking foul cigars throughout his interrogation, he bewildered the Congressmen with his convoluted and evasive answers about his relationship with Communism. The next day he left the United States, never to return.

Within a year, Brecht was back in Berlin. He made his home in the Soviet sector and set up the Berliner Ensemble there, with his wife Helene Weigel as the leading actress. The Berliner was lavishly funded by the East German government and gave him the stage on which to present the plays he had written in exile. It was extraordinarily successful, and Brecht's own 1949 production of *Mother Courage* was one of the seminal achievements of twentieth-century theatre.

The East German regime did well by Bertolt Brecht, endowing him with flat, car, chauffeur and a setting in which to present his work, but the circumstances of his life in Berlin became increasingly contradictory. He was a lifelong Communist, and he saw the regime as the last best hope for Germany. He knew that he ought to accept the Leninist view that violence was necessary to the transformation of society. But he had recognised the terrible facts of Stalinism in the 1930s. Now he was increasingly repelled by the East German regime's worship of Stalin, its cult of the leader's personality and its repression of the individual, the ordinary worker above all.

Then in June 1953 came the short-lived uprising in East Berlin. For a few days ordinary Berliners, most of them workers, rose against the regime. From the western sectors of the city the world looked on while Soviet tanks cleared the streets. It was a brief forerunner of what would happen in Budapest three years later.

Brecht wrote in his journal that these events 'alienated his existence'. In a truncated letter to the official *Neues Deutschland* he expressed support for the government, while calling for better communication between leaders and people. His enemies called this outright support for Stalinism. Retrospect sees it as an uneasy attempt to identify a middle way between the contradictions in which he was trapped. In private he expressed his real emotions in a poem (unpublished, of course) that captures his irony and anger:

> After the risings of the 17th June
> The Secretary of the Writers' Union
> Had leaflets distributed in the Stalinallee
> Stating that the people
> Had forfeited the confidence of the government
> And could win it back only
> By redoubled efforts. Would it not be easier
> In that case for the government
> To dissolve the people
> And elect another?

After 1953 Brecht stood increasingly aloof from the everyday issues of East German politics. He devoted himself instead to aesthetic questions. But his journals and letters show the regime interfering even in these uncontroversial waters. A great cycle of poems he wrote in that period, the *Buckow Elegies*, brilliantly illustrates his dilemma: the committedly political writer and artist who is confronted by what he knows to be the ultimate bankruptcy of the system he had supported, and yet is anxious not to give succour to its enemies.

Meanwhile the world continued to heap honours on Brecht. The Berliner Ensemble played triumphantly in Paris in 1954 and in London in 1956. He was hailed as the hope of postwar theatre. Yet his private life was becoming increasingly complex, his public position ever more compromised. His writing was turning introspective and his health was failing. Death at the age of fifty-eight gave him personal release. But three months after his body was laid to rest in that zinc coffin the violent repression by Soviet tanks of a workers' revolution shattered all the assumptions which had shaped the lives of Marxists like him. A radical intellectual tradition was eclipsed. It had tried to combine the popular with the intellectual and the political with the human. It stretched back to the French Revolution and now it was laid waste by Soviet action. Bertolt Brecht was both its practitioner and its ornament.

7

'Hungarians Arise!'

6 OCTOBER: RAJK REBURIED

The meetings of the Petöfi Circle in the early summer had shaken the Communist party and stirred the whole country, and with Rákosi's dismissal the opposition had tasted blood. But it still lacked the killer instinct. The intellectuals who led the dissenters had their holiday plans to consider. So men who had denounced the country's political leaders now took themselves off to Lake Balaton, the Danube Bend or the Bükk hills. Ernö Gerö, the man who had succeeded Rákosi, was left to reassert party authority. Through August and September some degree of calm descended on Budapest.

It was ended by a reburial, a class of event with even more potential for political theatre than a statesman's sixtieth birthday party. The date of the reburial was 6 October, which every Hungarian schoolboy knew was the day in 1849 on which the Austrians had executed the thirteen generals of Arad, who had fought against them in Hungary's war of independence. It took place in Budapest's state cemetery, the Kerepesi, where a line of graves of the heroes of the workers' movement had been planted among earlier burial plots when the Communists came to power. The man reburied was László Rajk.

Rajk's story is a prize exhibit among the brutal records of East European Communism in the early postwar years. During the war he distinguished himself as an activist of the small workers' movement, daring to agitate and trying to organise opposition to Hungary's Right-wing government. After it he emerged as a determined Communist leader. In the coalition government formed immediately after the war the Communists seized control of the Ministry of the Interior, responsible for police, security and justice. In 1946 they put Imre Nagy into the job, but he hated the work, lacked the toughness to use it against his party's enemies, and within six months moved on to gentler pastures. Rajk, younger and much tougher, took his place, and used his powers brutally against his party's enemies. The Prime Minister of the day, the Smallholder leader

Ferenc Nagy, wrote of him afterwards that he was 'the very personification of the half-educated Communist, a resolute and fanatical exponent of the most violent moves precipitated by Communist ideology. If the latent evil in this gentle-seeming schoolteacher had become evident sooner, I would never have accepted him as a member of my cabinet.'[1]

Ferenc Nagy himself was driven out of office and took himself off as a defeated refugee to the United States. The Communists took absolute control of Hungary and on Christmas Day 1948 they arrested the last man to stand out against them, the country's Roman Catholic primate, Cardinal József Mindszenty. The torturers of Rajk's security police took only a month to prepare that proud and cantankerous prelate for a show trial, at which he was sentenced to life imprisonment. And in May 1949, in elections orchestrated by Rajk, 95.6 per cent of the electorate voted for the Communists.

Then the Communist party turned on its own. Two weeks after the election Rákosi had Rajk himself arrested. He was held in the secret police cellars throughout a summer in which the streets of the capital were given over to the progressive politics and youthful junketings of the International Youth Festival. They took four months to break his will and in the end a party colleague, János Kádár, was sent to complete the job.

Kádár passed for a personal friend of Rajk's, and had stood sponsor for his baby son. He went to Rajk in his cell and urged him to confess his guilt for the party's sake, promising him his life in return. Rajk agreed, and at his trial he confessed to the implausible charge of plotting with Yugoslavia's Tito to bring down Communism in Hungary. He was condemned to death and hanged. Macabre legend has it, true or false, that his wife Julia was obliged to watch her husband's execution.[2] She got a long prison sentence, her baby son having been taken from her for adoption by an unnamed party member. Before long Rákosi had Kádár arrested too, and despatched him into Hungary's own Gulag archipelago.

By 1956 the times they were a-changing. We have seen Nagy in one of the essays he wrote in retirement showing up Rajk's trial for the travesty it was. Then, as Gerö strove to better his relations with Tito, Julia Rajk was released from prison. She demanded rehabilitation for her husband – and a state burial for what was left of his bones. The party first prevaricated, then yielded.

The day of the reburial was bleak and windy, but it attracted anyone who was anyone in Hungarian political circles, as well as many thousand anonymous mourners. Rajk's remains, recovered from the unmarked grave in which they had lain since his execution, were placed under the mausoleum of Lajos Kossuth, Hungary's archetypal nineteenth-century hero. The coffin was watched over by a guard of honour and flanked by candelabra. Julia Rajk stood beside it, her eight-year-old son at her side. Acquaintances, old enemies and old friends came to greet her, Imre Nagy and his wife prominent among them. Gerö, the man who had succeeded Rákosi, was in Moscow on the day of the reburial. Kádár, Rajk's treacherous friend, now released from prison and making his way back into party favour, was flying back from an official visit to Beijing. It was left to two case-hardened Communists of the old school to represent the regime. One of them, Ferenc Münnich, spoke of Rajk's murderers as 'sadistic criminals who had crawled into the sunlight from the stinking swamps of the "cult of the personality"'.[3] Stirring words they might have been, but they came nowhere near satisfying Julia Rajk. She was intent not just on rehabilitation for her husband but on revenge. 'Murderers should not be criticised,' she said, 'they should be punished.'[4]

21 OCTOBER: GERÖ'S WAY AND GOMULKA'S

When Mikoyan so unceremoniously deposed Rákosi on 17 July and sent him into oblivion in the Soviet Union, he faced a choice over whom to put in his place. Imre Nagy had been Rákosi's rival ever since 1953. Even after his disgrace in 1955, their rivalry had continued, if on a profoundly unequal basis, and in his essays Nagy had precisely targeted Rákosi's evil record. If the Russians wanted a truly different Communist leadership in Hungary, Nagy was the man to provide it.

It would however have been a major step to bring Nagy back into power and to Mikoyan it seemed a step too far. He chose instead to put in Rákosi's place a Communist *apparatchik*, Ernö Gerö, who had been an active Communist since the days of the Spanish Civil War (and, it is said, had been taken as a model by Ernest Hemingway for his portrait of an army commander in *For Whom the Bell Tolls*). Gerö knew the Marxist texts backwards and the corridors of Communist power in all their dangerous sinuosity. But he was a man without the skill and perhaps the wish to get the party's message across to ordinary Hungarians. To Mikoyan, Nagy must have looked like a dangerous, cantankerous oppositionist, and Gerö like a safe pair of hands. But in playing safe, he deprived Hungary of constructive leadership at a time of looming crisis.

The country remained relatively quiet through the rest of July, all August, and into September. Gerö kept effective power close, within a small circle at the top of the party, but the rehabilitation of former political prisoners continued. János Kádár advanced further towards the centre of affairs. Economic concessions were promised and mass outings to Vienna organised – the first opportunity most middle-class Hungarians had had to get outside their country since 1948. But Gerö seemed to find an understanding of the opposition beyond his powers of imagination. No effective action was taken to respond to or to silence the demands for freedom and reform that revived as the summer holidays came to an end. Gerö's political performance in those critical months was wooden and inept. He did not even respond effectively to the emotion of Rajk's reburial. The safe pair of hands brought revolution nearer.

Things were playing out differently in Poland, where the revelations in Khrushchev's secret speech had opened the way to the same kind of unrest as in Hungary. In June, the month in which Nagy celebrated his sixtieth birthday and Hungarian dissidents were showing their courage by exposing their faces to the cameras of the security police, strikes in the Polish city of Poznan had exploded into anti-Soviet and anti-government demonstrations. Generations of Western businessmen knew Poznan for its trade fairs, dispiriting events at which they had to put in an appearance if they were to win a share of East-West trade. Now from the windows of their hotels they saw clashes between stone-throwing crowds and police as violent as the demonstrators. Fifty-three people were killed, security men as well as rioters. The clashes could have spread across the country but the Prime Minister of the day came to Poznan to talk to the demonstrators and the Army was held well back from the fighting. The riots were contained, but the Polish temper remained aroused.

Meanwhile, an old Communist who was to play a central role in what followed was emerging from the disgrace in which he had languished since 1948. Like Rajk, Poland's Wladyslaw Gomulka had been suspected of sympathy for Tito. In 1951 he had gone to prison, and in the tense months in 1953 before Stalin's death he had been in danger of following Rajk to the gallows. Now, like Nagy, he started to circulate analytical political articles; and like Kádár, he began to show himself again in party circles. Finally, on 21 October, a meeting of the Central Committee unanimously elected him First Secretary of the party. Gomulka had come in from the cold, and he pledged himself to reassert Leninist principles in state and party life, just the principles for which Nagy had argued in his essays at the beginning of 1956. So in Poland one man, Gomulka, found himself playing the roles which, in these critical days of October, three men were playing in Hungary – Gerö the new party leader, Nagy the philosophical critic of what the Communist party had done to Leninism, and Kádár, the Communist victim of Communist oppression returned from the political dead and beginning to find a place once again in the leadership.

In embarking on this new and more liberal course Gomulka faced an immediate challenge from the Soviet leaders. To them the Poznan riots in the summer had spelt danger. 'They see in this', the Yugoslav ambassador in Moscow, Micunovic, recorded in his diary at the time, 'the beginning of the counter-revolution which, as they put it here, the West, led by the United States, has organised with the object of splitting the "camp" and separating Poland and the other socialist states from the Soviet Union.'⁵ Since the summer they had been making precautionary military moves. Soviet units stationed in Poland were moved nearer to the capital, the Soviet fleet staged demonstrative manoeuvres off the Polish coast, and troops outside Poland's borders were brought to a high state of readiness. Now the Soviet leaders took umbrage at Polish temerity in appointing Gomulka without consulting Moscow first. To voice their concern and put a personal face on their menaces, Nikita Khrushchev arrived at Warsaw airport. To crown everything, he had drunk too freely on the flight from Moscow and when he went to meet Gomulka he was still much the worse for wear.

Like everyone in the Kremlin, Khrushchev had always taken it for granted that the fraternal parties in the Soviet bloc accepted Moscow's authority even over their domestic affairs. Gomulka's return to power was the first time since Tito's defection that this assumption had been challenged. Khrushchev raged, but the Poles were not to be cowed, and this time the boldness with which they have confronted stronger enemies throughout their history came to their aid. They had deployed commandos of the security forces in combat gear around Warsaw. They put about a rumour that if attacked the Polish Army would invade East Germany and so undermine the whole Soviet presence in Central

Europe. Now Rokossowski, the Soviet marshal whom the Poles had removed from his old office as Poland's Minister of Defence, told the Russians that he could not be sure that Polish officers would obey Soviet orders. 'If Khrushchev insisted on removing Gomulka, major bloodshed could not have been avoided. The Poles were prepared to fight, and the Soviets respected Polish courage if nothing else ... So Khrushchev blustered and then relented.'[6]

Faced with Polish defiance Khrushchev blinked first. He backed away from the showdown he had contrived, saying that the Polish leaders would be left to tackle Polish problems in their own way. The Poles' courageous defiance of Khrushchev that day is one of the forgotten dramas of 1956 – forgotten because it was almost immediately eclipsed by the grander, more public drama of Hungarian defiance of Soviet tanks in the streets of Budapest. As for the Soviet leadership and the Red Army's generals, they suffered that day an unprecedented affront to their authority and self-esteem. They would not want to swallow their pride again when within a matter of days the focus of events shifted to Hungary.

23 OCTOBER: THREE STATUES AND A REVOLUTION

By that fourth week in October, emotions in Hungary were boiling over. Whereas in the summer the lead had been taken by writers, academics and journalists, now the baton passed to university students. By 22 October they were getting together to formulate and publicise their demands. In the words of the United Nations committee report of 1957 on the Hungarian tragedy: '... a number of student meetings took place in Budapest. At the most important of these, held by students of the Building Industry Technical University, the students adopted a list of sixteen demands which expressed their views on national policy. These demands contained most of the points put forward during the uprising itself. They included the immediate withdrawal of all Soviet troops, the reconstitution of the Government under Imre Nagy ... free elections, freedom of expression, the re-establishment of political parties, and sweeping changes in the conditions both of workers and peasants.'[7]

Hungarians had seen nothing like these meetings since the Communist seizure of power. For eight years the dictatorship had silenced any expression of political opinion outside the party. The summer meetings of the Petőfi Circle had broken through that wall of repression, but had then died away. This sudden tumult in the universities seemed to paralyse the regime. Gerö returned from Belgrade only on the morning of 23 October. He gave orders that demonstrations were to be banned; then he wavered; soon he repeated that the students were to be prevented from assembling; finally he recanted. The police chief of Budapest, Sándor Kopácsi, is in the room when a junior minister receives Gerö's orders over the telephone: 'Yes, Comrade Gerö. I agree, Comrade Gerö, your orders will be executed, Comrade Gerö.'[8] He goes with the minister to a student meeting in the School of Engineering. 'I will profit from the presence of police officers in the room', says a speaker, 'to tell them that the students of Budapest have decided to do without your authorisation. The demo will take place anyway. We will shout in the face of the leadership that we want change.' 'Tell them not to get worked up,' Kopácsi says. 'The ban is lifted.' 'Brilliant idea,' says the student leader sarcastically. 'We would like to announce it ourselves,' says Kopácsi, and at once the minister is on the platform announcing that the party organisation of the Ministry of the Interior, the most sinister of all totalitarian ministries, agrees with the students' 'noble determination for renewal'.[9]

The students' march begins, along the Buda bank of the Danube to the bridge that will take them into the heart of the city. As they advance they chant rhyming slogans. 'We do everything, but always too late. Nagy to power, and without delay' is one. 'The leadership must change, and Nagy shall be our leader' is another. Increasingly they turn to more formidable demands: 'Imre Nagy to the Government, Rákosi into the Danube.' Finally they dare to proclaim the unutterable: 'Russians, go home'.[10] At the approach to the bridge, traffic is halted. An official from the Soviet embassy asks Kopácsi's help in getting his ambassador across on his way back to his embassy in Pest. Kopácsi obliges, and is rewarded by a frosty question from the ambassador, relayed by his interpreter: 'Comrade Andropov asks whether, in your opinion, things aren't going a bit far. Some of the banners are insulting to the Soviet Union.'[11] In the next fortnight Andropov was to see worse, as the young people of Budapest hurled Molotov cocktails at Soviet tanks.

The demonstrators reached the statue of Sándor Petöfi, after whom the Petöfi Circle had been named. A precocious young poet and symbol of Hungary's will to be free, Petöfi vanished in Hungary's revolutionary battle armies in 1849. His body was never found, but gallant death in mysteriously romantic circumstances brought him enthronement as

Hungary's eternal poet laureate. Every year on the anniversary of that earlier uprising against oppression, his statue on the Pest embankment of the Danube had been garlanded with flowers. Now student orators recited his poems and declaimed their political opinions. The students applauded, the general public listened, the secret policemen in the crowd took discreet notes of this unprecedented indiscipline.

The crowds remember another hero of Hungary's nineteenth-century struggle against the Habsburgs and Romanovs, the Polish general Bem. Now, after Warsaw's rebuff to Khrushchev, everything Polish is the flavour of the moment in Budapest: 'To the Bem statue' is the cry. Bem's statue stands on the other bank of the Danube, a mile and a half upstream. The students, their numbers now greatly increased by onlookers, move on, passing Parliament on their way. At the Bem statue the President of the Writers' Union reads a manifesto. The students' sixteen demands are proclaimed again. Behind the Bem statue stands an army barracks. Soldiers join the crowd, carrying the Hungarian tricolour. Someone in the crowd notices that the Communist symbol has been cut from the centre of one flag, then from another, then from all of them. Someone else tries to garland old General Bem with a red flag and a tricolour. 'Not the red flag,' shouts an elderly man in the crowd. 'What have you got against the red flag?' he is asked. 'We have our own flag, the flag of Hungary,' he replies.[12]

Again the demonstrators move on, once again crossing the river, back to the Pest side. By now the marchers have been reinforced by 800 officer cadets from the Petöfi Military Academy. They cross the Margaret Bridge. Many turn along the river towards Parliament, others continue towards the boulevard around the eastern side of the centre of Pest. At Marx Square they meet industrial workers coming off the day shift in their factories in the north of the city. Many of the workers join them, particularly the young ones, and at once the demonstrations turn more formidable. They march up Stalin Avenue, past the Soviet Embassy. The route brings them to Heroes' Square, in which Hungary's ninth-century founding fathers are commemorated by a vast semi-circle of stone Magyar horsemen. From there they march on, drawn ineluctably to the statue of Stalin, towering high on its pedestal between a bleak parade ground and the trees of Budapest's City Park.

By now it is evening. 'A demand for the removal of the statue was one of the students' sixteen points, and some enthusiastic young people

climbed the huge monument and set to work on it.'¹³ The police do not
interfere, and Kopácsi tells us why. He gets a message from the police
post near the statue: 'The crowd is knocking down Stalin – request
orders immediately.' Kopácsi asks the man in charge the size of the
crowd: '... there may be as many as two hundred thousand. All of
Heroes' Square and all along the park, it's jammed with people.' How
many men has he got? 'Twenty-five, Comrade Colonel.' 'I suppose that
with twenty-five men you're not about to break up a crowd of one
hundred thousand people?'

There are 'specialists' among the crowd, workers with equipment
brought from their factories. They have blowtorches and cables. Now
Kopácsi fears the physical consequences of Stalin's fall. He orders his
man on the spot to get the crowd back. The statue weighs hundreds of
tons: 'Make sure they're at least a hundred metres back while the specialists are on the job,' he orders. An hour later Stalin comes crashing
down: 'His fall caused not the slightest injury to anyone.'¹⁴ Only his massive bronze boots are left, still planted on the plinth. The crowd rejoices,
and Hungary has taken another step down the road to revolution.

Patriots and poets still gather on Hungarian national holidays at the
foot of Petőfi's statue. General Bem still stands on the other bank of the
Danube. In the end, Stalin's boots went the way of legs, torso and head,
but there is a postscript to the story of his fall. After the defeat of the
revolution some of those who brought him crashing down were
executed. Kopácsi himself spent years in gaol for his equivocal role in
the uprising. He meets political prisoners whose first question to one
another is why they are there. Often he hears the answer, 'I'm a sculptor'. A sculptor was a man who had helped bring Stalin's statue crashing down on that first night of the uprising against the system that
Stalin had imposed on Hungary.

24 OCTOBER: NAGY TAKES OFFICE

Imre Nagy spent the weekend of 20–21 October staying with the owner
of a small vineyard beside Lake Balaton. He visited a wine festival,
pottered in the villages on the low hills overlooking the lake and
enjoyed what was left of the autumn sunshine. Photographs show us a
man who has not a care in the world. Yet in the capital and throughout
Hungary, in Miskolc, Szeged, Pécs and Sopron, the students were calling for marches and demonstrations. Either Nagy was sadly out of

touch with the real world or he was a man who knew how to bide his time. He lingered beside Balaton through Monday, 22 October, and set off for home only next morning.

By that time the students in Budapest were already at odds with the authorities. Gerö, just back from Belgrade, was wrestling with the decision whether he should allow or ban the march from the university into the centre of Pest. By the time Nagy got back to his home in Buda, the outcome was clear to those involved. The march would take place.

Some of his associates quickly gathered, men who had gradually associated themselves with him during his period of disgrace and who shared his conviction that what was left of Stalinism in Hungary must give way to a truer version of Leninism. The most prominent of them was Géza Losonczy, who went to prison with Nagy after the revolution and who died in prison while their trial was being prepared. At forty-six Ferenc Donáth was older than the others, standing midway in age between them and Nagy himself. József Szilágyi became Nagy's secretary during the revolution and was executed afterwards. Miklós Gimes was a journalist who had been close to Nagy for years and was to die with him. His son-in-law, Ferenc Jánosi – Protestant clergyman turned minor Communist politician turned adjutant to his father-in-law – was another member of the group. So was Miklós Vásárhelyi, Nagy's press spokesman who went to prison with him and, thirty years afterwards, formed the Committee for Historical Justice which secured Nagy's rehabilitation.

That meeting on the afternoon of 23 October soon turned acrimonious. His friends told Nagy what had been happening in Budapest: the students' plans, bitter arguments with the authorities, the party leaders aggressive yet indecisive. They were convinced that the time had come for Nagy to act. He remained reluctant to make any move outside party orthodoxy. By his logic, it was time for Gerö to invite him to party headquarters, but no word came from Gerö's office. Eventually the group dispersed, to the university, newspaper offices and party headquarters in Pest. Nagy and Jánosi remained in Orso utca, three miles from the centre of the city. From there they got news of the students' march only at second hand. It was like trying to understand the significance of demonstrations in Trafalgar Square and decisions being made in Whitehall from the discreet distance of Hampstead Garden Suburb.

In the end Losonczy returned to the house and persuaded Nagy to go to the Parliament on the Pest bank of the Danube. They crowded with Jánosi into a small car and drove down into the city. On the way Nagy saw with amazement that the Communist emblem had been cut out of the Hungarian flags along the way. Inside Parliament he got a cool reception. The frightened comrades feared that he had come to take authority from them.

Yet they needed Nagy's help in calming the emotions boiling in the square outside. He allowed himself to be pushed out onto a small balcony to address the crowds. There had been no discussion of what he should say, no attempt to set the stage for him. He was on his own. It was nine o'clock on a dark October evening and at first no one noticed the figure on the balcony above the crowd. Then someone called for silence. Nagy started to speak, and opened with the familiar vocative: 'Comrades'. 'There are no comrades here,' some of the crowd called back. Nagy asked them to go home, vaguely promising that the party would attend to their grievances. It was a pathetic performance, and he scrambled back into the building shaken. Gerö himself could scarcely have done worse.

From Parliament Nagy went on foot to party headquarters in a side street a few hundred yards away. At the door he irritably dismissed his companions, taking only Jánosi into the building with him. To the friends he left outside Nagy seemed to be going to join his enemies.

He found only uncertainty inside. Gerö was huddled with a small group of intimates, still reluctant to accept that Nagy must be called into the leadership. Eventually those members of the Central Committee who were there went into formal session. Nagy and Jánosi were kept waiting in an anteroom.

The news reaching party headquarters was bad. Kopácsi's 'sculptors' were at work on Stalin's statue. Demonstrators were jamming the narrow side street in which the radio building stood, insisting that their demands should be broadcast to the nation. Already there was fighting there; the security police had opened fire on the crowds; army units, summoned to protect the place, were handing over their weapons to the demonstrators. For the Central Committee the only question was whether they should summon Soviet forces to rescue the regime from what looked increasingly like the active majority of the people. In the late evening they decided, or acquiesced in a decision taken elsewhere, to bring Soviet troops into the city.

The first tanks entered Budapest between one and two in the morning of 24 October. They roamed the streets, their hatches closed, their guns silent. Determined men with improvised Molotov cocktails could have made things hot for them, for tanks on their own are vulnerable. But as yet what was happening in Budapest was demonstration, not uprising, certainly not revolution and far from outright war.

Nagy was not present when the Central Committee endorsed the Soviet intervention, but at some stage in the early hours of 24 October Gerö and his comrades recognised that they needed him if they were to quieten the demonstrators and restore order in Budapest. They called him into their meeting, a meeting dominated by men who distrusted and hated him. Gerö proposed that Nagy should become Prime Minister and his old rivals and enemies grudgingly agreed. Nagy accepted – and we shall never know whether he did so fearfully, or with a naïve enthusiasm that at last he could do something to save country and party. At 8.13 am Radio Budapest told the nation that earlier that day a new Political Committee had been formed and that Imre Nagy had been appointed Prime Minister. Half an hour later it reported the imposition of martial law and at 9 am it announced that the government had asked for Soviet help in keeping order.

So now Nagy was back in the office from which Rákosi had driven him in 1955. He assumed responsibility in the worst of circumstances, with the city in arms and the whole country in confusion. He had cut himself off from his natural allies and was trapped in party headquarters among men who until this morning had been his enemies. He had failed to command attention, let alone respect, outside Parliament, and the radio announcement made it look as if he had been involved in the call for Soviet troops. Nagy had accepted responsibility without securing power, the prerogative of the fall guy throughout the ages. Power still lay in the hands of the party leaders, the security police and the Russians – and increasingly in the hands of the demonstrators who that morning still roamed the streets of Budapest.

25 OCTOBER: A MUDDLE AND A MASSACRE

By the middle of the morning of 24 October, the insurgents of Budapest were celebrating three triumphs and nursing three disappointments. They had brought down the statue of Stalin, forced their way into the radio building and heard that Imre Nagy was once again

Prime Minister. Against that, Nagy had sadly failed to respond to their mood when he spoke from the Parliament balcony, their demands had not been broadcast to the nation, and the news of Nagy's return to office had been followed by the announcement of martial law. Above all, Soviet troops were out on the streets of the capital and their very presence protected the Gerö regime. So now the demonstrators who still had the stomach for it milled aimlessly around the streets, looking for drama, looking for events, telling each other that this uprising stood comparison with Hungary's revolt against the Habsburgs in 1848, but unsure what to do next. Individuals obsessively telephoned around the city, asking one another for news – the Budapest telephone service, so erratic in normal times, never failed throughout the revolution. Small groups of insurgents made themselves secure in individual buildings, on strategic street corners and in back alleys. Soviet tanks prowled the main boulevards but could not get into the back streets. Budapest radio, operating now from a stand-by station, broadcast patriotic music and popular music. And after the early morning's announcements, nothing more was heard for a time from the authorities.

Within party headquarters, shut away from the drama of the streets behind a guard of security policemen, the leadership – Nagy now included – debated how to bring the situation under control. Two basic choices were available. They could use force to crush demonstrations and armed resistance, promising to look into popular grievances once order had been restored. This was Gerö's choice. The other course, advocated at first by Nagy alone, was to reach out to the insurgents, listen to their demands, accept them where they could, and get their leaders talking about the nation's options. At this time of crisis Nagy wanted to take the line which he had followed when he was last in office and had advocated in his disgrace. The fact that it involved some surrender of the party's traditional monopoly of the political initiative was unimportant to him. His concern, now as in less critical times, was to rebuild bridges between party and people.

Gerö's view prevailed that morning, but to implement his policy, reliable, usable force would have to be found, and the night's events had swept much of it away. The security police had fought stubbornly at the radio but had been overwhelmed. A few still fought around the city, but most were changing out of uniform and melting into the crowds. Soldiers sent to reinforce them at the radio had instead given their weapons to the attackers, and the army clearly could not be relied on. Faced with thousands of demonstrators, Kopácsi's policemen had had no chance of saving Stalin's statue. Only Soviet forces could do Gerö's dirty work for him, and in this early phase of the intervention they were under orders to avoid action if they could. So armed insurgents – probably no more than 2,000 of them at the beginning – still controlled key points around the city.

At noon Nagy spoke on Budapest radio as Hungary's new Prime Minister. The broadcast was the first the whole nation had heard from him since his disgrace almost two years earlier. In it he called for 'order, calm, discipline' and promised an amnesty to insurgents who ceased fire within the next two hours. It was an uninspiring speech, and the rumour spread that Nagy was to all intents a prisoner in Gerö's hands. Certainly he was a lonely figure at party headquarters that day.

Later on 24 October Mikoyan and Suslov, the Kremlin's troubleshooters, arrived. Three days earlier Khrushchev in Warsaw had yielded to Gomulka; now they faced an even more dangerous situation in Budapest. They tackled it by accepting Nagy's advice that Gerö should go, despatched into exile like Rákosi three months earlier. Party hardliners moved out, reformers like Nagy and Kádár (who took Gerö's place as party leader) moved in. But still none of Nagy's old associates joined him. At noon on 25 October the changes were announced on the radio. Now Nagy had a chance to build his bridge to the insurgents.

A massacre got in his way. It took place in Kossuth Square, the open space in front of Parliament where the crowds had heard Nagy speak two nights earlier. On one of Pest's broad boulevards a crowd of demonstrators had encountered Soviet tanks. The soldiers and the demonstrators looked one another in the eye and on both sides there was a feeling of good fellowship. The Russians agreed to escort the crowd to Parliament. As they entered Kossuth Square security policemen on the rooftops opened fire. They killed a number of demonstrators, but the Soviet tank crews decided that they themselves were the targets. They fired back and in the crossfire more than 100 demonstrators died. It was one of the bloodiest incidents of the whole uprising and among the most significant. Immediately, the insurgents' attitudes hardened. Just as the killings at the radio had diminished the value of Nagy's appointment as Prime Minister, so the massacre in front of parliament devalued the significance of Gerö's dismissal. Where once the call on the streets had been 'Nagy to power', now the crowds united in chanting 'Russians go home.'

23 OCTOBER TO 4 NOVEMBER: A LEGATION UNDER SIEGE

By the time I joined the staff of the British Legation in Budapest in 1958 only the Minister, Sir Leslie Fry, remained of the diplomats who had been with him during the revolution. But he and the Legation's Hungarian staff had vivid memories of the uprising. All of us newcomers lived under its shadow, and at first my principal task was to log the rumours that reached us of the arrests, trials and executions of freedom fighters which still continued, two years after the end of the fighting.

The Legation was a massive, four square, six-storey building that had once been a bank, providing far more accommodation than any small diplomatic mission in normal times could require. It stood on the corner of one of the main squares in the centre of Pest, a hundred yards from the Budapest police headquarters, from where Sándor Kopácsi had tried in vain to grapple with the march to the Petöfi, Bem and Stalin statues in 1956. It was a handsome building, but dirty and the worse for wear, and it still showed the odd scar from the gun battles fought between police and insurgents during the revolution, as well as older scars from the siege of Budapest in the Second World War.

By the time I arrived the story of the Legation's role in the revolution had become almost a folk memory. The Minister showed me the drafts of the telegrams he had sent to London. They described horrendous events, but every full stop was neatly circled in what in those days was still British military style; and the ink was the Minister's personal prerogative red. He told me of the trouble he had had with the Foreign Office, which repeatedly warned him that if he gave asylum to Hungarians he would find himself saddled with difficult guests ever afterwards (as the Americans were when, on 4 November, they gave refuge to Cardinal Mindszenty). So while he took in British and Commonwealth citizens, he turned away Hungarians who came to him for asylum, telling them that if the Russians or the secret police forced their way into the building in search of fugitives he would have no way to stop them. But he had once bent the rules, and he proudly showed me his telegram about it: 'I have this day given political asylum to two Hungarian citizens, aged respectively two years and seven months.' Like all the others, the full stop was firmly circled in red ink.

In the years before the revolution, as long afterwards, the security police kept a watchful eye on the Legation. Opposite the main door was a dry cleaners. There was a well-supported rumour, confirmed when the photographs came to light long afterwards, that the central 'O' of the shop sign concealed a police camera, which recorded the features of everyone who entered the legation. But on the day the revolution began the security policemen vanished, quietly returning to duty only when the revolutionaries had been routed.

Those who were in the Legation during the revolution remember what happened on 23 October. Barriers to contacts with Hungarians suddenly fell away and the telephones rang incessantly, with callers reporting developments. 'The lights in the Legation burned late that night,' wrote someone who was there. 'By the time that most of us went home at midnight the demonstrations were out of control … After the lifting of the curfew at 9 that morning [24 October] all the staff, British and Hungarian, managed to get to work… Movement became dangerous. The bridges were blocked. We were forced to stay in [the Legation] for a week while our families were marooned [in their homes] widely scattered over Buda and Pest.'[15]

Like all the staff of the legation during the revolution my predecessor as third secretary, Mark Russell, had been out and about gathering material for the minister's telegrams to London. He had been on the scene as quickly as the ambulances after the massacre in the square in front of Parliament on 25 October. Yet more than everyone else in the Legation he had a pressing personal matter of importance on his mind – a baby son, born just three weeks before the revolution broke out. For a week, while the fighting raged, his mother nursed the baby alone in their flat in Buda. At last it became possible to get them and all the other families into the Legation, to camp out in dormitories on the empty upper floors of the building.

British journalists too were camping out there in what looked like relative security. Among them was Edith Bone, who had been the *Daily Worker* correspondent in Budapest as the Communists took over in the 1940s. Her paper's politics had not saved her from the security police, and she had spent the years from 1948 to 1956 in a Hungarian prison. The revolutionaries released her into an astonishingly different world, in which it appeared that the people were at war with their Communist rulers. As astonishing was what she saw in the Legation. 'Is that a *baby?*' she asked when she saw Neil Russell.

The Legation was full of strangers that autumn. The Consul had been out in her Morris Minor to round up the small British community. Most of them were elderly ladies, usually widows, astonished to see fighting in the streets of this foreign city in which they had spent their lives. They settled in, camping like the Legation families on the upper floors. The British journalists who came to join them were more demanding. They clamoured to be allowed to use the Legation's diplomatic wireless to get their copy home. After working forty-eight hours non-stop the sole wireless operator collapsed.

There was euphoria in the Legation when, by 28 October, the revolution seemed to have succeeded, with the Russians withdrawing and Hungary revelling in its freedom. But by 1 November it was clear that the Russians were coming back. A convoy was formed, to take all non-essential staff to Vienna. It drove away on 2 November, with Mark Russell in charge, and under the protection of a giant Union flag it reached Vienna that evening. A skeleton staff remained in the Legation, to witness and report on the devastation which descended on Budapest when the Soviet tanks returned.

25–30 OCTOBER: 'RUSSIANS GO HOME!'

There was fighting in provincial centres also as well as in the capital, and one place in particular became for the world a symbol of the revolution. When the revolution broke out Western journalists flocked to Budapest, most of them by road from Vienna. In the first town inside Hungary they found evidence of a massacre. In Mosonmagyaróvár, which was then no more than a modest country town, demonstrators had gathered on 26 October outside the barracks of the security police. The police fired on them, killing scores of people, most of them unarmed. Journalists arriving in the town found bodies laid out for identification, and the bodies too of security policemen lynched in retribution. The unpronounceable town in western Hungary became an early symbol of the tragedy of 1956.

Observers at the time and Hungarian émigrés in the West long afterwards tended to exaggerate the numbers of armed men and women who fought in the Hungarian Revolution. They probably never numbered more than 15,000 people, most of them young. Some were students but more were working people. All of them hated what Communism had done to Hungary, and their reasons for that hatred were as mixed as those of any disparate group of people in any situation. They all wanted personal freedom, and some wanted revenge. A few of them were people of bourgeois, even gentry origin, and some of these may have imagined that in a world from which Communism had been driven they might recover family property. A few may have fought for personal power, as a gang leader, or for personal psychological release There were no-gooders among them, people with little to lose who were attracted by the idea of violence. But there is no evidence to support the charge that came later, that the mass of the revolutionaries were thugs or reactionaries, let alone fascists.

Middle-class men and women were prominent among the masses of people who gave the revolution peaceful support, but they were conspicuous by their absence among the fighters. Communist propaganda claimed that aristocrats and capitalists were behind the uprising, pulling the strings, and that they were rushing back to Hungary from the West to reclaim their old estates. But the uprising was turning out to be dominated by working-class people, still committed to the collectivist ideas that had been introduced into Hungarian politics in the postwar years. It was taking shape as a phenomenon new to the world, an anti-Soviet Socialist revolution.

Inside party headquarters Nagy gradually asserted himself, assisted by Géza Losonczy and Ferenc Donáth when they were brought into the Political Committee, and then he moved the base of his operations to the Prime Minister's traditional office in the north wing of Parliament. There followed a slow – at first too slow and sometimes almost imperceptible – shift in attitudes towards the revolutionaries. But on 27 October Nagy announced a new government, still all-Communist but excluding the most unpopular hard men. On 28 October he announced a truce, and later that afternoon he made a broadcast of real significance. The uprising, he said, was a national democratic revolution – and, by implication, not the 'counter-revolution' the party had labelled it. The AVH, the hated security police, would be abolished. And Soviet troops would be withdrawn from Budapest. Over 29 October the truce held, and on Tuesday 30 October, perhaps the best day of the whole revolution, there were signs of a return to ordinary life. There were signs too that the Russians really were withdrawing from the capital, and Mikoyan and Suslov returned yet again to Budapest and seemed to bring good news with them.

But on 29 October Israeli forces launched a sudden attack on Egyptian troops and set off on their storming march across Sinai towards the Suez Canal. Britain and France quickly called on them and the Egyptians to stop fighting and pull back from the canal, threatening military action if they did not. At once events in the Middle East stole world attention away from Hungary, and you can find old men in Budapest today who are still convinced that it was the Suez crisis alone which prompted the destruction of the Hungarian revolution.

In fact events in Hungary too gave an excuse, and perhaps a reason, to anyone in Moscow or Budapest who believed that things were going too far and had to be reversed. On 30 October an armed gang attacked the headquarters of the Budapest Communist Party. A garrison of young security policemen resisted, but appeals for reinforcement went unheard. Exhausted, the garrison surrendered and came out with their hands up. They were innocent conscripts, but they wore the hated uniform of the security police. At once they were lynched, and photographs of the scene, showing broken bodies dangling from trees, went round the world. Half the world misunderstood and thought they showed Communist misdeeds. But this was the doing of men who called themselves freedom fighters. Like Suez, the massacre offered a reason for the Kremlin to think again about what was happening in Budapest. The revolution, hitherto unmarred, had clean hands no longer.

On that same day, 30 October, Nagy announced the formation of yet another new government. For the first time, the Communist monopoly of office was broken. Now the democratic parties – the Smallholders, the Social Democrats and the Peasant Party – which had been formed in 1945 and driven out of business by the Communists soon afterwards would have a share of power. To most Hungarians it was gloriously good news. To hard-line Communists it sounded like the wilful surrender of the people's power. And inside the Kremlin it sounded like yet another reason to think again.

Nevertheless, after a week of astonishing developments it seemed by 30 October that what was left of Stalinism had been rooted out of Hungarian soil. State terror was gone, Hungary was free, and so were Hungarians. From now on Communism would have to take its democratic chances in free elections. And the Russians, who had conquered Hungary in 1945 and garrisoned it ever since, really were going home.

8

Collusion, Confusion, Collision

As Dulles and the neutrals gutted SCUA at the London conference, the French became disillusioned with the whole idea, for it would not give them the *casus belli* they hoped for. They feared that Britain too might let them down and turned to the possibility of cooperation with Israel. Bourgès-Maunoury, the Defence Minister, who still fancied that he, not Mollet, should have become Prime Minister back in February, talked to Shimon Peres, then a young Israeli civil servant with close links with the French defence establishment. Through Peres he invited the Israelis to send a delegation to Paris to discuss the possibility of acting together against Nasser. The British, he said, knew what was proposed and consented. Thus was taken the first step in the great saga of tripartite collusion of 1956, whose entrails have been examined ever afterwards. What follows is a mere summary of what happened, drawn in the main from Keith Kyle's essential account of the whole Suez adventure.[1]

Even so, it is a complex story, for while the French were toying with *de facto* alliance with Israel, in another part of the forest the Israelis were moving not towards collusion with the Allies but towards a war that might find them fighting British forces. On 11 September an Israeli battalion had entered Jordan in retaliation for an earlier Jordanian incursion. It attacked a fortified police station near Hebron, destroyed the building (as well as a nearby school run by the United Nations) and killed sixteen Jordanians, ten of them soldiers of the Arab Legion. Three days later the Israelis struck again and towards the end of the month yet again, this time killing thirty-nine Jordanians. The Jordanians appealed to Iraq for military backing and a general Arab-Israeli war looked possible. Britain warned the Israelis that it was bound by treaty to support Jordan in the event of war. There seemed to be a real possibility that autumn that Eden was about to get not the war against Egypt that he wanted but a war instead with his French ally's new Israeli friends.

On 30 September those friends arrived in Paris. The team was led by Golda Meir, the Foreign Minister, status-conscious, edgy, uneasy, supported by Israel's most dashing young soldier, Moshe Dayan, and by Shimon Peres. They went at once into secret conversations with the French Foreign Minister, Christian Pineau, and with Bourgès.

The French were proposing that the Israelis should join them in an operation which, if all went well, would at a stroke remove the Egyptian threat to Israel and to the French position in Algeria, and restore the Suez Canal to the people to whom, before Nasser's coup, it had belonged. Pineau tried to convince them that the British, despite their concern with legal niceties, would in time commit themselves to action. As for the Americans, he argued, as long as they were taken up with their own election, they would not intervene.

On the other side of the table Dayan, self-confident and hawkish, half-convinced the French that he could lead an Israeli strike to quick success in Sinai. But the Israelis feared bombing attacks on their cities, perhaps by Soviet bloc volunteers. Only the Royal Air Force had the capacity to destroy Egyptian bombers on their airfields, but could the British be relied on to protect the vulnerable little country which, over Jordan, they saw as a potential enemy? Pineau said that they could, and Bourgès offered the Israelis more fighters, and the possibility of basing French fighters in Israel – which would, of course, have risked getting involved against the Royal Air Force if the British had intervened to help Jordan in a war against Israel.

So far so good for the French and Israelis. The conspirators had at least reached a provisional agreement that they could take to Mollet, Ben-Gurion and the British. The Israelis were delighted that at last they had a Western ally prepared to break away from the strict neutrality between Jews and Arabs to which the Tripartite Declaration bound them. For the French, the Israelis seemed serious co-conspirators who meant business against Nasser and who had few of Britain's curious inhibitions. The French flew the Israelis home in a military aircraft, accompanied by a French military delegation. It was led by General Maurice Challe of the French Air Force, who reappears later in this narrative.

Once on his home ground, Dayan demonstrated that his military confidence was well founded. To the French officers the Israeli Defence Force rag-tag soldiers might look like a bunch of gypsies, but Dayan convinced them that he could lead this people's army to victory. A tank attack could quickly break through Egyptian positions in north-eastern Sinai, while a brigade of parachutists led by one Ariel Sharon quickly moved west and south. In a matter of days the attackers would seize every key point in Sinai. The Israelis would not advance to the banks of the Canal itself, but from Sinai their very presence would threaten Egyptian troops along the waterway. If the French and British played their hand with half the vigour the Israelis promised to bring to the operation, Nasser would face overwhelmingly powerful enemies.

But there remained the question whether the French and British, or the French alone, would ever got to the point they had been working towards since July – an attack on Egypt and the seizure of the canal. From the beginning the French had talked of acting alone if necessary, but in reality only British involvement could clinch matters. And as the French well knew, the British were bound to be skittish about any commitment to the extraordinary enterprise which was taking shape. Whatever they told the Israelis, the French still faced the difficult task of coaxing their allies to join the conspiracy with Israel.

Things got worse for the French before they got better. The Israelis continued to brawl with the Jordanians, and when Iraq threatened to come to the support of Jordan they convinced themselves that Britain was set on gathering Jordan and Syria into an enlarged Baghdad Pact. On 11 October they attacked the Jordanians yet again, this time using artillery to soften them up and aircraft to direct the fire. King Hussein invoked the Anglo-Jordanian Treaty and called for air support from RAF bases in Jordan. The British consul-general in Jerusalem told the Israelis that if they did not call off the attack they would find themselves at war with Britain. The following day Britain promised to send more Hunter fighters to the bases in Jordan. With every Israeli's compulsion to see the mote in Britain's eye rather than the beam in his own, Dayan wrote in his diary, 'At the very moment when they are preparing to topple Nasser, who is a common enemy of theirs and Israel's, they insist on getting the Iraqi Army into Jordan, even if such action leads to war between Israel and Jordan in which they, the British, will take part against Israel ... they will leave Nasser gobbling up his prey while they rush off to start a new Israel-Britain-Jordan conflict.'[2] A Middle East war seemed imminent, on quite different lines from the one which the British and French had envisaged.

It did not come to that. Britain's top soldier, Gerald Templer, told ministers that 'we could either go to the aid of Jordan against Israel with sea and air power or we could launch Musketeer [the attack on Egypt]; we could not do both'.[3] And Lord Mountbatten, the First Sea Lord, added the egregious thought that if a French and British attack on Egypt were to go ahead in alliance with Israel and if, during it, Israel attacked Jordan, then the Americans would go to Jordan's aid and the British would find themselves at war with the United States. Even history's mind boggles, and so perhaps did the minds of the men involved.

Things had to be reordered, first things put first. The Prime Minister would allow nothing to distract Britain and France from their campaign to bring down Nasser, and soon we find him cooling in his support for Jordan. He dismisses the Foreign Office's loyalty to the alliance with Jordan as prejudice rather than pursuit of what it thought was British policy: 'I will not allow you to plunge this country into war,' he says to Anthony Nutting, 'merely to satisfy the anti-Jewish spleen of you people in the Foreign Office.'[4] When warned that King Hussein can still be expected to invoke his treaty with Britain he replies that by dismissing Glubb the young King has brought his troubles on his own head. From here on we can sense that Eden is subconsciously willing to allow the French to draw him into their conspiracy with the Israelis.

14, 21 OCTOBER: THE BRITISH JOIN THE PLOT

Sure enough, two weeks after that first meeting of the French and Israeli conspirators, the Prime Minister received French visitors at Chequers. They were led by a close confidant of the French Prime Minister, his Minister of Labour Albert Gazier, but the visitor who mattered was General Challe. He was introduced not as a gallant airman but as a member of Mollet's personal staff, and he was included in the delegation because of his involvement in the plot with Israel.

The meeting started by considering the problem of Jordan versus Israel. This was a subject which by now Eden wanted to put behind him and the discussion languished. But soon Challe floated the idea that perhaps France could encourage the Israelis to attack not Jordan but Egypt.

The idea of involving Israel in action against Egypt had been put to the British before – we have seen Pineau airily talking about it with Lloyd and Murphy over dinner in the Carlton Club back in July. But

Whitehall's received wisdom (and perhaps real wisdom too) had always remembered Nuri's advice that this was a sure way to incense the Arab world, set the oil pipelines across the Middle East alight and get the Suez Canal blocked to shipping. Now, however, almost three months into the crisis and as far from a solution as ever, Eden was tempted. He promised to study the idea.

In fact he did much more than that. He recalled the Foreign Secretary in haste from New York. Lloyd came unwillingly, because he felt that his talks with the Egyptian Foreign Minister, Mahmoud Fawzi, were going well, and that a peaceful settlement of the whole dispute might almost be within reach. By the time he got back, however, the Prime Minister's mind was made up. Lloyd found him at a meeting in No.10 at which Anthony Nutting, his deputy at the Foreign Office, and a handful of Foreign Office officials who knew what was in the wind were putting to the Prime Minister the manifest dangers of conspiring with France and Israel behind the backs of the United States and the West's remaining Arab friends. Eden brusquely overruled them, and Lloyd, doggedly loyal, rallied to his Prime Minister.

Prime Minister and an exhausted Foreign Secretary flew that evening to Paris, to meet Mollet and Pineau. Officials, even Britain's formidable ambassador Gladwyn Jebb, were excluded from the meeting. Though Eden said that he would have to consult his colleagues at home, to all intents and purposes he committed Britain there and then to the crucial decision at the heart of the whole collusion story. Yet throughout the short and inglorious history of the plot, the British were to be far more concerned than the French and Israelis to make the political and diplomatic cover story as convincing as they could. Hence all the glorious complications which were gradually built into the conspiracy. When the Israelis advanced into Sinai the Allies would detect an imminent danger that fighting on the canal banks would close it to shipping. As the Israelis approached the waterway, Britain and France would therefore call on both sides to cease fire and pull back. If they agreed, British and French forces would move in to safeguard the waterway, coming not as invaders but as saviours of the peace. If the Egyptians did not, they would be battered into submission by the Allies.

The whole thing was a pretty fantasy, which never had any serious prospect of carrying conviction. Yet to the British its complications lent a fig-leaf of respectability to what even its advocates could see as a devious piece of *Realpolitik*. They insisted on developing their cover story and they stuck to it through thick and thin. So in the interests of making it a shade more plausible they were to heap, as we shall see, extra political, diplomatic and military burdens on their own shoulders and those of their co-conspirators.

After Eden's meeting in Paris with Mollet, all that remained was for the British to meet the Israeli conspirators and look them in the eye, and for all three conspirators to tie up the details. This the French were happy to arrange. On 21 October Ben-Gurion himself flew to Paris and settled down in a private house in Sèvres on the city's outskirts for a crucial meeting with Mollet, Pineau and Bourgès-Maunoury. On the face of things their subject was the timings at which the various parties would move as the attack on Egypt unfolded. But behind the question of timings lay the question of the cover story for the attack, and behind the cover story the diverging concerns of the conspirators. The French wanted quick effective action, but they knew that if they were to carry the British with them the plan must provide a cover of diplomatic respectability. That required Israel to appear to be out in front of the other two. But the Israelis were determined not to risk Egyptian counter-action against their cities without Allied air cover.

Time pressed, yet at Sèvres Ben-Gurion showed no sign of urgency. He had come a long way in a long lifetime of building a Jewish state. Now, admitted into the company of French ministers, he waxed expansive, regaling his hosts with the story of the ancient Jewish people and its relevance to Israel's hopes for the future of the Middle East. One gets the feeling that acceptance into the counsels of a leading European power had gone to his head. Time and again the French tried to bring him back to present realities and above all to the vital necessity of winning British agreement to the plan which the French and Israelis had devised. Ben-Gurion continued to take his time.

Finally Selwyn Lloyd arrived to represent the third conspirator. He was tired, he was confused, and he hated what he was doing. The background from which he came to the conspiracy was very different from those of the French and the Israelis. He was convinced that ten days earlier in New York he had come close to a peaceful settlement of the Suez crisis; they were set on war, and wanted no diplomatic success to get in their way. They had plotted the conspiracy; he was coming late to it. They believed in it, convinced that it could bring them the supreme prize of removing Nasser from the Egyptian scene; he was profoundly sceptical. The French saw the meeting as a triumph for their diplomacy, and Ben-Gurion rejoiced to be at last received as an equal by the Western powers; Lloyd's concern was with technicalities and above all with secrecy, determined that every trace of the conspiracy which the others saw as a triumph should be expunged from the diplomatic record.

Loyal to Eden, Lloyd waded manfully through the mire. But instead of focusing on the conspiracy alone, he took the French and Israelis round every angle of the Middle East crisis, with an attention to detail that must have tried French patience almost as much as Ben-Gurion's grand historical and strategic dreams. French and Israelis alike soon found themselves hating him. Very English they thought Lloyd's attitude, crabbed, evasive, cold, the epitome of the islanders' hypocrisy. But they needed him, and the military and diplomatic strength Britain could bring to the operation. For his part, he clearly longed for a different, more honourable way of tackling the Suez problem, but having spoken his piece he did his duty by his Prime Minister, took note of what was planned, and flew back to London to report to the one Englishman whose heart really was committed to this, perhaps the strangest of all the international stratagems in which a British government involved itself in the course of the twentieth century.

22 OCTOBER: THE PLANNERS PREPARE

So by the fourth week in October French, British and Israeli ministers had agreed that they would act together to bring Nasser down, but all of them, and the British most particularly, were determined to conceal the fact. The British Cabinet was given a very selective account of what had been agreed. Documents were destroyed, ministers took even the details of action into their own hands, and knowledge of what was happening was kept within a small circle of officials. Yet military planning for the assault had to accommodate these new political and military realities, and the planners were far away, in Cyprus.

Right to the end of the Suez adventure, Keightley was not told the whole story of what had been agreed at Sèvres on 21 October, but even in that maddest of years he had to know the military concept to which the political leaders had committed themselves. But even when he knew what was envisaged, the requirements of politics still dogged the planning and execution of operations. The Israeli march into Sinai was to provide the excuse for an Allied ultimatum, calling on the Egyptians as well as the Israelis to pull back from the canal. But the British were convinced that if that ultimatum was to carry any kind of conviction as an even-handed intervention, the Allies issuing it could not be seen to be on the brink of war against Egypt. It was therefore essential that when the Israelis attacked they should appear to do so on their own. There had to be time once the fighting had started to issue the ultimatum to both parties and for them to reply. Only then could the Western allies commit their men to the enterprise.

By now, in late October, the doubts of August and September about where the troops should land had been resolved. They would go in, as originally envisaged, at Port Said and Port Fuad at the entrance to the canal itself. The soldiers had lived through repeated postponements, but the timetable seemed at last to be settled. British officers still knew very little about the conspiracy with Israel. The French commanders were rather better informed but they were under instructions to keep what they knew from the British. So the British noticed mysterious comings and goings to the French headquarters in Cyprus, and there were rumours that Israeli officers were among the visitors, but no reliable information about what was happening.

Uneasy and confused, the force commanders got on with the task of preparing to wage war against Egypt and seize the whole length of the canal. The plan envisaged the destruction of the Egyptian Air Force, if possible on its airfields; the advance of a major armada of ships and landing craft from Malta to the Eastern Mediterranean; and an airborne and seaborne assault on Port Said and Port Fuad. All this they understood. What the British officers did not know was the complication which the politicians had agreed.

The United States, like everyone else, was to be kept in the dark while this plot unfolded. But from as early as August the Americans had been flying their U-2 spy planes over the eastern Mediterranean, one of them piloted by Gary Powers, who was to come so spectacularly to grief in 1960 when a missile brought his aircraft down deep inside the Soviet Union.[5] They had the Sixth Fleet in the immediate area of the assault, and a capacity to pluck messages out of the ether all over the world. Many sources told them that something was afoot, though to this day we do not know for certain whether they were reading the texts of French, British and Israeli signals or making more general deductions from the patterns of signal traffic and the physical evidence that began to unwind as the Israelis and their new Western allies – those unlikely allies, whose soldiers as yet did not even know that they were allies – prepared to go to war. Certainly Eisenhower showed every sign of being surprised when he got the news of the Israeli attack and the Allied ultimatum. He was not alone; and the final charge against the whole collusive enterprise is that the secrecy, deception and downright lies which were thought necessary to maintain the fiction intensified the political storm when it finally broke, in New York and Washington, in the Commonwealth and in the House of Commons, lending it a personal and moral bitterness that the world of politics and diplomacy had not experienced since the end of the Second World War.

The Allies added yet another complication to the difficulties with which their policies had saddled them. It reads like a comedy to lighten the Greek tragedy of collusion and bad faith.

It was essential, the Allies believed, to preface the military assault on Egypt with a propaganda onslaught. The British in particular remembered the triumphs of their wartime propaganda machine and were eager to repeat them. The venomous words of Cairo Radio must be challenged. Leaflets must be prepared, to be showered when the time came on the Egyptian population. The devious arts of black propaganda, too, must be brought to bear to defeat the magic of Nasser's name. Bernard Fergusson, a literary soldier who later became governor-general of New Zealand, was put in command of a psychological warfare operation based in Cyprus and went energetically to work.

The BBC had an existing Arabic-language station, Sharq al Ausat, which could be used to carry Fergusson's message. But as in the course of the crisis the nature of British intentions towards Egypt gradually emerged, the Palestinian staff of the station walked out in protest, to be joined by its British director-general. There was an urgent need to establish an Arabic-broadcasting radio station in Cyprus in its place. Sharq al Britania – Voice of Britain – would take over where Sharq al Ausat had left off. To do the job a motley group of journalists, diplomats and technicians was quickly assembled. A friend of mine was among them.

He remembers mysterious orders reaching him when he was on leave in England to report to the RAF station at Lyneham. His wife drove him there, where an almost empty aircraft awaited him. Away they flew, until, two hours into the flight, he was invited to join the pilot on the flight deck. There they opened sealed orders: in effect, 'fly to Gibraltar and turn left'. They did so, and in due course arrived in Cyprus. Other members of the team were waiting there, most of them as confused as he was. They found themselves installed in a hutted, makeshift broadcasting station, equipped with all the appropriate broadcasting paraphernalia of the era, reel-to-reel tape machines and a vast library of Arab songs and Koranic readings, and above them the transmitter masts themselves. They said they needed Arabic-character typewriters and a consignment was rushed to them. When the crate was opened it revealed Urdu-character typewriters instead.

None of the team had ever seen the inside of a broadcasting station before, but gradually Sharq al Britania got on the air. Technicians would take care of the transmissions, but on content everything was still to play for. They broadcast news in English and Arabic, talks with a social, political or even theological flavour, readings from the Koran, Arab music. From time to time bloodcurdling pieces of propaganda recorded in London reached them, the messages to be conveyed inextricably muddled, some designed to frighten, others to woo, none of them well calculated to make any Egyptian listener love the invader.

We can see looking back that they had hardly a prayer of success. Nasser commanded all the Arab world's sex appeal. The British and French were imperialists, and without American support they promised to be losers too. Rightly or wrongly the average member of an Arab audience thought that the British and French were in the Middle East to serve Israeli interests. Even properly equipped the propagandists could never have competed successfully with Cairo Radio. As it was, they were singularly ill-equipped, voices crying vainly in the Middle East wilderness.

16, 24 OCTOBER: POLICE AT SEA, PIRATES IN THE AIR

In the course of 1956 the French made their relatively peaceful exits from Morocco and Tunisia. Success there provided no model for French rule in Algeria, trapped as it was between the obduracy of the French settlers and the demands of the Arab and Berber majorities. In February, Mollet had looked the settlers in Algeria in the eye, then blinked; and his attempts to mollify the *pieds noirs* had increased the anger of the native Algerians, an anger which Cairo Radio inflamed. He looked to success against Nasser over the canal to solve the Algerian problem as nothing else could.

Throughout the summer of 1956, therefore, the French government was on the watch for evidence of sinister Egyptian contacts with the Algerian rebels. By the autumn there was talk in Paris of Egyptian arms being smuggled into Algeria and on 16 October hard evidence was found to back it up. On that day French warships in the Mediterranean arrested a former Royal Navy minesweeper, now Sudanese owned. In the *Athos* they found six Algerians who had been trained in Egypt, and seventy tons of arms which they said had been put aboard at Alexandria by Egyptian officers. It was not a very surprising discovery, but the French played it up for all it was worth. It proved, as if proof were needed, that Egypt was supporting the Algerian uprising.

So on the very eve of the attack on Egypt the French withdrew their ambassador from Cairo. French ministers were already frenetic with excitement about the coming attack and this looked to them like a masterly propaganda coup to justify what was coming. Six days later they pulled off what they thought was another.

On 24 October a Moroccan aircraft took off from Rabat. It was carrying delegates from the capital of one sovereign North African country to another, Tunis, to attend a conference on the solidarity of the Maghreb – Algeria, Morocco and Tunisia. Among the passengers were four Algerian rebels, most notably a freedom fighter whose deeds had already won him iconic status, Ahmed Ben Bella.

The flight was civilian and entirely legitimate, but the French air officer commanding in Algeria ordered the French pilot to divert to Algiers. He did as he was told, and there Ben Bella and his colleagues were arrested. It was an act of pure piracy, an assault on the very idea of Maghreb solidarity, and it was well calculated to destroy any hope of fruitful negotiations between France and the Algerian nationalists.

French public opinion insisted on seeing it as a success to put beside the seizure of the *Athos*. Mollet had knuckled under to the settlers in February. Now he defended piracy and kidnapping. The French minister responsible for relations with Morocco and Tunisia resigned in protest and so did the ambassador to Tunisia. That was the limit of French honour in the affair. Mollet said that the kidnapping illustrated France's resolve and reach. Outside France, opinion was scandalised, and any propaganda benefit the *Athos* coup had brought was immediately obliterated. When a Moroccan mob rioted in protest and murdered thirty French settlers the authorities did not intervene.

The damage to France's reputation was great. It would have been the greater if the incident had not been overtaken within days by the gigantic affront to Arab, Third World and liberal sensibilities which the Allied attack on Egypt represented.

29 OCTOBER: COLLISION

In the late afternoon of 29 October a force of about 400 soldiers of Colonel Ariel Sharon's parachute brigade was dropped just to the east of the Mitla Pass in western Sinai. They were only 45 miles from the southern end of the Suez Canal and 150 miles inside Egypt. Just before the drop the rest of their brigade crossed the border and set out across the desert to join them. Till that relief arrived they were exposed and on their own.

We have seen that the Israelis had assurances of French naval and air cover for their advance. But the Israelis remained anxious that at the last moment the alliance with the British (and French military subordination to them) would block the promised French support. So the Israelis wanted to preserve as long as they could the appearance of being as concerned with their eastern as their western border; and the pretence that their assault was no more than a border raid, rather than all-out war against Egypt. Moshe Dayan had devised his plans accordingly, plans more cautious (the matter of the parachute drop apart) than those which Israeli subordinate commanders were used to.

Once success had been achieved (with a good deal of unpublicised help from the French) the Israeli operation became for the world a classic example of courage and improvisation, but it could very easily have failed. The troops travelled mainly in commandeered civilian trucks and vans, which could not cope with desert conditions. A consignment of French cross-country trucks was delivered on the day the operation began, but without the tools to keep them mobile. By heroic improvisation the column got to the rendezvous with the airdrop. It arrived late in the evening of 30 October, seventeen hours after the landing from the air.

Two other columns crossed the border on 29 October. One was to go south from Eilat at the head of the Gulf of Aqaba, the full length of the gulf to Sharm al-Sheikh at the tip of the Sinai Peninsula, which it finally reached on 5 November. The other, which crossed the border just inland from the Mediterranean coast, was to advance across northern Sinai towards Ismailia on the canal. Immediately after it entered

Egypt this second column got itself involved in serious fighting with a resolute defence. Its commander ignored his orders and called forward tanks which Dayan had intended should be held back inside Israel until British bombing had destroyed the Egyptian Air Force. Dayan came close to sacking him, but finally he got his column to a position in the desert just east of the canal by 2 November. Another column, still further north, attacked on 1 November, bypassing Gaza and advancing along the Mediterranean coast towards El Cap. It too stopped just short of the canal on 2 November.

Even in the midst of victory, the Israeli Army encountered stiff resistance in some places. The Egyptian Army was at a loss in a war of manoeuvre but tenacious in fixed positions. When Nasser ordered the abandonment of such positions in Al Arish and Abu Agheila the commander on the spot remained convinced that he could have continued to hold them, and withdrew only under protest. And at the Mitla Pass a piece of insubordination got the Israelis into serious trouble. Sharon's orders were to deploy his brigade in the open desert to the east of the pass, where his parachutists had landed. He was unhappy doing nothing, and claimed that his position was vulnerable to an Egyptian tank attack.

At this point a friend of mine takes up the story. Erich was a young reservist officer in the Israeli Army. He had just completed a spell of refresher training and was about to go back to his kibbutz when he was hauled back to the company office. Get aboard a two-seater Piper aeroplane and fly to join Sharon at the Mitla pass, he was told, there to act as his communication link to higher command. Erich and his pilot took off in search of Sharon, and found themselves approaching the Suez Canal instead. They turned back just in time and found their way to Sharon's brigade at the Mitla pass.

Erich knew Sharon's reputation. So for that matter did the whole Israeli army: 'His orders had to be obeyed immediately,' Erich told me, 'and if possible before he barked them out. Orders he was given, on the other hand, could be disregarded if he didn't believe them to be right.' Sharon's trouble with orders was, Erich added, 'a sort of Israeli disease. "I can do anything better than you and I am always right".'

This is what happened at Mitla. When Sharon grumbled about his exposed position, Dayan authorised him to send a patrol into the pass. Sharon decided to go his own way and despatched a fighting force. Egyptian troops, dug in and well concealed, ambushed it and Egyptian aircraft came in to take a hand. It took seven hours' fighting and 150 casualties to get the Israelis out of the trap into which Sharon had sent them.

Everywhere else Israel had played its military part in the attack on Egypt with complete, almost contemptuous success. By 2 November its forces could have reached the canal in a matter of hours. By 5 November they controlled all key points in the vast wilderness of the Sinai desert. The Israelis could happily accept their allies' ultimatum that called on them to cease fire. They had real estate in their possession to strengthen their hand in the negotiations that would follow the cease-fire. And they had played their part, near impeccably, in the game of collusion whose script they had agreed with the French and the reluctant British at Sèvres a bare fortnight ago.

Another friend of mine took part in that advance. She is an old lady now, but fifty years ago she played her part in history as a strapping member of the Israeli Defence Force doing her national service as a cartographer with an armoured brigade. Describing her adventures she told me how her unit generated copies of battle maps by exposing photosensitive paper to the desert sun, a technique that seemed to me quite as unrealistic as the dreams of instantaneous graphic intelligence which the mad major and I had been propounding in distant England only a matter of weeks earlier.

Ruth's unit advanced in the usual Israeli jumble of vehicles, improvising repairs as they went. Along the way they captured an Egyptian supply dump. Among the supplies they found hundreds of bottles of Coca-Cola. These Zionist warriors had heard of Coca-Cola. For them, as for the whole postwar world, it was on the one hand a symbol of American luxury and sophistication, almost as heady in its effects as the latest Hollywood romance, and on the other an objectionable example of American cultural imperialism. But Israel's balance of payments did not then stretch to importing luxuries; none of them had ever tasted Coca-Cola. Now there was enough for every man and woman in Ruth's victorious unit, a quaffable trophy of war. They popped off bottle after bottle, but each had been gently cooked under the desert sun. The fabled nectar proved to be a revolting soup.

The cartographers had better luck with other spoils of war. Along the desert road they found abandoned cars, most of them with full fuel tanks, many with a key waiting in the ignition, each of them abandoned by fleeing Egyptians. For a few days they enjoyed the luxury of driving their own Fords and Chevrolets, disputing among themselves which of them had acquired the best set of wheels. 'It's like America,' they said.

A Bedouin family crossed the path of their advance. They exchanged greetings, the Israelis saying they were going to war, the Bedouin that they were on their way to Mecca. It was, said Ruth, a brief heart-warming moment, a moment of peace on the eve of battle, but to the Bedouin women the idea of a female soldier was a concept too far. But they prodded Ruth in all the right places and confirmed that she was indeed a woman. They went on their way towards Mecca while Ruth continued her advance into Egypt, the Arabic incantation 'A woman, a woman' still ringing in her ears.

30 OCTOBER: ULTIMATUM

On the afternoon of 30 October the Israeli and Egyptian ambassadors in London were summoned to the Foreign Office. There they were received, first the Israeli and then, ten minutes later, the Egyptian, by the French Foreign Minister and the Foreign Office Permanent Under Secretary, Sir Ivone Kirkpatrick. A note containing an ultimatum was handed to each.

The notes addressed the consequences of the hostilities which had broken out the previous day, when the Israeli parachutists landed at the Mitla Pass and Israeli tanks crossed the Egyptian border. They noted that these hostilities threatened freedom of navigation through the Suez Canal, and called on both Israelis and Egyptians to cease fire and withdraw ten miles from its banks. That to Egypt also required the Egyptian government to accept temporary occupation by British and French troops of key points the length of the canal. Both notes called for a reply within twelve hours, failing which British and French forces would take action to secure compliance.

These were the documents which finally touched off the explosion of the world's anger which had been in the making since July. They broke decisively with the United States' efforts to put together a tripartite response to the crisis, as the terms of the Tripartite Declaration of 1950 required. They lent confirmation to suspicion, rapidly becoming conviction, that the Israeli attack had been contrived to provide the occasion for this Allied ultimatum – that Israel, France and Britain had colluded together to get to precisely this point.

Shortly after 4.30 pm, before the Egyptian ambassador had left the Foreign Office, Anthony Eden began a statement on the situation to the House of Commons. He started by announcing that he had just received reports that Egypt, Jordan and Syria had formed a joint military command. He noted, judiciously, that Israel might reasonably see this as a threat to its security. He went on to describe incursions by Egyptian irregulars into Israel and then, coming at last to the real flashpoint of the last twenty-four hours, turned to the Israeli attack in Sinai and advance towards the Canal.

Eden then went on to describe the action that was being taken to deal with this grave situation. There had been tripartite discussion in Washington on 28 and 29 October, he said. Now Britain and France were joining the United States in asking for a Security Council discussion of the situation. And at the very end of his statement – low key, almost matter-of-fact – he described the notes that Britain and France had just addressed to Israel and Egypt. He did his best to make what was planned sound reasonable and statesmanlike.

Eden had a high House of Commons reputation as a man who had devoted his working life to foreign affairs, spending thirty years in the search for peace. Retrospect shows us that his statement was as misleading as any that has ever been made in the House of Commons. Yet at the time it was received with attention, and by many even with respect. The House listened carefully to what had been said and needed time to reflect on its significance. The explosion of anger would come soon, raging against the government's duplicity, hypocrisy and aggression, consuming British political life for weeks, and some individuals for a lifetime. But it did not come that afternoon.

There was no such moment of reflection in the United States. The American ambassador had been given copies of the two notes while the Prime Minister was still speaking. He flashed them to the State Department and Dulles telephoned the news to the President. Both were shocked and Eisenhower fired off notes to Eden and Mollet, dissociating the United States from their actions. In New York the American ambassador had already opened Security Council discussion of the crisis with a plea for prompt action to stop the Israeli attack. Then the Soviet ambassador read out a press flash of the Prime Minister's statement in the House of Commons. Pierson Dixon, the British ambassador, could only ask for an adjournment until the afternoon while they considered Eden's words – and while he burnt the transatlantic telephone wires with a plea for an explanation, for a line to take.

That evening the House of Commons came back to the topic, to the only issue of the hour. Opening, Eden had little more to say. Winding up, Selwyn Lloyd was heckled and ineffectual. It was Hugh Gaitskell, the leader of the opposition, who spoke the decisive words of the debate. There was no United Nations cover for what the government had done, he said, no justification in international law. For five years Britain had relied on the Tripartite Declaration, which it now seemed to treat as nothing. And the ultimatum itself was profoundly inequitable, facing the Egyptians with a demand that they pull back still further within their own country, while leaving the Israelis 160 miles inside it, and only ten from the canal. He divided the House. 270 members supported Eden, 218 voted against the government.

The consequences of the British political explosion that Eden touched off that day haunted him for the rest of his premiership and the rest of his life. The storm raged until, a week later, he agreed to stop the invasion in its tracks; it persisted until, more than a month later, British troops were at last withdrawn from Egypt; it sent him, a broken man, to convalesce in the Caribbean; and it wreaked its final damage when, early in January, he resigned the office he had sought throughout his political life and occupied for a mere twenty months of crisis, frustration and defeat.

9

The Assault on Egypt

From the early days of planning for action against Egypt, bombing of airfields had been part of the equation. It seemed the easy way to win air superiority over Egypt. Once the plotting that led to Sèvres had begun, bombing assumed a more urgent political significance as well, for Ben-Gurion was mortally afraid of Egyptian air attack on Israeli cities. When the British and French argued that, for purposes of verisimilitude, it was essential for the Israelis to attack before the Allies, he insisted that they must put the Egyptian Air Force out of business at the latest on the day after the Israelis crossed the frontier. So once the Allies' ultimatum had expired the bombing began.

It was supposed to be a joint operation, but only the British had the aircraft to do it effectively. The new V-bomber force had been designed to strike at Soviet targets; it would launch its Valiant bombers from Malta. The Canberra tactical bombers would attack from Cyprus. On 3 1 October the first squadrons set off for their Egyptian targets.

The operation, like almost everything else in the Allied campaign against Egypt, was beset by changing orders. The worst example occurred when the Valiants were within ten minutes of their target. The British Embassy in Cairo reported by flash telegram that the Americans were evacuating civilians to Libya along a road that passed near the target airfield. The political danger of inadvertently killing Americans screamed alarm. The Prime Minister himself despatched the order that the attack must be switched. The Valiants' navigators sweated to establish new attack coordinates. They failed to find the new target and attacked Cairo's civil airport in error instead.

There was muddle about other targets too. The psychological warriors had argued that if their broadcasts were to be listened to, Cairo Radio must be put out of business. Its studios were added to the target list. But at the last moment someone remembered that the studios were in the city itself, where any attack would cause civilian casualties. So the attack was called off, and no one thought of hitting the radio's transmitters out in the desert, where only a passing camel might have fallen victim to collateral damage.

So the airmen faced many difficulties, some of them imposed by their own side. They did their best, but their performance seems unimpressive from a service which, twelve years earlier, had so comprehensively pulverised the Reich. Yet air attack achieved what it was supposed to achieve. Rather than see them destroyed on his airfields, Nasser despatched his most modern aircraft to safety in Sudan and Syria. Aircraft which remained were steadily destroyed, mostly on the ground, mostly by strafing rather than bombing. Egyptian aircraft and anti-aircraft batteries proved unable to put up effective defence. In a day and a half the bombing campaign was over.

It might have been a different story if Communist-bloc trainers, or volunteers flown in from the Soviet Union or Eastern Europe, had taken a hand – a possibility that the planners could not exclude from their calculations. They could have intercepted the attackers or, still better, destroyed British and French aircraft crammed onto the few airfields in Cyprus, three-quarters of an hour's flying time from bases in the Nile Delta. But while Moscow rattled its sabres, it showed the same caution over Suez as the Western powers over Hungary. The Allied air forces were left to go about their work essentially undisturbed.

There were fears in London that the bombings might provoke mob attacks on French and British citizens in Egypt, but few of the individuals concerned had any sense of danger. A friend of mine who was employed by the British Council to teach at Cairo University went to Suez the day before the Israelis attacked to help appoint a new headmaster for a boys' school in the town. That evening he sat drinking on the terrace of a flat overlooking the canal. The only sign of the storm to come was a solitary Egyptian soldier guarding the famous waterway. 'You'd never think we were in the middle of an international crisis,' someone remarked. The next day the Israelis struck and the balloon went up, but even then private Egyptians remained friendly. One of John's neighbours in Cairo came round to ask him, in curiosity rather than anger, what on earth the British thought they were doing bombing Cairo airport. And when John went to fill his car with petrol the attendant asked him where he was from. 'Britain,' he replied. 'Ah,' was the answer to that, 'British people good, but Eden, bad like Hitler.' It was, my friend reflected, an exact mirror image of what Eden was saying about Nasser.

All the same, even when less provoked than by aerial assault, the Cairo and Alexandria crowds had a famous reputation for volatility that could easily turn vicious. The Egyptian authorities wanted no outrages. Embassy staff were confined to their homes and offices, Western businesses guarded, the Western employees in the bases along the Canal taken into a protective custody where they were to stay, uncomfortable but safely, until they were evacuated when the shooting was over, in December. Nasser's government demonstrated that, even under attack, they were in complete control of Egypt.

1–5 NOVEMBER: SLOW BOATS TO PORT SAID

Once the bombers had destroyed the Egyptian Air Force it seemed reasonable to expect that British and French parachute and sea landings would quickly follow. After all, the ultimatum had been supposed to keep Israeli and Egyptian forces away from the canal while Allied troops took charge and secured safe passage for shipping. But for four clear days there was no sign of landings. The British concern to lend colour to the fiction that they were intent on stopping the fighting between Egypt and Israel, not looking for an excuse to join in the attack, had delayed the departure of the invasion fleet from Malta. Now it steamed at the speed of its slowest ships, half the length of the Mediterranean from Malta towards the Egyptian coast, while the aircraft carriers shadowed it from a distance. Senior officers were alert to the possibility of attack by Soviet submarines, but to their sailors and their passengers it seemed that they were at the tranquil eye of a storm which raged in Sinai, in the air over Egypt and in London, Washington and New York.

Yet throughout the voyage to Port Said the power of the United States Sixth Fleet loomed over the armada. Dulles wanted a demonstration of American concern and naval might, and the fleet was ordered to shadow the British and French ships closely. It flew its aircraft close to, sometimes directly over the armada; at night it illuminated its ships with its blinding searchlights. The British and French thought that they were at war, while the Sixth Fleet made mock of them. After the event the British naval commander submitted a shocked statement of the obvious: 'I considered it quite possible', he wrote, 'that they were obstructing us on purpose as their aircraft flying in the area rendered our air warning virtually useless.'[1] There was a constant danger of collision, of something going wrong that would produce the ultimate international incident. But the Americans went on harrying the armada, gung-ho naval warriors playing chicken, and there is a curious blend of arrogant triumphalism mixed with practical frustration in the words of the United States' most senior sailor when Dulles asked him if the Sixth Fleet could not do something to prevent the invasion: 'We can defeat them – the British and the French and the Egyptians and the Israelis – the whole goddam works of them we can knock off, if you want. But that's the only way to do it.'[2]

5 NOVEMBER: THE PARAS LAND

Despite the delay, Nasser was under no illusions. He knew that a land attack was coming. In a voice half-choked by laryngitis he went on Cairo Radio in Churchillian mode: 'Today we face British cunning ... we shall fight a bitter battle. We shall fight from village to village, from house to house ... we shall fight, fight, fight and never surrender ...'[3].

At last, at 7.15 in the morning of 5 November, the first Allied troops landed in Egypt. At that hour, almost 700 men of the 3rd Battalion, the British Parachute Regiment, leapt from their aircraft above Gamil airfield west of Port Said. At 7.30 am 500 men of a French Colonial parachute regiment landed just south of the city. It was a long thirteen weeks since the British and French governments had decided for their different reasons that if they must, and if they could, they would use force to bring Nasser down and recover control of the Suez Canal.

The British attackers had been scattered the length of the airport as they landed. Some encountered no resistance, others a 'bloody good reception committee'.[4] Slowly they regrouped, got on top of local resistance, gathered up their equipment, and started to move along the airfield towards Port Said. They took the control tower, an Egyptian coastguard barracks, and the better part of a sewage farm. They could call on air support from a 'taxi-rank' of fighter-bombers, but that apart they were on their own, lightly armed if highly motivated men against Egyptian forces of uncertain size and unknown fighting quality.

They encountered steadily increasing Egyptian resistance, reinforced by four self-propelled guns dug in beyond a chain of war cemeteries that were reminders of an earlier occupation of Egypt. Soon the parachutists' ammunition was running short. They held an airfield, but its runway could handle only Dakotas, and the Royal Air Force had no Dakotas in the eastern Mediterranean. Ahead of the troops lay the crowded buildings and narrow streets of a Port Said slum. They decided to settle down to hold the sewage farm (and so the airfield) and await the seaborne attack scheduled for the following day.

The French who had landed south of the city centre were set the task of capturing two bridges which would open the way for an advance down the canal to Ismailia and eventually the town of Suez itself. The Egyptians destroyed one bridge but the French captured the other and set about readying it to take the tanks that would come ashore on the following day. A British reconnaissance troop that had dropped with the French set off southwards down the causeway that ran parallel to the canal and came back reporting that little stood in the way of an advance. In the afternoon a second French parachute regiment descended on Port Fuad across the canal entrance from Port Said and took control there. The first French attackers, however, faced an anxious night, on the edge of a major and hostile city, with no prospect of reinforcement or air support until the dawn.

Looking back one is still left with a feeling that the French parachutists brought greater aggression to the assault than the British out to the west of Port Said. Like the British Parachute Regiment they thought themselves an elite. Unlike the British they had recent first-hand experience of all-out war, first in Vietnam and now in Algeria. Their commander, Brigadier-General Gilles, overcame the communication difficulties that otherwise plagued the whole of the Suez operation by supervising his troops from a slow-flying aircraft circling overhead. His colonels on the ground led their men from the front. In action, the British fought by the book, the French by instincts which had been honed by violent experience. And though they would never have admitted it, their officers were driven by a need to reassert French military honour, so disastrously lost in the debacle of 1940. Already they were the ruthless fighting men who, in the years of fighting in Algeria that lay ahead, would earn themselves such a terrible reputation as killers and torturers. For the moment they thought they were about to bring down the man, Nasser, whose enmity was destroying France's inheritance in North Africa. They had no patience with anyone, hostile fighter or peaceable civilian, who got in their way.

In the course of the night of 5–6 November, while Egyptians and attackers alike awaited the coming onslaught from the sea, the Egyptian commander on the spot, General Moguy, asked for a cease-fire. He was invited to the French headquarters on the edge of the city, to meet the British officer commanding all the Allied troops ashore and his French subordinate. He was looking for an informal truce, the Allies for his surrender. In the threatening presence of an Egyptian police officer, whom the Allied commanders called a 'political commissar', Moguy insisted that he needed Cairo's authority to sign anything other than a truce. The terms of anything approaching a surrender must be referred to his superiors. It was agreed that he would cable Cairo. Each side may have believed that it was hood-winking the other, but it was the Egyptians who did the better out of the confusion.

There was a long delay before Cairo's reply arrived. Meanwhile the local police and civilian activists (aided by a very active Soviet consul) got busy urging ordinary Egyptians to resist the invaders, and distributing weapons to any who would take them. And when at last Cairo's orders came through, they forbade Moguy to yield – indeed, it is said that when he read Moguy's report Nasser wanted to order him to reply that if the British commander wanted a ceasefire 'he should be peremptorily told to give himself up with all his troops'.[5]

The result of all this was that when Tuesday, 6 November dawned the Allied troops faced an excitable and armed civilian population, as well as unbroken military and police resistance. But the abortive negotiations with Moguy did wider harm to the allied cause as well. Reported over unclear radio links and garbled by wishful thinking, the fact that Moguy had asked for a truce became a conviction that the Egyptians were ripe for surrender. A top priority signal went to London from the commander in chief, General Keightley: 'Governor and Military Commander, Port Said, now discussing surrender terms with Brigadier Butler. Cease-fire ordered.'

The signal was brought to Eden in the House of Commons where members were baying for his blood. He read it out to cheers and congratulations: 'It seemed as though Anthony Eden, through keeping his nerve, had pulled it off after all.'[6] Back went a congratulatory signal to Keightley: 'Our most sincere congratulations to you all. If surrender in Port Said is complete, your immediate and urgent aim should be to occupy Ismailia and Suez as quickly as possible and with minimum loss of life. If you consider this can best be done by direct approach to the

Governors of Ismailia and Suez, you have authority to go ahead. You should now cease all air bombing unless you receive special authority from us.'[7]

It seemed like a famous victory. Yet at dawn on 6 November only 3,000 lightly armed soldiers were ashore in Egypt. The Egyptian military in Port Said was as yet scarcely bruised, and now they were supported by armed civilians. Cairo's reply to Moguy's report put a firecracker up the defenders' tails. This was not going to be a walkover for the Allies, and now they were inhibited in their use of air and naval firepower. But the reinforcements for which the parachute regiments were waiting went ahead, with two British Commandos sweeping in from the sea, a third by helicopter. Tanks and more parachute troops came in later waves. The French launched similar landings in Port Fuad.

The British went ashore looking for a bloodless walkover. 'Do you know if they drive on the right or the left in this country?' a Centurion tank driver asked his commander; and a moment later: 'Sir, there's a traffic light at red. Do we stop?'[8] But in places they encountered stiff resistance: there was no panic-stricken Egyptian flight of the British imagination. Egyptian troops fought hard in the streets that led back from the waterfront and at the Canal Company offices, and unwisely gallant Egyptian civilians imagined that they could engage Centurion tanks with their newly issued rifles. At Navy House, where the British occupiers had handed over to the Egyptians before they sailed away four long months earlier, the new occupants fought so well that only when the British brought in rocket-firing aircraft did the firing cease. When the defenders came out on the following morning, 7 November, only twenty men surrendered, leaving thirty dead inside.

Somewhere in the fighting General Moguy was captured. The Allies got hold of the idea that, as a prisoner, he might be able to bring about an unconditional surrender. A farce that could easily have become a tragedy now ensued. All three British task force commanders and the French land force commander got into a naval launch together and went ashore 'to insist on a firm surrender this time'.[9] An Egyptian gunner who succeeded in sinking their boat under them would have made himself a national hero. When they tried to get ashore at the

Canal Company's offices, they were shot at for their pains. Once ashore, they wandered aimlessly around the city, looking for someone to negotiate with. No amount of rationalisation can make it seem like anything other that a feckless expedition, as little thought through as the invasion of which it formed a pendant.

The great men found no Egyptian officer in a position to offer an unconditional surrender. But the battle of Port Said was an uneven contest, and gradually the Egyptians gave ground. Many of them attacked the French parachutists who had been holding the bridges since the previous day and who blocked their escape down the canal road to the south. Other Egyptian army and police units faded away into the civilian anonymity of the back streets and many soldiers and policemen joining the civilian flight across open country between the lakes to the south west of the city. When the fighting stopped the Allies had lost 23 dead, 121 wounded; the Egyptians, according to later calculation, between 750 and 1,000.

For the Allies, the way down the canal towards Ismailia and Suez now lay open. British tanks and parachute troops advanced along the canal road. It looked as if, left to themselves, they could be in Suez by the middle of the next day, 7 November, and the French inevitably complained that if the job were left to them they could do it even quicker. Control of the canal from end to end would have conferred some kind of sense on the whole operation. But the soldiers were not to be left to themselves. Political pressures were growing at home and diplomatic pressures in Washington and New York. The British government yielded, dragging the French along with them. A ceasefire was ordered, to come into effect at 2 am on 7 November. The troops were told to seize control of the canal as far south as they could get in the time available. When 2 am came they were two miles beyond El Cap, where the narrow causeway which forms the banks of the canal gives way to the open spaces of the Egyptian desert.

The operation to free the canal had ended up in possession of a quarter of its length. The Israelis had played their part in the charade that was meant to justify the Allied intervention; now they waited off-stage in the eastern desert. The Egyptians had never agreed to withdraw from their own waterway; now they were steadily reinforcing their control of the rest of the canal. Already ships filled with cement were being scuttled to block it to shipping. And far away the political kettles were boiling, in London, Washington and New York.

31 OCTOBER–6 NOVEMBER: IKE IN A RAGE

Eisenhower was in the south on election business when he heard that
war had broken out in the Middle East. On his way back in *Columbine*
– the aircraft that had so impressed Eden's party when they came to the
United States back in February – he was told that the Israelis were
attacking in Sinai with all their strength. That evening he discussed
developments with the Dulles brothers, Hoover and the Secretary of
Defense. The British and French were about to intervene, Dulles
averred. 'They appear to be ready for it, and may even have concerted
their action with the Israelis.'[10] Collusion was becoming unmistakable,
and the President was about to move against the British, French and
Israeli conspirators. 'We cannot be bound by our traditional alliances,'
an aide records him as saying, and then, with that wounded vanity
which seems to have driven Eisenhower throughout the crisis: 'Nothing justified double-crossing us.' He brushed domestic political
concerns aside: '...he did not really think that the American people
would throw him out in the midst of a situation like this, but if they did,
so be it.'[11]

Then, on the afternoon of 30 October, Eisenhower heard the news
of the British and French ultimatum to Israel and Egypt. The hypocrisy
of treating aggressor and victim alike was blatant. Eisenhower sent
messages to Eden and Mollet begging them to withdraw the ultimatum.
To his advisers, he fumed: 'I've just never seen great powers make such
a complete *mess* and *botch* of things.'[12] The following morning he
heard how narrowly Eden had survived the vote of confidence in the
House of Commons: 'I could not dream of committing this nation on
such a vote.'[13] But the attack on Egypt was going ahead and on 31
October the bombing of Egyptian airfields began. That night the President made a televised address to the nation. He had not been consulted
in any way on the attack on Egypt, he said. Britain, France and Israel
had the right to make such decisions, just as the United States had the
right to dissent. Its policy was to support the United Nations in seeking
peace, and to support the rule of law.

On the morning of Thursday, 1 November, Eisenhower held a meeting of the National Security Council. It looked briefly at what Dulles
called the 'miracle' of the Hungarian uprising, but Eisenhower brought
it firmly back to Suez. Dulles would be speaking to the General Assembly that evening. The United States must take the lead there and prevent

the Russians seizing the initiative with a false exhibition of concern for smaller nations. Dulles went off to New York and Eisenhower to Philadelphia, for the last speech of his presidential campaign. 'We cannot subscribe to one law for the weak, another law for the strong,' he said there, 'one law for those opposing us, another for those allied to us. There can be only one law – or there shall be no peace.'[14]

The weekend of 3–4 November came, and with it a strange inactivity in the White House. The Israelis had conquered Sinai, British and French troops were about to land in Egypt and Soviet tanks were massing to reoccupy Budapest and destroy the Hungarian uprising. Eisenhower faced the greatest challenge of crisis management of his Presidency and on the Saturday the indispensable Foster Dulles was suddenly taken to hospital for an urgent operation on a hitherto unsuspected cancer. On Tuesday, 6 November, the United States would be going to the polls. Yet Eisenhower spent the weekend with a group of intimates, watching a televised football game, playing bridge and telephoning his farm manager at Gettysburg to talk about cattle. On the Sunday morning he heard the news that the Russians had seized control of Budapest and went to church. On the Monday morning he heard that British and French parachute troops were landing in Port Said and Port Fuad. It seems a strange way to spend one of the most critical weekends of twentieth-century history.

Then, on that Monday morning, 5 November, Bulganin sent ferociously abusive messages to Eden and Mollet condemning the assault on Egypt and implying that the Soviet Union was ready to use force to protect its interests in the Middle East. Simultaneously he wrote to Eisenhower inviting him to join the Soviet Union in intervening in Egypt to stop the war. That message brought the President off his high horse and down to the realities of power politics. He summoned his advisers and agreed that Bulganin's proposal was preposterous. Hoover, standing in for Dulles, was instructed to announce that if the Russians tried to put troops into the Middle East the United States would resist with force – and Eisenhower inquired whether the fleet in the Mediterranean was equipped with nuclear depth charges. America might be impotent in Hungary, but it had an overwhelming strength in the Mediterranean.

Election day, Tuesday 6 November, came and the Eisenhowers went to Gettysburg to vote. Back in Washington, the President spoke on the telephone with Eden. The British had just declared that they were ready to accept a ceasefire. Now Eden faced another vote of confidence. 'If I survive here tonight,' he said, 'I will call you tomorrow.' He asked about the Presidential election. 'I don't give a damn how the election goes,' Ike replied, 'I guess it will be all right.'[15]

The voters justified his confidence. More than 35,000,000 votes were cast for Eisenhower, just under 26,000,000 for Adlai Stevenson. At a stroke the question of the President's electoral prospects was removed from the diplomatic equation. Now America could turn its full attention and bring all its strength to bear on international issues. The President's victory came too late to save Hungary, but his hands were free to tackle the Middle East crisis. If he wished he could ease the pressure on the invaders, or he could dictate terms to Eden, Mollet and Ben-Gurion.

3–4 NOVEMBER: EDEN UNDER FIRE

From the moment of his announcement of the ultimatum on Tuesday, 30 October, Eden was under ever-mounting pressure in Parliament to stop the assault on Egypt. Members may have contented themselves with anxious reflection that day, but as the bombing began, anger grew, until on one occasion the Speaker had to suspend the sitting for half an hour while tempers cooled. As the invasion convoys moved so slowly towards Egypt and Eden stuck to his plans there was a real danger of a vote to overthrow him.

His Cabinet gave him only cautious support. Selwyn Lloyd, stolid but confused and profoundly unhappy, stood by him. So did Macmillan at first, till financial pressures from the United States began to build up. At that point, he panicked. Butler had never been one of Eden's confidants, and he had made little secret of his doubts about the Suez adventure. Other members of the Cabinet, uneasily conscious that Eden had shut them out of much of the real story, were loyally correct, but they did not rush to his support. Anthony Nutting resigned and so did Edward Boyle, the Financial Secretary to the Treasury. Mountbatten drafted a letter of resignation and only a sharp rebuff from the Minister of Defence, who told him that as First Sea Lord he should concern himself with his duties rather than with politics, stopped him sending it.

Popular concern grew too. It was never unanimous – this was a nation divided down the middle by the government's adventure – but many were passionately critical. On Saturday, 3 November, Eden broadcast a message to the nation, recalling his credentials as a man of peace: 'I have been a League of Nations man and a United Nations man, and I am still the same man.' He was doing what the United Nations could not do in time, he said, and when it could take action, Britain would welcome and support it. It was an argument which swayed some, but on the following day, 4 November, a Cabinet meeting called exceptionally on the Sabbath took place against the clamour of 30,000 demonstrators gathered in Trafalgar Square and spilling down Whitehall. Very early on that Sunday the Russian onslaught on Budapest began, and to all the folly of the Suez adventure was added the additional horror that it seemed to stand in the way of any effective Western response to the Hungarian tragedy.

On the Monday the parachutists landed at Port Said, and on Tuesday the Commandos and the tanks followed. By Wednesday, American and United Nations criticism, and the financial pressure which accompanied it, was too much for Eden – he ordered the ceasefire and the halt to the advance, so removing the last scrap of practical purpose from the attack on Egypt.

OCTOBER–NOVEMBER: EGYPT AT THE UNITED NATIONS

Throughout October the United Nations had been the scene of efforts to find a non-violent solution to the Suez crisis. Until Eden recalled him to play his part in the plot with France and Israel, Selwyn Lloyd did his best to argue Britain's case there. But on the very day he arrived in New York, 2 October, determined to mobilise pressure against Nasser, Dulles yet again cut the ground from beneath his feet. 'The United States', he told a press conference, 'cannot be expected to identify herself 100 per cent either with colonial powers or the powers uniquely concerned with the problem of getting independence as rapidly and as fully as possible.' The implication was that the Suez issue was nothing more than a scrap between colonists and peoples yearning to be free. Then, as if to ensure that the SCUA plan should bring no pressure to bear on Nasser, he added: 'There is talk about teeth being pulled out of the plan, but I know of no teeth: there were no teeth in it so far as I am aware.' 'Dulles did not exactly make my heart rejoice,' wrote Lloyd long afterwards.[16]

But Lloyd was nothing if not persistent. On 5 October he opened the Security Council debate and spent the next seven days in discussion, negotiation and frustration. He tried everything, but everything seemed to conspire to undo him. Sometimes it seemed impossible to unravel the meaning of Dag Hammarskjöld's statements. Krishna Menon, the Indian representative, was still as self-serving and malignant as he had been at the London Conference. Worst of all were the contradictory words that continued to emanate from Dulles, the United States delegation, and the President himself.

Lloyd fought on doggedly. 'The impression that we were coming to the Security Council as a formality had to be dispelled,' he wrote afterwards. 'We genuinely wanted a peaceful settlement, provided it restored the international element in the working of the Canal.' And by the time Eden called him away he had persuaded himself that intense discussions with Mahmoud Fawzi, the Egyptian Foreign Minister, had brought him close to a breakthrough. But after his departure the Security Council debate on the canal came inconclusively to an end. Attention turned briefly to Hungary, to swing back to Egypt only when on 29 October the news of the Israeli march into Sinai reached New York.

Then, on 1 November, Foster Dulles arrived in New York, to make the speech to the General Assembly which set the tone for everything else that would be said about Suez in the United Nations that autumn. He spoke extempore, but for once without confusion or ambiguity. '...the United States', he said, 'finds itself unable to agree with three nations with which it has ties of deep friendship, of admiration and respect, and two of which constitute our oldest and most trusted and reliable allies.'[17] He went on to set out the long, sad story of the Suez crisis, saying 'Surely ... we must feel that the peaceful processes which the Charter requests every member of the United Nations to follow had not been exhausted.'[18] He proposed a resolution calling for an immediate ceasefire, which was carried by sixty-four votes to five (Australia and New Zealand voting with the three aggressors) with six countries – European and Commonwealth, plus Laos showing its sympathy for France – abstaining. 'You should know', Pierson Dixon, the British ambassador, reported to London, 'that even our closest friends here are becoming intensely worried at the possible consequences which might follow if we and the French remain for long in open defiance of the UN.'[19]

At that time Douglas Hurd had just arrived in New York. He had been transferred from Peking, to serve as private secretary to Dixon. This was to be his first experience of big-time multilateral diplomacy. He started work when the delegation was in turmoil, and as his colleagues became ever more involved in the developing crisis he felt himself almost as useless as I felt in Levant Department at exactly the same time. His superiors, he wrote in his memoirs almost half a century afterwards, 'had little time to explain to me what was happening and how things worked, let alone what I might do to help. For several weeks I felt unhappily idle while those I was meant to support bustled furiously about me.'[20]

For Hurd, things suddenly came into focus on the evening of 29 October. The British and American ambassadors were sitting in adjoining boxes at the Metropolitan Opera when the news of the Israeli march into Sinai reached them. Maria Callas was singing Norma in the Bellini opera of that name, but there was as much drama going on in the boxes as on stage. A telegram was brought to Dixon hot from London. It instructed him not to go along with any motion to take Israel to the Security Council. Yet to the Americans that was the obvious response to aggression; and, recalling the Tripartite Declaration, they wanted Britain and France to join them in it. So in the interval Cabot Lodge, the American ambassador, came to Dixon's box to agree on procedure. Dixon could only tell him, in the words that Lodge reported to the President, that the Tripartite Declaration 'was ancient history and without current validity'.[21]

The storm which had been grumbling in the United Nations since the end of July burst. Now it began to become clear that Britain and France were acting in collusion with Israel, and that the Israeli assault was a put-up job. Eisenhower was determined to punish the British and French for what was in his eyes the ultimate offence of deceiving him, the President of the United States. The American mission to the United Nations went to work to put that determination into effect. 'It was not simply that they frustrated what we were trying to do,' Hurd wrote of the Americans' activities. 'They destroyed the intimacy of Anglo-American cooperation. They cut us out of their lives on all subjects for several months. We spent humiliating hours trying to find out what had happened at meetings which they had called, from which we had been excluded.' Eisenhower had insisted that the United States should take the lead in the attack on the Allies. He told intimates that he was doing so to prevent the Russians scooping all the credit in the Third World for rebuffing colonialist aggression. But he was not averse to receiving the

Third World's plaudits. Lodge sent him excited messages about the gratitude which greeted American policy: from Third World ambassadors to Haitian lift attendants, all were pressing Lodge's patrician hand and telling him to thank the President for them. All this showed the American electorate that Eisenhower, the war hero, really was a man of peace. By comparison the interests of two countries which remained, when all was said and done, America's closest allies were featherweight considerations.

So as the Israelis advanced towards the canal, as Britain and France called on them and the Egyptians to pull back and as their invasion armada steamed steadily from Malta to Port Said, Cabot Lodge led the pack against Dixon, the French and Israeli missions and those rare allies, Australia and New Zealand. 'We sit in the General Assembly', Hurd wrote in his diary, '…hearing the world crumbling around us. Dulles very solemn and impressive and unscrupulous about Suez. Poisonous attacks on us by the Afro-Asian ranks – gallant worried attempts by Aust. and N.Z. …Louis de Guiringaud [the French mission's deputy ambassador] calm and euphonious. Ludicrously massive vote against us.'[22]

Those who were in New York never forgot the tension of those days. In the course of them the French ambassador, recently arrived and struggling to combine chairmanship of the Security Council with defence of his own government's position, physically and mentally exhausted, succumbed to an old malaria. His deputy was left to stand, almost alone, beside Dixon. On 3 November the news of Anthony Nutting's resignation reached New York. Those who had seen him in action at the United Nations earlier knew him for something less than a heroic figure, but to the British government's critics he became, however briefly, a warrior for truth.

Pierson Dixon, a very much more substantial man than Nutting, also contemplated resignation. He was horrified by what Britain was doing, and as Britain's advocate at the United Nations uniquely exposed in defending the indefensible. Hurd watched him struggle with his conscience over reports that British bombs were hitting civilian targets. 'Dixon,' he wrote, 'facing a hideous personal dilemma, believing that the British Government's policy was tragically mistaken, needed to find a test for that Government which would decide whether he continued in its service.'[23] In the end Dixon decided to soldier on. 'Britain's most distinguished public servant', in Anthony Eden's words, persevered at the United Nations, diligent, wise, conciliatory. In doing so he saved what was left of Britain's international reputation for fair dealing, and rescued what could be rescued from the wreck.

When he came to write his memoirs in 2003, Douglas Hurd ventured a judgement which is worth recording here for the sidelight it throws on Britain's partnership with the United States in a modern Middle East adventure quite as wrong-headed as Suez ever was. He drew a parallel between the Americans' behaviour in 1956 and their equally brutal treatment ten years earlier when Britain was asking for a loan to save it from postwar bankruptcy: '... no rhetoric about a special relationship influenced on either occasion the chilly American calculation of US interests,' he wrote. Hurd offered no third example of American ruthlessness, but one senses that his conclusion draws on the wealth of experience of working with the United States which he accumulated over forty years in public life. 'Too often we British clothe the Anglo-US relationship in a warm, fuzzy haze,' he wrote. 'Its basis is the real usefulness of one country to the other. If that usefulness dries up, no amount of speech-making will prevent the relationship from withering.'[24]

IO

Hungary Attacked

On 30 October Mikoyan and Suslov, the Kremlin's most assiduous
travellers, returned again to Budapest. They brought with them the text
of a new Soviet government declaration. It dealt with relationships
between the Soviet Union and its Socialist neighbours, and with the
nature of the Warsaw Pact. It brought Nagy further encouragement just
at a time when he seemed to be getting the changing situation within
Hungary under control.

The declaration is a remarkable document. In 1,300 words of
straightforward prose it makes calm and sensible proposals to improve
relationships between the members of the Warsaw Pact.[1] It seemed to
call for exactly the kind of relationship which Nagy had envisaged in
his essay nine months earlier, one of equality based on the Bandung
principles of independence, sovereignty and non-interference. It
confirmed that orders had been given to withdraw Soviet forces from
Budapest and that Moscow was ready for negotiations about their
presence elsewhere in Hungary. It offered to look with an open mind at
ways in which Warsaw Pact arrangements and relationships could be
adjusted to take into account the realities of the positions of member
states. There were worrying passages, such as the allegation that reactionary elements in Hungary had taken advantage of legitimate discon-
tent, and the way in which it seemed to prejudge the Hungarian
people's political wishes by saying that it was up to them to safeguard
their own socialist gains. But it read like a vote of confidence in Nagy's
ability to keep control. Even more important was the way it set the
Hungarian question in the much wider context of equal and free relationships between all the members of the Warsaw Pact. If it had been
allowed to stand it would have provided a basis for an enduring friendship between the Soviet Union and its East European neighbours.

With the declaration as background, Mikoyan and Suslov settled down with Nagy and Kádár to an anxious discussion of the situation in Hungary. By now, 30 October, the worst of the revolutionary disorders seemed to be behind them. The fighting had ended and Soviet troops had pulled out of Budapest. The leaders of the revolutionary fighters were talking to Nagy and his colleagues. It looked as if Nagy had at last caught up with events and was imposing order on them. The Russians left, and as they said goodbye an onlooker heard Mikoyan say to Nagy, 'Comrade Nagy, save what can be saved.' Kádár took them to the street door of Parliament. When he came back he said to Nagy: 'Imre, have we done it?' 'We've done it, János,' Nagy replied.[2] At that moment they believed that they had convinced the Soviet visitors that Hungary could safely be left in their hands – and perhaps they had. It was the high point of the Hungarian Revolution.

Mikoyan and Suslov flew back to Moscow, where the Central Committee had been holding a two-day meeting. They found the situation there fundamentally altered, for the Kremlin wind had swung around since the 30 October declaration was written. Now the Soviet leaders were convinced that they could not let the Hungarian uprising live. They may have feared that reaction was taking charge in Hungary – though there is next to no evidence to support that fear. There was a danger of infection spreading to the other satellites, the more so because the Poles had so successfully defied Khrushchev only ten days earlier. The Kremlin may have seen events in the Middle East as threatening, or as helpful in distracting the West's attention from Hungary. Whatever the cause, Mikoyan and Suslov encountered a very different mood in Moscow when they returned.

'We discussed the mutiny', Khrushchev recalled long afterwards with a rather sickening unction, 'and came to the conclusion that it would be inexcusable for us to stay neutral and not to help the working class of Hungary in its struggle against the counter-revolution. We passed a unanimous resolution to that effect.'[3] Whatever hopes they may have had in Budapest, the returning travellers could only fall in line. By 31 October free Hungary was doomed and the Soviet declaration which they had taken to Budapest had become no more than a scrap of paper.

The Soviet Union was not pursuing nationalist goals, Khrushchev writes, still oozing unction, but 'the internationalist goal of fraternal proletarian solidarity. To make sure that all countries understood us correctly on this point we decided to consult with the other Socialist countries – first and foremost with the fraternal Communist Party of

China.' So on the night of 31 October–1 November Khrushchev settled down with a visiting Chinese delegation in one of Stalin's dachas. They talked all night, first deciding for intervention, then against, as if the Russians had not yet taken the decision that had settled the fate of Hungary. In the morning, Khrushchev says, he went to report to the Central Committee leadership that they had decided against intervention. Eventually, they decided (yet more unction here) 'that it would be unforgivable, simply unforgivable, if we stood by and refused to assist our Hungarian comrades'.[4] The entire Soviet leadership trooped out to the airport to tell the departing Chinese what they had decided: 'There were no arguments at all. The conversation proceeded in a particularly fraternal atmosphere ... We were all thinking about the well-being of the Hungarian working class and about the future of the Hungarian people.'[5]

The Chinese delegation said that they still needed to get Mao Tse-tung's agreement. From Peking they would relay China's formal position, but the Russians could assume that the Chinese would back them. It remained for the Russians to talk to the East European Communist leaders. Khrushchev and Malenkov flew off on this diplomatic mission, while the Soviet generals set about putting their military machinery into gear.

2–3 NOVEMBER: THE COMMISSARS CONSPIRE

On the night of 2 November four men gathered on a landing stage on the Adriatic island of Brioni. It was a foul night: 'It was pitch-dark outside, you couldn't see your hand in front of your face, there was a howling gale, and it was as rough on the little stretch of water across to Brioni as on the open sea.'[6] They shivered as they waited, until a motor launch eventually emerged from the darkness. Two men stepped ashore. They were half prostrate with seasickness; and long afterwards one of them, Nikita Khrushchev, recalled that his companion, Georgi Malenkov, was 'pale as a corpse'.

They had had a nightmare journey. They had flown in a small aircraft from Sofia 'to consult with Comrade Tito. The weather couldn't have been worse. We had to fly through the mountains at night in a fierce thunderstorm ... I'd never flown in conditions this bad ... During the storm we lost contact with our escort reconnaissance plane.' When at last the aircraft landed at Pula on the Adriatic coast, the airfield was nothing more than 'one of those primitive airstrips built during the war ... When we landed, we asked if our other plane had arrived. The Yugoslavs told us they didn't know anything about it. We were very distressed about the fate of the crew'.[7] The two Kremlin leaders could count themselves lucky to have survived.

From the airport they were taken to the motor launch for the crossing to Brioni. 'We had just landed after the roughest flight imaginable and now we were heading out into a choppy sea in a small launch. Malenkov lay down in the boat and shut his eyes. I was worried about what kind of shape he'd be in when we docked, but we didn't have any choice. As the old Russian saying goes, we couldn't sit on the beach and wait for good weather.' Khrushchev and Malenkov were paying a high price for their eagerness to consult the Yugoslavs.

Their hosts did nothing to make things easier for them. If there had been any suggestion that the Yugoslav leaders might return to Belgrade to receive the visitors, it had been rejected. Let them come all the way through an autumn gale to Tito's island retreat. 'For the sake of "security" the officers from the security service and Tito's guard had brought them from Pula to Brioni by a longer route than they needed, through very bad seas, strong winds, and pitch-darkness, so that Khrushchev and Malenkov had both felt very sick by the end of it.'[8] For the Russians, this was truly the road to Canossa.

Both sides did their best to put a good face on things. Tito 'welcomed us cordially. We embraced and kissed each other, although until recently our relations had been strained, and they were becoming more and more strained as the events in Hungary developed.'[9] Days afterwards Micunovic, the Yugoslav ambassador in Moscow, remembered that at Brioni the Russians 'behaved in an extremely cordial manner, as never before. This was a premeditated gesture intended to influence our whole attitude towards them ...'[10] He remembered the kisses too: 'I still seem to feel Malenkov's fat round face, into which my nose sank as if into a half-inflated balloon as I was drawn into a cold and quite unexpected embrace.' Khrushchev and Malenkov badly needed Yugoslav goodwill when they made their journey to Brioni.

They had come, of course, to discuss the revolution in Hungary. It had taken them a whole night to reach agreement with the Chinese in Moscow.[11] Then Khrushchev had flown to the Soviet-Polish border to tell the Poles what the Kremlin intended to do about Hungary. The Poles argued, but were wise enough not to push their luck for the second time in ten days. Then Khrushchev and Malenkov flew to Bucharest to brief the Romanians and Czechs, and to Sofia to talk to the Bulgarians. All agreed with the Russians.

How the Yugoslavs would react was more uncertain. Khrushchev records his surprise that their response was so unambiguous: 'I expected even more strenuous objections from Tito than the ones we had encountered during our discussions with the Polish comrades ... We reported to Tito on why we had come and confronted him with our decision to send troops into Budapest. We asked for his reaction. Tito said that we were absolutely right and that we should send our soldiers into action as quickly as possible. He said we had an obligation to help Hungary crush the counter-revolution'.[12]

Yet there was more at stake in the all-night meeting in Tito's villa than Yugoslav applause for a Soviet attack upon Hungary. The six men round the table that night – four Yugoslavs and two Russians – had spent seven years at bitter odds about the true nature of Communism and about the relationship between Moscow and the Socialist countries. In 1949 the Kremlin denounced Tito as a renegade and drove him out of the Soviet camp. For years the East European Socialist countries joined Moscow in waging a bitter ideological and economic war against Yugoslavia, and throughout Eastern Europe good Communists, like Rajk in Hungary, were hanged on charges of espionage for the Yugoslavs. But Tito had proved unyielding, and gradually he built himself a position as a leader of the non-aligned movement, distinct not just from Washington but from his old partners in Moscow.

After Stalin's death the new Soviet leadership had started to rebuild their bridges to Belgrade. It was for them a bitter process, and they resented the way Tito forced them to come to him, with scarcely a gesture of movement towards them. Micunovic, arriving in Moscow to take up his post in March 1956, entered a hostile world. Yet it was a world in which he, while still held at arm's length, was treated also as a socialist, almost as a comrade, an ambassador with a privileged relationship with Khrushchev and the other Soviet leaders, even when they used the relationship to abuse him and the government he represented. The process had continued when in September Tito accepted an invitation to spend a working holiday in the Crimea. His relationship with Khrushchev there was like Micunovic's on any working day in Moscow: intimate yet wary, friendly in a coarsely jocular way, but with a continuing undertone of menace and hostility.

So Micunovic gives us a subtler impression than Khrushchev's of the talks on Brioni on the night of 2–3 November 1956. Beneath the insincere good fellowship, brutal realities were ill-concealed. 'Khrushchev talked about the way events in Hungary were moving towards counter-revolution ... Communists in Hungary were being murdered, butchered, and hanged ... Whether Nagy was just a tool or had long been an agent of imperialism was not clear at the moment; what was important was that things had taken this course and that the outcome would be the restoration of capitalism.' Khrushchev had turned rhetorical: 'What is there left for us to do? If we let things take their course the West would say we are either stupid or weak, and that's one and the same thing. We cannot permit it, either as Communists and internationalists or as the Soviet state. We would have capitalists on the frontiers of the Soviet Union.'[13]

The Yugoslavs went along with this. It was clear to them that the Soviet leaders had made up their minds; they too feared the democratic contagion that could spread from a free Hungary; they may have feared that matters in Budapest were getting out of hand. At the same time they knew that the storm that had blown through Poland and Hungary was driven by the same reaction against Stalinism as had driven their own breach with Moscow in 1949. For them, Khrushchev's secret speech in February had been a signal of better times. So were the Kremlin's attempts to build better relations with the Yugoslavs, the old pariahs. So, for that matter, had been the Soviet declaration of 30 October, which had seemed to promise freedom and equality to the countries of the socialist camp. Now, two days later, Khrushchev was tearing up that declaration, preparing war against Hungary.

There was, Micunovic noted, something shamefaced about the secrecy of the meeting. On their side of the table, Khrushchev and Malenkov were alone, without even the support of the Soviet ambassador in Belgrade. Tito was accompanied only by Micunovic himself and by his two senior colleagues, Rankovic and Kardelj. 'There was nobody else in the room – no notetaker, no interpreter, and no "technicians"... There was nothing, not even a scrap of paper, on the table. Nobody made any notes; just occasionally one of us would jot down [something] on a piece of paper ... and when he had finished he would tear up the paper and drop it in an ashtray ... It is all very odd ... There is in fact a war going on ... And it is being waged by the armed forces of "the first and biggest country of socialism" against the people of a "fraternal socialist country" and a member of the "social-ist camp".'[14]

They discussed whom the Russians should put in charge in Hungary when they had unseated Imre Nagy. Khrushchev favoured Münnich, the Yugoslavs Kádár – and Kádár and Münnich were indeed the two Hungarian leaders who returned to Budapest in an armoured car on 7 November when the way had been cleared by Soviet tanks. There was, too, the question of Nagy's fate. Could Tito, the Russians asked, help them over that? It seems to have been agreed that the Yugoslavs should offer Nagy and his colleagues asylum in the Yugoslav embassy. There they could be isolated from the fighting in the streets and the politicking that would follow; from there, perhaps, they could be brought out to rally behind a government acquiescent in Soviet wishes. In the end Khrushchev and Malenkov went away early on 3 November satisfied, ready to order an all-out Soviet assault on Imre Nagy's Hungary.

The Yugoslavs were left reflecting on their changed relationship with Moscow. On the face of it, they had come out the winners from this strange encounter. Khrushchev and Malenkov had come to Canossa and treated the Yugoslavs as comrades and friends. They had revealed how much they needed Yugoslav help. An optimist could see the meet-ing as restoring the Yugoslavs to the Kremlin's favour. But a realist, let alone a pessimist, might worry at what Tito had let himself in for. The coming attack on Hungary was going to shock world opinion; the whole Socialist camp would join Moscow in the dock. The Yugoslavs had involved themselves directly by agreeing to take Nagy in. Would the world give them the credit for saving him from his enemies? Perhaps; but how long would the Russians tolerate Yugoslav protection of the men they were about to overthrow? And when the Yugoslavs gave up their guests, how would their reputation then fare? Everything depended on Nagy, once installed in the embassy, recanting, perhaps even accepting some token role in the new Hungarian regime. Tito, in short, had entrusted his policies and reputation to Imre Nagy's hands.

3 NOVEMBER: THE DYING OF THE LIGHT

While Khrushchev and Malenkov travelled round Eastern Europe making the diplomatic preparations, the Soviet generals were moving their troops into position for the assault on Hungary. There was going to be no messing with this second assault on the Hungarian Revolution.

It was impossible to hide all this preparation, much of it inside Hungary, and from the morning of Thursday, 1 November, Nagy knew that the fair words of the declaration which Mikoyan and Suslov had brought him on Tuesday were as good as dead. But he and his colleagues could still hope that Moscow might change course again and decide to let a free Hungary live. It was a faint hope, and it grew fainter over the first three days of November. But it was all that was left to Nagy and his supporters, and it was worth playing out to the end what came increasingly to look like a charade.

So at 9 am on Thursday, 1 November, Nagy summoned the Soviet Ambassador, Yuri Andropov, and complained about Soviet troop movements into Hungary. These breached both the Warsaw Pact and the very recent agreement that the troops would be pulled out of the country. Andropov checked with Moscow and two hours later assured Nagy that the newcomers were no more than reliefs for troops who had already gone; they too would be withdrawn in turn. At noon he telephoned Nagy to assure him that Moscow still stood by the terms of the 30 October Declaration.

But telephone reports continued to flow into Nagy's office in Parliament. They came from Hungarian army units, from mayors' offices and police stations, and from railway officials who saw their rolling stock being seized at gunpoint. Tanks and troops were pouring into Hungary at Zahony on the Ukrainian border. In the west the Russians were sealing off the border with Austria. Other units were seizing Hungarian airfields. Hungarian officers were asking for orders to fire on the invaders. Nagy rang Andropov demanding to know what was happening, and threatened to announce Hungary's withdrawal from the Warsaw Pact. The whole Cabinet endorsed that threat and Nagy summoned Andropov again. In a tense meeting at 5 pm Nagy told Andropov that Hungary was no longer bound by the Pact's terms and was going to protest to the United Nations. Kádár, in what was his last appearance at Nagy's side, threatened that if Soviet tanks entered Budapest he would fight them with his bare hands. Andropov repeated his promise that the troops would be withdrawn and begged Nagy not to take the matter to the United Nations. That evening Nagy despatched his appeal to the United Nations, sent messages to Western embassies in Budapest, and broadcast to the nation, announcing Hungary's withdrawal from the Pact.

Andropov went on playing on what was left of Nagy's hopes. Late on 1 November he came yet again to Parliament, urging a cancellation of the appeal to the United Nations and still promising a troop withdrawal. Nagy let the appeal stand, but he issued specific instructions that Hungarian forces were not to fire on the invaders.

On that same evening, Kádár disappeared from Parliament. Budapest Radio then broadcast a speech he had recorded in the morning, and his voice and words came across as defiant as those he had used with Andropov. But by now he and Münnich had joined Andropov in the Soviet embassy. The Russians flew them to Moscow. There Kádár conferred with Soviet leaders and signed a declaration, drafted in Russian and only belatedly translated into Hungarian, in which he undertook to form a new Hungarian government to replace Nagy's.[15] It was an undertaking which completed his transition from embattled patriot to servant of his country's enemies.

But the farce was not over yet. On the morning of Friday, 2 November, Andropov came back to Parliament yet again. He reported that the Soviet government had taken note of Hungary's withdrawal from the Warsaw Pact and proposed political and military talks between the two countries. As long as Soviet troops went on pouring into Hungary the proposal looked like nothing more than prevarication; but the Hungarians had nothing to hope for but hope itself. So they sent Andropov three diplomatic notes in reply. In the first they agreed to political talks on the assumption that the Russians recognised the principles of equality, sovereignty and non-interference – the very principles of Bandung, which Nagy had embraced so enthusiastically in his essay in January and which the Soviet declaration had seemed to endorse three days ago. In the second they named Pál Maléter, the colonel who had emerged as a national hero in the course of the uprising and who was now Nagy's Minister of Defence, as their representative at the military talks. In the third they protested yet again at Soviet troop movements into Hungary.

The military talks started in Budapest on Saturday, 3 November, and in a rather forced atmosphere of military bonhomie seemed to be going well. It was agreed that they would be continued that evening at a Soviet air base on Csepel island in the Danube on the southern fringes of the capital (the airfield from which, we now know, Kádár and Münnich were flown to Moscow). Meanwhile, whatever the threat that hung over it, Budapest seemed to be recovering its peacetime animation. Yet another new government was formed, this time with all four major parties of the postwar period included. Workers' councils in the industrial suburbs, Csepel and Ujpest, which spoke for men who had borne so much of the fighting in the uprising, announced that they would resume work on Monday, 5 November. It was assumed that all Hungary would follow their lead and in many places work was already beginning on the Saturday. There still seemed to be room for hope, and the less you knew the more hope you entertained.

Maléter and his delegation set off for the meeting with the Soviet delegate to the military talks, General Malinin. Nagy, waiting in Parliament, soon lost radio contact with them. When they arrived at the Soviet airfield Malinin pressed a banquet upon them. It was nearly midnight before the festivities were broken up by the arrival of Serov, the dreaded Soviet security chief, at the head of a hit squad of Soviet special troops and Hungarian security policemen. Malinin expressed real or feigned indignation, but Serov ordered him out of the room and arrested the Hungarians.*

Soon after Maléter's arrest, Soviet tanks and troops began to move into Budapest. They met fierce resistance in places, little or none in others, but nothing delayed them very long. At 5.05 am Kádár announced on a provincial radio transmitter the establishment of his renegade government. Fifteen minutes later Nagy broadcast a bleak little message to the nation and the world, announcing that Soviet troops were moving into the capital 'with the obvious intention of overthrowing the legal Hungarian democratic government' and declaring that the government was at its post and that Hungarian troops were in action. By dawn Soviet tanks and troops were in the centre of Budapest, 'in control of the Danube bridges, the Parliament Building and the central telephone exchange'.[16]

At some stage in the long night of 3–4 November Nagy and his principal Communist colleagues received an invitation, approved by Tito, to take refuge in the Yugoslav embassy. At dawn they went there, with wives and children a considerable little party. Soviet officers, penetrating into the long corridors and dark corners of Parliament, found them largely deserted. In one room, however, they came across one man, busy typing. He was in fact a minister of state in Nagy's government. István Bibó, a noted academic and a representative of the newly reformed Petöfi Party, was busying himself with the unworldly task of composing an official protest against the illegal overthrow of the Nagy

* Maléter was executed with Nagy in June 1958.

government and its replacement by Kádár's. They took him for a minor functionary and left him to his labours.*

4 NOVEMBER: THE CARDINAL SEEKS ASYLUM

Early on 4 November, while Nagy and the Communist members of his government set off for the Yugoslav Embassy, Cardinal Mindszenty and his secretary walked the couple of hundred yards from Parliament to the United States Legation and rang the bell. József Cardinal Mindszenty, Primate of Hungary, was seeking asylum. He stayed there for the next fifteen years, living in a sunlit upstairs corner room which the Legation made over to him.† It overlooked one of the city's central squares, and through the Venetian blinds he could see, if he cared, the unmarked police car that always waited there against the unlikely event that he might make a run for it. (In my time in Hungary in the late 1950s, an irreverent Italian diplomat suggested that the Americans should give a fancy dress party for the Western diplomatic corps. We would all go as cardinals, causing chaos among the police when twenty of the West's finest emerged simultaneously on the pavement dressed in red soutanes and sporting cardinals' hats.) Mindszenty took exercise (with an American always escorting him) in the small courtyard at the back of the building, talked to the occasional member of the staff who came to see him, and said Sunday mass for a few Western members of the Budapest diplomatic community.

Mindszenty was a controversial figure in 1956. Under the Nazis and at the coming of the Communists he had shown himself a brave and stubborn man who spoke out for the people of a largely Catholic country. In the last year of the war he did his best to stand up to the Germans and to Hungary's own fascist party, the Arrow Cross. In the early postwar years, when democracy still had a tenuous hold in Hungary, he spoke out for the property rights of his Church in language that could too easily be characterised as reactionary. He tried to protect the Church's schools from expropriation, and that too could be seen as a controversial defiance of the state. The Communists went on taking

---

* In 1958 Bibó was sentenced to life imprisonment. He was released five years later and died in 1979.

† Mindszenty remained in asylum in the US Legation until 1971, when he left Hungary under arrangements agreed with the Hungarian government by the Vatican. He died in 1975.

their salami slices towards power, the salami slices with which, Rákosi bragged, he was cutting away his opponents' ability to resist. Eventually they reached the Prince Primate and in February 1949 Mindszenty was arrested.

He was taken to 60 Andrássy Avenue, later renamed Stalin Avenue, then Avenue of the People's Republic and now Andrássy Avenue again. Passers-by used to cross the street to avoid the shadow of No. 60, for it housed the most dreaded interrogation centre of the security police. Men and women who were taken there through the sinister garage gates in a side street came out broken if they came out at all, ready to confess to anything when they were put on trial to show the people what crimes they had got up to against their People's Republic. In No. 60 Mindszenty faced implausible accusations of espionage and currency speculation. The security police quickly broke his powers of resistance, he was displayed in a show trial and sentenced to life imprisonment.

His day in court over, Mindszenty vanished into Hungary's Gulag. Over the years the conditions in which he was imprisoned improved, and when the revolution came he was living an isolated existence under house arrest in northern Hungary. On 30 October an Army officer found him and escorted him to his palace in Budapest. On the evening of 3 November he spoke on the radio in a speech whose ambiguities were fought over for years afterwards by propagandists, particularly Left-inclined propagandists, who wanted to find in it proof of the essentially reactionary nature of the whole revolution. Whatever Mindszenty may or may not have intended, it was all for nothing, since the Soviet tanks were already closing in on Budapest and the revolution's last hours were numbered. An impartial Hungarian historian sums up the Mindszenty of that time by saying that he stood at the centre of 'a conservative, mainly Catholic group ... oriented to an older historical model [than Nagy's] and accepting the post-1945 reforms only with reservations'.[17] My own judgement is that he was simultaneously a hero, a victim and a political babe-in-arms.

So on 4 November 1956 Mindszenty began his long stay as an honoured but increasingly embarrassing guest of the American Legation in Budapest. I got to know him when he had been there two years and we started to go to his mass on Sunday. We were never more than eight or nine Western diplomats in the congregation, but he would give us the benefits of his thoughts in full-blown sermons in scarcely comprehensible English. At first the Americans asked us not to enter into conversation with him, but gradually things changed, and when our third child was born we asked whether the Cardinal might baptise him. It was agreed that he could, but with only our family and an American godfather present. We took along our eldest child, the daughter with whom this book started, to witness her brother's christening.

By then Mindszenty was a benevolent old man in a red soutane, not the brave and cantankerous figure who had set out to defy Nazis and Communists in turn. He had sweets and a tangerine ready for Julia, then turned his attention to her baby brother. Stephen, he baptised him, after Hungary's eleventh-century king and patron saint, St István. We went home, and there our three-year-old showed her tangerine to our maid Eva, who certainly reported regularly to the secret police. Julia told her just where she had got her presents and from whom: 'Father Christmas poured water over Stephen in the Legation' she said. So out of the mouth of a babe flowed a secret of state.

4 NOVEMBER–10 DECEMBER: LAST STANDS

The second and more hard-fought phase of the Soviet-Hungarian war of 1956 began on 1 November, when Soviet troops started to re-enter Hungary. They came in from Zahony and Beregszász, just over Hungary's frontier with Ukraine in the extreme north-east of the country. They moved south-westwards, to Miskolc and Debrecen. From Miskolc, units of the Soviet 13th Army advanced on the capital from the east, while units of the 38th Army moved from Debrecen across the Hungarian Great Plain and then, via Kecskemét, bypassed the capital to the south. Some units then swung north, approaching Budapest and Györ (on the road from Vienna to Budapest, along which any notional intervention from the West would have to come) from the south. Other units continued westward, south of Lake Balaton, towards the Austrian frontier. Yet others came into Hungary from Romania, to guard the Yugoslav border. By early morning of 4 November, when Soviet intentions were made unambiguously clear by the assault on Budapest itself, the Russians had an armed presence in the whole country.

Outside Budapest and the industrial cities, they met little resistance. We have seen Nagy hoping that Moscow would yet take the political decision to let the revolution live, and ordering his troops to do nothing to challenge the Russians. So the invaders were able to proceed from garrison to garrison, disarming Hungarian soldiers in each. Some units tried to resist the advance, but were easily swept aside. In the major towns along the way freedom fighters resisted and were bloodily disposed of. Workers' councils tried to organise against the invasion, but their members were at once arrested.

And of course, no Western support came down that road from Vienna. For years the United States (and John Foster Dulles in particular) had talked, emotively and imprecisely, of 'rolling back' Communism. When revolution came, Radio Free Europe broadcast inflammatory material. But in so far as they could devise a coherent line in those fraught days of October and early November (and Britain and France were preoccupied with Suez, the United States with the Presidential election), the Western powers thought that the best contribution they could make to the cause of Hungarian freedom was to assure Moscow that it could safely let those troublesome Hungarians go – there would be no thought in the West of conscripting them into NATO when they were free. At the time it may have seemed a craven policy, but in the light of history it was clearly not just inevitable but also right. Whatever Radio Free Europe may have implied to the contrary, there was no way of getting Western military help to the Hungarians, and no rational case at all for using nuclear weapons in their defence.

Left to fight alone, the Hungarians' resistance was strongest in Budapest and one or two other industrial centres. In his last message to the nation on the morning of 4 November Nagy at last seemed to reverse his order that the Hungarian Army should not engage the invaders. 'Our troops are in combat,' he said, and a few of them were.

Civilian freedom fighters were active too. A group ensconced around a cinema in Pest fought effectively, and so did troops in a nearby barracks, blocking its main gate with a tank that for a time resisted Soviet fire. Insurgents calling themselves the National Guard Command tried to coordinate resistance, but with limited effect. In Buda groups of young people, some of them schoolchildren, some of them led by gallant old men, tried to hold city squares and road junctions. But by 8 November the fighting was over in the centre of the city, and by 10 November in the nearest industrial suburbs. The fighters in Csepel, an industrial centre and working-class district on an island in the Danube just south of the city, had got hold of a number of anti-aircraft guns, with which they held Soviet tanks at bay and even succeeded in shooting down a Russian aircraft, but by 11 November they too were silenced. Another centre of working-class resistance, the new industrial town of Dunapentele on the Danube forty miles south of Budapest, ceased fire on the same day. A few bands continued their resistance in the hilly north of Hungary, more often than not on their way to escape to Austria and exile. A few security troops aside, no Hungarians fought on the Russians' side. This really was a war between the Soviet Union and Hungary, the only war between two sovereign states to be fought in Europe between 1945 and the Balkan wars of the 1990s. But it was a terribly one-sided war, and inevitably a short one.

It was notable that in this second phase of the revolution as in the first, most of the fighting was done by working men and by very young people, schoolchildren, students and young factory workers. Once again the middle classes were conspicuously absent. This was an uprising of the working classes against those who claimed to speak in the workers' name – the Soviet Union and the Communist party.

An official report compiled in 1957 and kept secret by the authorities for over thirty years put Hungarian losses in the war against the Soviet Union at a minimum of 2,700 dead and ten times that number wounded.[18] Of the dead, 1,330 were workers, 44 students, and 196 children under fourteen years of age. The real total must have been higher, for many of those who died fighting or were shot out of hand when captured were buried where they fell. And figures for the provincial towns and villages were much less reliable than those for the capital. Soviet troops took their casualties too, and Soviet documents put their losses at 669 dead, 1,450 wounded and 51 missing. Dealing as they do with the losses of organised units, these figures are probably more accurate than those for Hungarian losses among freedom fighters, demonstrators and passers-by, few of them in uniform.

So some Hungarians fought to the end. Others set about organising unarmed resistance to the invaders – and once again the workers were in the forefront. In the heady days of the uprising, workers' councils had sprung up in individual factories and industrial districts. During the fighting some of them organised armed groups, others called strikes and demonstrations, and the major ones put their demands directly to the Nagy government. Now they started campaigns of passive resistance: strikes, demonstrations, marches.

At first the Kádár regime talked with them, claimed to welcome their opinions, and handled their demonstrations gingerly. Over November and December, however, the regime's attitude steadily hardened, and on

11 December martial law was proclaimed. The first trials and executions for armed resistance, for incitement to violence, and for concealing arms began. Demonstrations by workers were banned, strikes broken. The Workers' Guard was formed: hard-line Communists who were armed and deployed as a counterweight to the continuing influence of the democratic workers' councils. And in early 1957 came the first trials of councils' leaders.

11

Hungary Eclipsed

4 NOVEMBER: AT THE UNITED NATIONS

The United Nations never showed quite the enthusiasm to get its teeth into the Soviet attack upon Hungary that it so joyously displayed over Egypt. Almost all its members could agree in condemning Israeli, French and British aggression. The Soviet Union, on the other hand, had its loyal band of satellite supporters. To Third World delegations, Hungary was far away, Suez immediate. A firm American lead might have made a difference, but we have seen Eisenhower consciously giving priority to Suez, recognising throughout that he could do nothing effective for Hungary without risking war. In the end the Soviet Union was too powerful, its position as the occupying power in Hungary too secure.

Nevertheless, on 28 October, five days after the start of the uprising, the Security Council held a meeting to discuss the situation in Hungary. At that stage things there seemed to be going well, with Imre Nagy restoring order and reaching out beyond the Communist Party to the people at large. Soviet troops were being pulled out of Budapest, and no United Nations statement, let alone action, seemed required. Indeed, at that stage too much Western interest in what was happening in Hungary would probably have been unwise. So on 29 October the Security Council turned away from Hungary, to a French complaint of Egyptian assistance to the Algerian rebels. It was soon overtaken by the news of the Israeli attack in Sinai and on 30 and 31 October, the Security Council embarked on its four-meeting marathon discussion of Israeli aggression and the European Allies' ultimatum. That debate was then taken up by the General Assembly, which held three meetings on 1 and 2 November. Four vital days had passed without discussion of Hungary.

In those four days the trajectory of the Hungarian Revolution reached its zenith and then, as evidence mounted that Soviet forces were returning, plunged to earth. In his note of 1 November Nagy told Dag Hammarskjöld that Hungary was leaving the Warsaw Pact and declaring its neutrality. He asked the Secretary-General to include in the General Assembly's agenda 'the question of Hungary's neutrality and the defense of this neutrality by the four Great Powers'.[1] On the following day, Friday, 2 November, the Security Council duly turned its attention to Hungary again.

A friend of mine was a junior member of the British Delegation at that time. Like Douglas Hurd, Mary Moore was a second secretary and a newcomer to New York. She and he were learning the ways of multilateral diplomacy fast that autumn. But whereas he had come from a remote Peking, she had immediate, first-hand memories of Budapest, having left the legation there only in the early summer of 1956. 'I felt passionate about Hungary,' she told me, but she found a United Nations pretty well impotent to do anything about it. Of the atmosphere in New York at the time, she said it was 'dramatic, awful ... They were all hounding us over Suez, all except the Australians and New Zealanders ... There was confusion about everything, we were always meeting in the middle of the night, there were so few of us in the delegation, trying to cover so much ... above all I remember how desperately tired we were... Of course, there was so little we could do about Hungary.'

Debate in New York hung on news from Budapest. In the five days since the Security Council's first discussion of Hungary on 28 October the situation there had dramatically worsened. By now it was clear that only a political miracle could avert a Soviet assault, but on 2 November New York, like Budapest, was still waiting on that miracle. The meeting was fraught, agonising, but inconclusive. So passed the last occasion when the Security Council might have taken action – but what action? – to deter a Soviet attack. When it next met, on 4 November, at 3 am in New York but at midday by Central European time, the attack had gone in and Hungary was prostrate, its power to resist broken. The General Assembly passed what Hurd calls 'a noble, useless resolution' that afternoon.[2]

Yet Hungarian hopes still remained fixed upon the United Nations. The country had become a member only in 1955, during the thaw that followed Stalin's death and during Imre Nagy's first premiership. To ordinary Hungarians it was therefore linked with optimistic times. Though they knew little about how the organisation worked, they now hoped it could produce miracles. Nagy and his government in some small degree shared this national misconception. When he wrote his essays in late 1955 and early 1956 Nagy himself had invoked United Nations' principles. Back in office he had turned to it when he told the world of the Russian assault. And when his Minister of State, István Bibó, sat down in the deserted Parliament Building on 4 November to write that testament of his he still invoked the name of the United Nations. Hungary had 'shed its blood to show its insistence on freedom and justice ... Now it is the turn of the world's mighty to show the power of the principles laid down in the United Nations Charter and the power of the freedom-loving peoples of the world.'[3]

Everyone, in that embittered autumn, demanded that the world should do something more about Hungary – action, not words. You can still find old men in Budapest who are convinced that the West and the United Nations could have done something to save Hungary. But it is as hard now as it was then to see what even a West that was not divided over Suez, and a United Nations that was really eager to get to grips with the issue, could have done about the tragedy that was unwinding in Hungary. The Soviet Union had thousands of troops in the country and thousands more around it. The satellites, and even Poland, were not going to break ranks with Moscow. Yugoslavia was desperate to avoid straining its relations with Moscow further. The West's political and military strength was far away, and separated from Hungary by an Austria whose neutrality the United States, Britain and France had joined the Soviet Union in guaranteeing the previous year. And even if American and British tanks could have rolled down the road from Vienna to Budapest, as so many Hungarians expected that they would and should, no responsible government could have sent them into the jaws of Soviet superiority. For all Foster Dulles's talk of rolling back the Soviet empire in central Europe, the United States and its allies could never have done more than talk. Only nuclear weapons could have saved Hungary – at the price of destroying it, half Europe and much of the world in the process.

10 NOVEMBER: ESCAPE TO ANDAU

As Soviet troops wiped out the last hopes of Hungarian freedom, the trickle of people escaping into Austria turned into a flood. Many of the refugees escaped across the bridge at Andau.

Andau today is a sleepy market town in the small part of Austria that lies east of the Neusiedler See, the lake it shares with Hungary. In 1956 it was little more than a straggling village, not much different from the Hungarian villages dotted across the desolate plain to its immediate east and south. But as the revolution went down to defeat, thousands of Hungarians decided to make a dash for freedom. Some went to Yugoslavia, most to Austria. In the end, 200,000 people left Hungary, two per cent of its population. Many of them escaped over a little foot-bridge across an irrigation canal that ran beside the Austrian border. To a whole generation of refugees, settling into new lives in Australia, Britain or the United States, it was remembered as the bridge at Andau.

At the height of the exodus, in the first half of November, the American writer James Michener stationed himself at Andau and from interviews with fleeing Hungarians he constructed a book about their experiences in Communist Hungary which had provoked them to flee. In retrospect it is a rather terrible little book, with the understandably bitter memories of the refugees filtered through a very crass kind of political insensitivity. But for a time it was the thing to read, and readers snapped it up like everything about the revolution. Michener called it simply *The Bridge at Andau*.[4]

Michener identified three waves of refugees which flowed through Andau. The first came at the end of October and in the very first days of November, when the revolution seemed to be successful. These, he said, were the opportunists, with Budapest prostitutes prominent among them. They took the first chance in eight years to get to the West, where they thought the streets would be paved in gold. To Michener they were a shameless bunch, deserting their country precisely when it seemed set for better times. The second wave was a small group of perhaps 2,000 people, most of them young: these had fought in the revolution and were its heroes. Lastly came the great exodus, in the second and third weeks of November, of people who had not fought but had hoped for the success of the revolution. Once it was crushed they abandoned hopes for a better Hungary and made a dash for freedom before the Iron Curtain could be restored and the frontier with Austria sealed.

From the late 1940s until the uprising, the Hungarian controls on the Austrian border were as fearsome as any the length of the Iron Curtain, and they became so again when once order was restored after the crushing of the uprising. I crossed it for the first time in the summer of 1958, and by then it had been restored with all its lethal ferocity, with watch towers, barbed wire, ploughed strips, tracker dogs and restless border patrols. But in October and November 1956, that whole system of frontier control was swept aside. Frontier guards, customs men and immigration officers had better things to do than keep their fellow Hungarians in. Journalists and aid workers (and, Communist propaganda asserted, CIA-funded agitators and Hungarian Nazis) poured in from the West. There were no major natural obstacles along the border and the country was flat and open on both sides. It was easy to cross, at recognised crossing-points, on back roads and tracks, and across the open fields.

As the Russians prepared to seize control of Hungary from the revolutionaries, they moved to close the frontier again, but they could do no more than seize the major crossing points. For two weeks after the suppression of the revolt, escape across the border was open to anyone who had the guts to try.

In every Western country you can still meet Hungarians, most of them seriously old by now, who left then. An acquaintance of mine took a seductively easy but dangerous way out. He was a pilot of the Hungarian Air Force who got into his MIG fighter and flew it to the West. Western intelligence pored over the trophy for a month and he is still, half a century later, a bit nervous about talking for the record about the details of his escape. Most went out the harder way, on foot across the fields, and among these were the people whom Michener interviewed. When he found them they were cold, exhausted, hungry, but elated to be free. They told him horrifying stories about the oppressive police-state that they had fled, and they would have been more than saintly if they had not sometimes exaggerated for effect. As for Michener, he was a good American who hated Communism, and he had a nose for what would sell. The accounts which he recorded, basically truthful as they may have been, still carry with them fifty years afterwards the smell of particularly virulent propaganda. As a result they do less than justice to the real suffering that Communism brought into the lives of ordinary Hungarians.

Michener's account of the hardships and danger of the actual escape is also highly coloured, but it captures the nature of this area of open fields, marshes and drainage ditches along the flat Austro-Hungarian border. Escapers faced a long hard walk across fields, more often than not ploughed, usually by night. They could easily find themselves struggling in the marshes. They had to find bridges over the ditches, or wade across them. Most of them were young and relatively fit, but they were exhausted by the time they got close to the frontier, and many of them had children with them, some of them mere babies. If you could not find a bridge the larger canals were impassable if you could not swim them, in icy water in the depth of a winter's night. Hence the vital importance of the bridge at Andau, itself in Hungary but right up against the easternmost corner of Austria. Cross that bridge, stumble a few yards further and you were safe in friendly Austria – and Austrians in those days proved themselves models of hospitality to these escapers.

In the course of the first fortnight of November, the apparatus of control was gradually re-established along the frontier. In the Hungarian towns and villages in which the escapers arrived to start their march to freedom they found guides offering their services, occasionally for love of country, usually for money. But they increasingly encountered informants working for the security police; and there was a serious danger of bumping into Soviet troops or the patrols of Hungarian security policemen which the new regime hastened to reorganise. (On at least one occasion, Soviet troops crossed the frontier in pursuit of refugees. Near the village of Reichnitz, Austrian frontier guards found Soviet soldiers on Austrian soil. They arrested them. One of them made a run for it and a brave or foolhardy Austrian shot him dead.)[5] So escapers went to ground whenever a flare illuminated the night sky. They crouched in ditches as the guards went by. Young couples hushed their children, half-stifled their babies when they cried; and Michener tells tall stories of patriotic doctors back in Hungary giving babies just enough sedative to keep them quiet till they were safe in Austria. It was a tragic time, a romantic time, in the end a hopeful time for the majority who made it safely to Austria and freedom.

The Austrians were not left to cope with this flood of refugees alone. The Hungarians were heroes, and all the Western countries were eager to help them. My friend from the British Council in Cairo was redeployed to Vienna, where he tested refugee candidates for British universities. There were many young, bright men and women among them, eager for an education, and thousands more were immediately employable. The refugees settled in their thousands in the United States, Canada and Australia, and all over Europe. A friend of mine who escaped then became an eminent British engineer. And everywhere they settled the Hungarians brought, for a little time, an air of romantic heroism with them. So only the day before yesterday yet another friend, an old lady now, still had a sparkle in her eye as she told me about her experiences as a newly qualified nurse in a London hospital taking care of a notably frisky young Hungarian refugee. 'He was ill enough to be bed-bound', she told me, 'but not ill enough to be safe for one of us to go behind his bed-curtains on our own. So we made sure that there were two of us when he needed his wounds dressing.' And then she added a note of pure nostalgia for those days of her youth: 'Of course, we wore traditional uniform in those days: short skirts, starched aprons and black stockings!' Young János had come a long way from fighting Russian tanks in the streets of Budapest to hanky-panky in a London hospital.

The story of the Hungarian refugees adds a rare note of cheer to the tragic events of that year of crimes, blunders and disappointed hopes. Some, like my friends, still remember it vividly, most of us only at second or third hand, if at all. But if you go to Andau today you can drive down a long track which leads to a replica of the famous bridge, now solidly built in new timber. It takes you past a succession of art works, all of them modern, a few of them effective, which bear witness to such commendable things as human freedom, peace, mutual under-standing and good will to all men. They are well intended and within their limits well executed, but they seem a pale tribute to the famous exodus from Hungary in November 1956.

22 NOVEMBER: ABDUCTION

When Khrushchev and Tito discussed the fate of Hungary in Brioni on that stormy night of 2–3 November, they considered what should be done about Nagy and his government. Moscow had determined to use force. Nagy might see the uselessness of resistance, join the government they were agreed Kádár should form, or allow himself to be bundled back into the retirement in which he had been living until the uprising. But he had a stubborn streak, he was a passionate patriot, and he had held the nation together through the most traumatic days in Hungary's twentieth-century history. There was no guarantee that he would yield even to overwhelming force. An arrest, still more a killing, would add yet more anger to the brew; these were possibilities to turn to when passions in Hungary were calmer. For the time being he needed to be got out of the way.

So Khrushchev asked Tito to offer asylum in the Yugoslav embassy to Nagy and his closest Communist associates. Tito was hesitant. To take Nagy into asylum (or, seen through different-coloured spectacles, into custody) would involve Tito directly in events in Hungary. The West might see him as Moscow's accomplice. And he must have seen the opposite danger that when once order had been restored Moscow would turn on him, label him an accomplice of Nagy, a supporter of counter-revolution, once again the renegade he had been in the years before his reconciliation with Moscow. But he took the plunge and agreed that Nagy should be offered asylum when the tanks went in.

The Yugoslavs orchestrated matters carefully, and the embassy made early contact with Nagy's office. In the early morning of 4 November, as Soviet units converged on Parliament, Nagy was driven to the Yugoslav embassy. By midday forty-two men, women and children – all of them close associates of Nagy and their families – had taken refuge there. There they stayed through the tragic events of the next two weeks: Soviet occupation, desperate armed resistance, strikes, protests, arrests, shootings, retribution.

Nagy continued to behave as Prime Minister of his country. He called his colleagues to regular meetings of what they labelled the Executive Committee to consider what was going on outside the embassy and what course they should themselves adopt. It was of course play-acting, for they had only the information the Yugoslavs and the radio gave them, no power and only a passive kind of influence over events. The Russians quickly isolated the embassy with a ring of tanks. Then, on 6 November, a member of the staff was killed at a window by a bullet from a Soviet tank. It could have been a stray shot, but the embassy staff believed otherwise and talked about the victim's striking facial resemblance to Imre Nagy.

Other Yugoslavs were waking up to the fact that the Soviet attitude, at Brioni so accommodating, was changing. On 6 November Veljko Micunovic was on his way back to Moscow from Brioni. He recorded in his diary how things seemed to be changing. Khrushchev and Malenkov had come to Brioni as friends: 'They behaved in an extremely cordial manner, as never before.' Later he wrote: 'Whatever we proposed in good faith in an effort to ease their difficulties, so as at least to reduce the bloodshed in Hungary, in the interests of both Russians and Hungarians and ultimately of all of us, Khrushchev and Malenkov accepted at once.' But now he foresaw that 'the Russians and the newly formed Hungarian government will ... start accusing Imre Nagy of things for which he is not to blame... And Imre Nagy himself, whom they are accusing of counter-revolution, is now enjoying the protection of the Yugoslav Embassy in Budapest. It is not far to go from making such accusations against Imre Nagy to extending them to those who have taken him under their wing.'⁶

Soon Khrushchev was saying as much. On 7 November Micunovic went to protest to the Soviet Foreign Minister at the shooting of the diplomat in Budapest. Shepilov gave him short shrift: the gunner was responding to attack, was his reply. Later Micunovic met Khrushchev himself at the Soviet National Day reception. Khrushchev complained of the Yugoslavs' failure to hand Nagy over to the Hungarian authorities. 'Nagy had, right up to the last minute, appealed on the radio for a struggle against the Russians and had taken refuge in our embassy ... Could it be that we were trying to form a new government opposed to Kádár's?' Micunovic replied, 'It was not a simple matter for Yugoslavia ... to grant asylum to people, to render any further action on their part impossible and so help the new revolutionary government, and now to go back on their word and hand the people over. Khrushchev repeated that he didn't understand a Communist moral code which protected accomplices of counterrevolution.'⁷ There was no more of the affability of Brioni. This was Khrushchev the political thug; the man who, back in London in April, had left Richard Crossman recording the brutality with which he told the Labour leaders that 'we should join the Russians because, if not, they would swat us off the face of the earth like a dirty old black beetle'.⁸

But Nagy's fate, Khrushchev told Micunovic, was a matter to be settled between the Yugoslavs and the new Hungarian government. Kádár repeatedly sent messages to Nagy urging him to resign and recognise the new government. A Hungarian historian sums up his response. 'Nagy rejected these urgings emphatically. He was secure in this position because of the unqualified support of his political allies. Except for Kádár and Sándor Kopácsi, the police chief seized by the Soviets, Nagy had with him in the embassy the entire Executive Committee of the anti-Stalinist Hungarian Socialist Workers' Party [the reformed Communist party] founded [with Kádár at its head] on 31 October.'⁹ But if Nagy had justice and all his colleagues on his side, Kádár had the backing of Soviet troops and the old security police. He could starve the embassy out. It could be only a matter of time before the Yugoslavs' nerve broke.

They tried to extract from Kádár a guarantee of safe-conduct for the refugees, and the deputy Foreign Minister came from Belgrade to see him. In a long talk he got assurances, and then a formal note signed by Kádár and by Münnich promising safe conduct. When they came out of the embassy the members of the party would be allowed to return quietly to their homes. In a broadcast to the nation, Kádár talked soothingly about reconciliation. Nagy still remained sceptical: Kádár had betrayed him in October, as long ago he had betrayed Rajk. But the Yugoslavs were putting increased pressure on the group in the embassy; it was clear that they were no longer welcome guests; they agreed to leave and trust themselves to whatever value Kádár's word might have.

At 6.30 in the evening of 22 November the little party emerged from the embassy and anxiously boarded the bus that awaited them. It drove away past the Soviet tanks and the broken remains of Stalin's statue. Two Yugoslav diplomats came with them to see the party safely delivered to their homes, but soon Soviet vehicles stopped the bus and Soviet security men came on board. The diplomats were unceremoniously ejected and the bus went on its way, not to the Hungarians' homes but to a Soviet barracks on the outskirts of the city. Here Nagy and others were confronted by Münnich, who with Kádár had signed the note that promised them safe conduct. Münnich was one of Nagy's oldest comrades and friends but he came now as a man who had sold out to his country's enemies and become a committed leader of the post-revolutionary regime He brought with him a document for the men of the party to sign. They all refused. Whether their acquiescence would have helped them we do not know. That first guarantee had already been proved worthless, and Nagy and his companions would have been naïve indeed to hope that Münnich's new document would be any better.

At the time the Yugoslavs seemed innocent victims of deception, their faith abused as much as Nagy's by the false safe conduct. But in December Kádár told his colleagues that the guarantee of safe conduct that he had given to the Yugoslavs had been accompanied by an oral warning that it would not be honoured.[10] If so, and if he knew of it, Micunovic did not admit even in his diary to knowledge of the deception. He had been following the drama from his embassy in Moscow. 'Agreement has been reached in writing,' he recorded. 'The Hungarian Government has given first an oral and then a written guarantee that all the people who found refuge in our embassy can return freely to their homes.'[11] Later he added another paragraph: 'We rejoiced too soon at the successful solution of the problem of Imre Nagy and the others ... The same evening as they left our embassy they were seized by Soviet troops. The agreement signed by the Hungarian Government ... has become as usual a scrap of paper. Imre Nagy and the others have been taken off ... perhaps to Romania.'[12] To the words 'signed by the Hungarian Government' he might have added 'and accepted by the Yugoslavs'. There was a lot of perfidy about it in Central Europe, as in the Middle East, that autumn.

Nagy and his companions were indeed taken to Romania. On the day after their abduction the Workers' Councils of Budapest called for a silent demonstration of protest. For an hour all activity stopped in the city. There was no one to see the Russians' prisoners go as they were driven through the deserted streets to a Soviet air base. There three Soviet aircraft were waiting. Survivors remember how nervous their guards were, and that one of their own number was bundled onto the aircraft by force. The pilots refused to tell them where they were being taken but revealed that it would be a two-hour flight. When they landed at a snow-covered airfield the prisoners at first assumed that they were in the Soviet Union. But Romania it was, and an official came to welcome them to Romania. 'Thank you,' Nagy replied, almost light-heartedly, 'but we did not ask you to invite us.'[13] The party was taken to a lakeside resort not far from Bucharest. There they were prisoners, but they were still treated as guests, their food brought to them by an obsequious waiter who, they later discovered, was a Hungarian-speaking security policeman. And there they saw out what remained of 1956.

Early in 1957 Nagy and his associates were brought back to Budapest. There they languished in prison for a year and a half and it was there that in the end Nagy and his closest colleagues were put on trial. And it was in the central prison of Budapest in the early morning of 16 June 1958 that Imre Nagy and three of his companions were executed. They were the most renowned, but they were not the last of the victims of the Hungarian tragedy of 1956.

10 JANUARY 1957: THE UNITED NATIONS REPORT ON HUNGARY

As Hungary lay broken, there was worldwide anger against the Soviet Union and the Kádár puppet regime, an anger which in many countries destroyed for good the credentials and standing of the local Communist

parties. Refugees fuelled the anger with stories of the heroism of the revolutionaries and the oppression against which they had fought. Now
Khrushchev and Kádár were reimposing that oppression with a new
vigour. They were putting about allegations that the uprising had been
inspired by Western broadcasts and succoured by Western intelligence,
Western capital, clerical reaction and aristocratic Hungarian émigrés. It
seemed as if the least the international community could do was to document the facts. Minds turned to the idea of a United Nations Committee to pin down the causes of the uprising and the exact course of events.
Such a study would move in parallel with efforts to succour Hungarian
refugees and get humanitarian relief into the country.

So on 10 January 1957 the General Assembly voted to create a
special committee to 'report on the problem of Hungary'. A Danish
politician became its chairman, a notably vigorous and effective
Australian diplomat its rapporteur. The other members came from
Ceylon, Tunisia and Uruguay. The committee held its first meeting on
17 January, submitted an interim report on 20 February and unanimously adopted its final report on 7 June, 1957, a year to the day after
Imre Nagy's birthday party. The printed report extends to 139 quarto
pages.

From the beginning the Soviet Union and the new Hungarian
government refused to have anything to do with the committee and
would not admit its members into the country. To gather evidence, they
therefore visited Geneva, Rome, Vienna and London, holding meetings
in each city as well as in New York. In the course of their work they
interviewed 111 witnesses, most of whom had taken part in the uprising. Verbatim records of the evidence cover 2,000 pages. The committee heard terrible stories about Hungary's interrogation centres,
political prisons and detention camps, and more about the events of the
revolution. Coloured as some of the evidence may have been by anger,
prejudice and the desire to traduce the revolution's enemies, the report
itself nevertheless gives a dispassionate yet vivid and often very moving
account of the uprising, its causes and its suppression. So though the
United Nations was unable to do anything to save the Hungarian
people it was able to document, with an authority that has never been
seriously called in question, the revolution which was perhaps the
single most important event in Hungary's twentieth-century history.

12

The End of the Road

By 2 am on Wednesday, 7 November, British and French troops controlled Port Said and Port Fuad, and the first twenty-three miles of the Suez Canal. The Egyptians defiantly still held the rest of it. Nasser was as popular as ever among his people, the more enthusiastic for the indignity that had been done to their country. They basked in Arab support, and the active attention of the United Nations and most of the world. As for the Israelis, they had halted their advance and waited just over the eastern horizon from the canal; at the Mitla Pass; and at Sharm-al-Sheikh, at the southern tip of the Sinai peninsula.

The British and French had found the fighting in Port Said and Port Fuad much tougher than they had expected. The fiasco of senior officers on the spot twice convincing themselves that the Egyptians were on the point of surrender illustrates how over-confident they were. Now they were warned from London that a ceasefire was to take effect at midnight GMT, 2 am their time. Meanwhile they were to seize as much of the length of the canal as they could. The British troops in the lead set off on a last dash down the canal, parachute troops riding on Centurion tanks, with Qantara, thirty-five miles from Port Said, as the goal. When 2 am came they were just short of El Cap. For twenty minutes more they turned a blind eye to their orders and continued the advance as far as El Cap, but Qantara was beyond them. Meanwhile the leading French troops, seeing the cup of victory dashed from their lips, talked wildly of going on without the British, of operating in conjunction with the Israelis, even of putting Israelis into French uniforms or French ones into Israeli. But from 2.20 am local time on 7 November, the ceasefire held

The Allies were in a tactically very difficult position. They were not even in complete control of Port Said and Port Fuad, through which all supplies and reinforcements must come. Some Egyptian troops and police remained there, capable of resuming the battle; and the civilians, with hidden arms available, were restive, their patriotism played upon by Cairo Radio. The Allies had reached El Cap along a single road running between the canal and marshes, and now at the tip of the advance they held little more than the road and its verges: 'a one-tank front', as a British officer complained. The Israelis were standing well back, ten miles away. There was nothing to stop the Egyptians reinforcing their positions facing the British forward troops, and their performance in the fighting in Port Said had demonstrated that these were far from the chocolate soldiers the British and French had envisaged. There remained a danger that the Russians might re-equip the Egyptian Air Force or send in volunteer pilots; and Port Said, like the air bases in Cyprus, was desperately vulnerable to air attack. All the British and French invaders could do was to settle down in Port Said, Port Fuad and El Cap and await further orders.

7 NOVEMBER: WAUGH'S ASSESSMENT

Also on 7 November, Evelyn Waugh wrote to Ann Fleming to give her his view of the Suez adventure. The woman who, before the month was out, would be giving Anthony Eden a roof over his head in the Caribbean was told:

Dearest Ann,
    I have studied the Suez expedition with interest. These are the important facts:
(a) it cannot be justified on moral or legal grounds
(b) practically no recent action of any British government can be justified morally, e.g. Death duties
(c) Any troup of Boy Scouts can defeat the Egyptian army
(d) No one can govern Egypt now that Nasser has armed the school children
(e) No one can manage the canal without governing Egypt
(f) If Jerk [Anthony Eden] really wants to increase the traffic in this country by importing more petrol through the canal, he must depopulate Egypt. This can very simply be done by destroying the Nile barrages. The wogs would starve to death in six months.
(g) A more humane solution is to stop motor traffic – particularly buses & charabancs in England

(h)   Our long occupation of Cyprus proves fatuous since its justification was to keep a holding force ready for immediate
police action in just this situation.[1]

Allowing a certain amount of licence for Waugh's reactionary instincts
and more for fantasy, it remains a persuasive summing up of the
adventure.

9 NOVEMBER: EDEN *IN EXTREMIS*

It had been American pressure that had done most to bring Anthony
Eden to the point of accepting the ceasefire and Mollet could not
persuade him to delay it until the Allies could take control of the whole
canal. Now he hoped for his reward from Eisenhower. If the British and
French could quickly restore relations with the Americans and bring
back into play the Tripartite Declaration they had so briskly dismissed
when they launched their ultimatum, there was still a chance that the
will of the West could be imposed on Nasser. Eisenhower's election was
behind him, and he had won by a huge majority. Surely now he would
see the wisdom of the course on which his European erstwhile friends
had embarked.

Eden spoke to Eisenhower and suggested an immediate three-man
summit meeting in Washington. Eisenhower agreed, and authorised
Eden to tell Mollet so. For a moment hopes were high in London and
Paris. But then his advisers pulled Eisenhower back. He had put his
faith in Hammarskjöld's ability to get Nasser's acceptance of a United
Nations force to police the ceasefire. The Secretary-General was trying
hard, but Nasser was haggling every inch of the way. Hammarskjöld
believed that even the possibility that tripartite discussion might lead to
tripartite action would make his task impossible. In any case, Eisenhower's advisers reminded him, there was no need for the United States
to rush to rescue the British from the disaster they had brought on
themselves. They needed American help, at the United Nations, over
sterling, perhaps over oil. They could be left to stew a little while yet,
'stew in their own oil', as Eisenhower put it. And meanwhile the United
States could devote itself to doing what only it could do with real
conviction, frightening the Russians off from meddling further in the
Middle East.

This rebuff from Eisenhower added still further to Eden's burdens.

The months in which he and Macmillan could delude themselves that the Americans did not mean what they said were over. The biggest gamble of his political life had failed. Physically and psychologically he was at the end of his tether. There seemed to be nowhere sensible for him to turn.

Eisenhower's rebuff of Eden meant that the way remained clear for Hammarskjöld to devote his phenomenal will, ingenuity and energy to getting the idea of a multinational force under United Nations command (UNEF) accepted and the force itself established in Egypt.

When Dulles had first called for a ceasefire in his speech to the General Assembly on 1 November, Lester Pearson, the Canadian Minister for External Affairs, moved quickly to propose a United Nations force to supervise it and safeguard the canal. He quickly developed the idea into one that would have teeth, and which might give the British and French the beginnings of a way out of the diplomatic corner into which they were advancing.

Hammarskjöld's response at that stage was sceptical, but Pearson persisted. By 4 November the Canadian proposal had been adopted by fifty-seven votes to none, but with nineteen members abstaining, Britain, France and Israel among them. The vote did not stop the British and French sending in their parachute troops the following day, but with the ceasefire Hammarskjöld went to work on converting the proposal into a reality.

He faced enormous difficulties, for every national interest involved pulled in a different direction. Britain and France wanted UNEF's intervention to be seen as a natural follow-up to their own. For that reason, and for reasons of speed and effectiveness, they wanted their own troops to be involved; and they wanted the Americans in too. Hammarskjöld knew that he could never sell such a force to Nasser. Now Eisenhower came out in his support, and persuaded Eden that if any of the major powers contributed troops 'the Bear' would insist on sending Soviet soldiers too.

So the Secretary-General put to Nasser the concept of a force provided by smaller, generally neutral nations. Nasser tried to rule out the participation of Canadian troops: they wore the same uniforms as the British, owed allegiance to the same queen. But it was a Canadian proposal, and psychologically they seemed to stand midway between Nasser and the allies. In the end Hammarskjöld sold a reluctant Nasser the idea of a Canadian commander for the force.

On 21 November the first United Nations troops – a Scandinavian company – arrived and four days later the Canadian General Burns himself flew into Port Said. General Keightley met him. Their khaki battledress, red tabs and hat bands were identical, just as Nasser had complained, Burns's distinguished only by an improvised United Nations arm band. Keightley had the wit to make a joke of it or the grace to be embarrassed: 'Well, at least we wear the same cap, Burns.' But Burns came to supervise a ceasefire, not enforce an ultimatum. He came by agreement, however reluctant, not behind a naval and aerial bombardment. And he represented the collective will of the United Nations, not two outlawed and isolated invaders.

23 NOVEMBER: EDEN FLEES

Things looked as grim for the government in London as for British and French troops on the canal. From the moment of Eden's acceptance of the ceasefire it knew it was fighting for its life. Its members were exhausted. Respected junior ministers had resigned. Washington still withheld its favour. The economy was teetering. The Conservative party in the House of Commons was divided, the opposition cock-a-hoop. Eden limped along, his health and nerve broken, keeping himself going with stimulants and with what passed in those days for tranquillisers.

Then on 18 November the Prime Minister's doctor gave him the politically fatal advice that he must get away from politics and from London, to a prolonged break in the Caribbean sun. On 23 November he flew to Jamaica, to a remote villa owned by Ian Fleming, the creator of the 007 novels, and his wife Ann, recipient of Waugh's fantasies and confidences and herself a well-known and in some circles faintly notorious political hostess. It was a most extraordinary desertion of troops, party and nation at a moment of supreme need. Reminiscing long afterwards, Eden recognised that as the doctors were convinced that he could not continue, he should have resigned there and then, leaving someone else – and at that stage it would have been Butler – to take his place. As it was, what looked like panicky desertion of his post effectively wrote off what was left of Eden's political career.

Nevertheless, he went off to recuperate, far from the preoccupations of the government of which he was still Prime Minister. The press were told that 'Mr Butler will be in effective charge of affairs so long as Sir Anthony is absent'. Rab, who had bound himself, if with many an equivocation, to the wheels of Eden's chariot, found himself in charge of efforts to salvage what could be saved from the wreck of the Prime Minister's policies.

22 NOVEMBER: MAC KNIFES RAB

Washington was glad to see Eden gone and Butler in charge, but as determined as ever that the Allies must withdraw from the canal before it would relax its political and financial pressure on Britain and the pound. Yet the Conservative Party and many, perhaps a majority, of the British people were incensed by the United States' betrayal of its old ally, and longed for a transatlantic showdown that Britain could only lose.

To a party that felt like this, Butler himself was suspect. Throughout the Suez crisis, party and nation had regularly reminded themselves of the consequences of appeasing a dictator, with Hitler and Mussolini still vivid in their minds; and in the eyes of the Tory Right, Butler remained one of the guilty men of Munich. On the record he had rallied to Eden's policy over Suez, but in the Commons tea-room and at Tory dinner tables he had got up to his old tricks and made little secret of his doubts. Now he faced the almost impossible task of holding the Conservative party together while bending to Washington's will and bringing the troops home from Suez. On Thursday 22 November, the day before Eden's flight to Jamaica but four days after his withdrawal from the political scene, he went to the House of Commons to make the best of things.

The world was witnessing, he said, an attempt by the United Nations to organise an effective intervention in Egypt. 'This intervention', he asserted, 'has been made possible by Franco-British action.' If it succeeded, it would set a precedent 'which will give mankind hope for the future'.[2] Meanwhile, Britain was ready to demonstrate its good intentions by withdrawing an infantry battalion from the Canal Zone at once. That gesture clearly pointed to a complete withdrawal in due course.

Under Butler's leadership the government was, in short, preparing itself to drain the cup of its humiliation while pretending to have achieved something by the attack on Egypt. The Tory party was close to mutiny. That evening Butler went back to the House of Commons to address a meeting of the Conservative Parliamentary Party, the 1922 Committee. It promised to be a more difficult occasion than the Parliamentary session earlier that day.

Butler was never a man for histrionics. Somehow, he got through a brief and low-key statement without serious interruption. It seemed as if his words had succeeded in steadying things, in holding the party together. But Butler had taken Harold Macmillan with him to address the 1922 Committee. Macmillan spoke immediately after Butler, and he did not share Rab's distaste for drama. Long afterwards he claimed in that lofty way of his that 'I held the Tory Party for the weekend, it was all I intended to do',3 but in the words of Butler's biographer he 'turned in a veritable political organ voluntary lasting thirty-five minutes – pulling out every stop and striking every majestic chord in his well-practised repertoire, including a *tremolo* on his own advancing years'.4

Between them, Macmillan and Rab succeeded in keeping control of the Conservative Party that evening, and the press praised both – but particularly Macmillan – the following day. Yet before their Parliamentary Party audience, Macmillan had stolen the show. His performance had spectacularly upstaged Butler. It was, Enoch Powell recalled, 'one of the most horrible things that I remember in politics ... seeing the way in which Harold Macmillan, with all the skill of the old actor manager, succeeded in false-footing Rab. The sheer devilry of it verged upon the disgusting.'5

The speech served Macmillan well. It bound to him what Reginald Maudling later called 'the blue blood and thunder group' of the Tory party.6 It took him a decisive step further towards the goal which he reached less than two months later – the Premiership. For however bitterly several of his colleagues might remember his performance in Cabinet and in private throughout the Suez crisis, they had to follow him once he had established such a leading position for himself in the party on 22 November.

Yet the record shows us just how erratic Macmillan's performance had been in the months of the Suez crisis. In many ways he bears as large a responsibility as Eden for the whole fiasco. At the very beginning of the crisis Macmillan, who as Chancellor of the Exchequer had no *ex officio* role to play in its handling, had muscled his way into the small inner circle of ministers around Eden who were dealing with it. At once he had proved himself the most hawkish of the hawks, demanding firm action against Nasser, wanting, in Brendan Bracken's words, 'to tear Nasser's scalp off with his own finger-nails'.[7] Soon he emerged as the first member of the Cabinet to toy with cooperation with the Israelis to bring Nasser down – and got himself rapped over the knuckles by the Prime Minister for his pains.

Unabashed, when in late September he went to the United States, primarily on Treasury business, Macmillan got himself invited to a long talk with Eisenhower in the White House – something which, he pointedly noted in that feline way of his, the Foreign Secretary, Selwyn Lloyd, had failed to achieve when he too was in Washington.

It was a strange, almost inconsequential conversation and accounts of it differ widely. What Macmillan said he heard the President say and what the British ambassador heard seem to be quite different things. In retrospect it seems clear that Macmillan wilfully misinterpreted Eisenhower's remarks. The President believed, Macmillan recorded, that 'the United Nations had destroyed the power of leadership of the great powers', so that 'small nations like Egypt could do the most outrageous things'. Eisenhower seemed to be saying, Macmillan asserted, that 'the great powers ... should get together to maintain order, peace and justice, as well as mere absence of armed conflict'.[8]

All this Macmillan reported to Eden, who liked what he heard. The implication seemed to be that, whatever Dulles might say, the President himself would look on benevolently if Britain and France took military action against Nasser. By seeing Eisenhower, it seemed, Macmillan the magician had conjured a major obstacle out of Eden's path.

So from July until October, Macmillan had played a major part in leading the Cabinet to war. Yet the man who as Prime Minister later presented himself as the old unflappable Supermac was the first to panic in November when Washington, far from nodding benevolently as British troops went ashore in Egypt, turned up the pressure on sterling. To quote Brendan Bracken again: 'Today he might be described as the leader of the bolters. His Treasury officials have put before him the economic consequences of the Suez fiasco and his feet are frost-bitten...'[9]

Even Antony Head, the Minister of Defence during the attack on

Egypt and a far kindlier observer of Harold Macmillan than Bracken ever was, told Macmillan's biographer that his volte-face was 'the one thing he could not understand about Suez'. Head ruled out 'naked ambition' as the key to Macmillan's behaviour, 'though if you had a nasty mind you might have thought so'.[10] Fifty years later, most of us looking at Macmillan's record in 1956 may find ourselves entertaining nasty thoughts and interpreting it (and the speech to the 1922 Committee above all) with something less than Head's generosity of judgement.

23 NOVEMBER: CHURCHILL PLAYS A HAND

Winston Churchill played a very small part in the Suez crisis, and that only peripherally. Nevertheless, three things about his role are worth remembering.

First, it is hard to resist the conclusion that Churchill's endless procrastination in handing over power to his heir apparent contributed to the nervousness and tension which Eden eventually brought to No.10, and to the crisis itself. It is even clearer that early in the crisis, when Macmillan was trying from the Treasury to insinuate himself into its management and orchestrate diplomatic and military policies which were not his business, Churchill let Macmillan use him as a stalking horse, putting Macmillan's ideas to Eden as if they were his own. The pretence was transparent, but it could only rattle still further a Prime Minister of Eden's fragile temperament.

Second, in the aftermath of Suez, when the relationship with the United States to which he had dedicated his political career was on the rocks, Churchill made a moving attempt to draw Eisenhower back into a warmer relationship with Britain and a better understanding of what Eden had been trying to achieve.

'There is not much left for me to do in this world', he wrote in a letter to Eisenhower from Chartwell on 23 November, 'and I have neither the wish nor the strength to involve myself in the present stress and turmoil. But I do believe, with unfaltering conviction, that the theme of the Anglo-American alliance is more important today than at any time since the war.' But there was 'misunderstanding and frustration on both sides of the Atlantic', and if it was allowed to continue it was the Soviet Union that would benefit. Churchill went on to paint a vivid picture of Europe's fate if the Middle East and North Africa fell under Soviet control.[11]

Other old British friends of Eisenhower were writing him personal letters that autumn. Most were more bitter than Churchill, intent on re-fighting the arguments of the immediate past. Eisenhower gave them firm answers, and not even Churchill, old as he was and great as was his reputation, shifted him on the substance of the matter. Replying to Churchill on 27 November he acknowledged that 'the Soviets are the real enemy of the Western world, implacably hostile and seeking our destruction'. But that did not alter the fact that Britain was in the wrong over Suez, and 'even by the doctrine of expediency the invasion could not be judged as soundly conceived and skilfully executed'. Only when he had laid all this down did Eisenhower admit a sentence of sentiment. 'Nothing saddens me more', he wrote, ' than the thought that I and my old friends of years have met a problem concerning which we do not see eye to eye. I shall never be happy until our old-time close-ness has been restored.'[12]

For all the British delusions to the contrary, Eisenhower never was a softie.

Lastly, there is Churchill's famous aphorism shortly after Suez, which sums up the politics and diplomacy of the whole mad adventure perhaps better than any other: ' I would never have done it without squaring the Americans', he said, 'and once I'd started I would never have dared to stop.'[13]

FRIENDS' EYE VIEWS

When I told friends of my age about this book some of them offered me their memories of the period. They were all young men in 1956, and they saw very different aspects of Suez from the ones that engaged Winston Churchill's attention. These are some of their stories.

A neighbour spent the early months of the year in Egypt as a very raw officer of the Parachute Regiment. They lived in the Suez Canal base and patrolled the canal-side roads; but as often as he could their colonel got them out into the Egyptian desert on exercises. Robert's introduction to it was a parachute drop somewhere between Cairo and the Red Sea. Injured on landing, he got away from the immediate drop-ping zone just before the heavy drop – the trucks, jeeps and Ferret scout cars – rained down on it.

In the course of the next few days he learned the hard way how to survive, march and fight in the desert. His first failure was over all-important water discipline for his men and himself. He let them empty their water bottles too soon and he and they faced the agony of thirst as they stomped the desert miles. 'Suck a pebble', the major told them, 'and when you do at last get to water, sip it and swill it round your mouth.'

Robert encountered few Bedouin on the march, but one he saw was like a figure out of *The Seven Pillars of Wisdom*, 'belonging to nature as no man I have ever seen before or since'. And when the troops yomped to St Catharine's monastery in Sinai he experienced 'a night when the heavens were alive with shooting stars and those that hovered over us seemed so close that we could reach up and touch them'. The desert had majesty and purity: 'I knew why it was known as the "Holy Desert".' It was a far cry from the squalor and tedium of the canal base.

By the time the Suez crisis broke Robert was out of khaki and in drama school. 'But your regiment dropped at Port Said?' I asked him. It did. 'And how did you feel about not being with them?' I asked. Badly, he said; and then, in blind contradiction, 'But I would have refused to jump. Cowardice, they'd have called it. But I'd seen in the base area that we had no right to be in Egypt. I couldn't have fought to get it back.'

A man I met on holiday told me that he was working in GCHQ in Cheltenham in 1956. I asked him what he could tell me about it. At the end of a working lifetime of infinite discretion he was still a man of few words: 'We worked for seventeen hours a day, for what must have been six weeks. When we came out we looked the colour of finely cooked turbot.'

Martin was in Dusseldorf, about to exchange his Grenadier uniform for a place at Cambridge. He and two other ensigns went out on the town to celebrate their escape from the Army that was due on the morrow. The party got noisy, and they ended up in the hands of the Military Police. All releases of national servicemen were being stopped, the Redcaps told them (quite wrongly, as it turned out), and the official confirmation would be in the their adjutant's in-tray in the morning. So the three of them decided to do a Nelson and not stay to see the signal. In the grey dawn they set off to drive to the Channel ports: one in a Jaguar that was unhappy at anything under 60, one in an ancient Mercedes that could touch 60 only with a following wind behind it, and Martin in a Ford Popular that might or might not make it to the Channel, Britain and escape to the courts of Cambridge University.

David was a member of the British diplomatic mission in Peking. When Britain attacked Suez, Chinese indignation, real or synthetic, rose in pitch and volume. He and his colleagues found themselves besieged by a Chinese mob. Meanwhile, a Hungarian countess to whom he had become engaged was bombarding him with letters of reproach at Britain's failure to ride to the rescue of her gallant rebellious countrymen. How could he serve such a government, she asked; he must choose between them and her. He resigned from the Foreign Service, voting with his feet against his government and for his girl-friend. Soon afterwards she left him.

Erich got to St Catharine's monastery from the other side from Robert's. The Israeli campaign ended at Sharm al-Sheikh at the tip of Sinai. Erich and two friends demobilised themselves on the spot and set off in a jeep 'which seemed to be surplus to the requirements of the regiment' towards Mount Sinai. 'It was rather a dangerous venture. For a start none of us had a driving licence or for that matter could drive properly.' But they found their way to the gates of St Catharine's, whose monks 'must have thought God had sent three holy ghosts to punish them'. The next morning Erich and Co set off to climb Mount Sinai. They got to the top as the sun rose, and 'Moses standing there a solitary figure those many centuries ago couldn't have imagined a better spot to meditate and then produce ten of the most famous sentences of all time'. As for Erich, I couldn't help thinking he had come a long way from the four-year-old boy who had come to Britain on the last Kindertransport out of Hitler's Europe in 1939.

Philip is another ex-diplomat. In the autumn of 1956 he completed a tour of duty in the British Embassy in Vientiane. His next post was to be Paris, and he took passage from Saigon in a liner of the French Messageries Maritimes headed for Marseilles. She was fifteen miles off Suez, her passengers happily homeward bound, when her captain heard the news of the Allied attack. There was no way home through the canal for them now and with Gallic drama he violently reversed his helm, sending revellers, champagne flutes and coffee cups flying into the scuppers. The passengers spent the next week, marooned in Djibouti:

'It was worse than Aden,' Philip told me, 'we stayed for a week and it felt like a month.'

Eventually he succeeded in making his way to his new post in Paris. Ever since the Suez crisis started he had been longing for a convincing explanation of British policy. He could not find one in Vientiane, still less in Djibouti. 'Yet we thought it could not', as he said to me fifty years afterwards, 'be as mad as it seemed.' Over a welcoming lunch in Paris he sought the answer to the mystery from Sir Gladwyn Jebb, Her Majesty's Ambassador to France and a hard intellectual diamond of the Foreign Service. 'I was told nothing, I understand nothing, I can explain nothing,' Jebb replied. That most senior of ambassadors, most experienced of public servants, the man whose job it had been to interpret the two Suez allies to each other, professed himself as mystified by the events of the last few months as the naïve and ignorant refugee from Djibouti and Vientiane.

Another friend of mine, John, had another take on Suez 1956. He was in Jordan as a young officer of the Royal Air Force Regiment, guarding Venom fighters on the British airbase at Amman. He and his men were in a hot spot: Israel seemed to be moving towards war with Jordan. Yet Britain, while professing itself committed to defending Jordan, was joining Israel to threaten Egypt. Then came an order, on the eve of the Suez landings, to fly the aircraft to the base at Mafraq out in the desert of eastern Jordan, to be followed by road by ground crews and RAF Regiment. John and his men left for Mafraq in the small hours, and when they got there they spent the rest of the day and the following night digging gunpits.

On the next night a very weary John was duty officer. The corporal commanding one of the gun sites called in: 'I can hear tractors.' Dawn revealed the Soviet T34 tanks of a Syrian armoured brigade hull down surrounding the airbase. A long stand-off followed, with the British expecting an attack at any time, their gun positions constantly alert. Eventually a Saudi armoured brigade arrived, invited in by King Hussein to warn off the Syrians. The Syrians went home, but the British were still there at Christmas, in that rarest of years in which snow fell in Jordan.

John spent the most memorable Christmas of his life at Mafraq and then was ordered back to Amman to recover equipment that had been left there. He arrived to find a young Arab officer of what had once been Glubb's Arab Legion, directing his men to strip the British base. 'That's ours,' said John. 'We've got it,' said the Arab. 'All the same, it's ours,' John replied. 'It's no use to you,' said the young officer. 'I have my orders,' said John. 'But why do you need it?' he was asked. John dredged out of his troubled memory something he had heard about the Arab mind. 'My honour is at stake,' he said. The Arab knew when he was beaten: 'Take it, it's yours,' he said.

We have seen another John, the British Council teacher in Cairo, earlier in this story. When things got hot for British subjects in Egypt he feared a long internment, for the Council staff had no diplomatic immunity and his wife and a new-born daughter whom he had never seen awaited him in Britain. He decided to take his chances, leaving Egypt on the train that was to carry embassy staffs to Libya, running the risk that frontier guards might turn him off it at an inhospitable border post in the desert. But he made it to Libya, and soon he was in Vienna, where we have seen him issuing visas and university places to young Hungarian refugees.

John was, he reminded me, one of the relatively few people to be directly involved in both the great crises of October-November 1956, and I asked him how, looking back, he saw the dramas in which he had played a part. 'I suppose both of them showed the crumbling of empires,' he said. Nasser saw himself as a doughty warrior against Western imperialism. Dulles was acting out the Americans' narrative that saw themselves as enemies of imperialism, though before very long they were to go about building an empire of their own in the Middle East, complete with Israel as a client state. As for the Hungarians (and in a way the Poles a few days earlier), they had risen against Moscow's Marxist-Leninist empire, to reassert the civilised values of Central Europe. And then, perhaps reminded of civilised values, John added a thought that might almost form the epigraph of this book: 'I suppose', he said, 'that Suez was *HMS Pinafore* and Hungary *Fidelio*.'

2 DECEMBER: CASTRO INVADES

Early in December, as the Middle Eastern and Hungarian dramas were winding down, another opened on the coast of Cuba. It reminds us that not all the political passions of 1956 were being played out in Hungary and the Middle East that autumn.

On 2 December, a ragged group of men landed in eastern Cuba. There were eighty of them, all armed, and they came in a small ship, the *Granma*. At their head was a twenty-eight-year old who had already made a modest name for himself in the violent world of Cuban politics. Some called him a freedom fighter, others a desperado. His name was Fidel Castro.

With Castro aboard the *Granma* and in the ranks of this little army of revolutionaries were his brother Raul and a close ally who in time attained a more glamorous revolutionary reputation than Castro himself, Ernesto 'Chez' Guevara. Their aim was to set the Oriente province alight, move on and overthrow Cuba's dictator, General Fulgencio Batista, and seize power for the revolution. Almost at once Batista's army ran them down and killed or captured most of them. Only twelve of the eighty escaped, the Castros and Guevara among them. They retreated into Cuba's Sierra Maestra uplands.

Born one of seven children of a prosperous sugar-cane farmer, Castro was educated at a Jesuit boarding school in Santiago de Cuba and at the University of Havana. He went there to read law but found himself in a university consumed by political emotion. At once he got himself involved in political activity, little of it legal, and by the time he was twenty he had taken part in an unsuccessful attempt to invade Cuba's near neighbour, the Dominican Republic, and overthrow its dictator, Rafael Trujillo, a man as notorious an enemy of Left-inclined revolutionaries as Cuba's own Batista. A year later he moved on to Colombia, and set about fomenting rioting in the capital, Bogota. The Castro brothers had become dedicated revolutionaries, set on bringing their personal version of social justice and their own brand of power politics to all Latin America.

Yet there was still something indecisive about their plans for revolution. Castro went back to his studies at Havana University and in 1950 he graduated. He took up law and reformist politics, looking forward to winning a seat in parliament at the next election. It never came; in March 1952 Batista turned Cuba's civilian government out and cancelled the election.

Denied his chance at the ballot box, Castro turned again to the bullet. On 26 July 1953 he led 150 men in an attack on a barracks in Santiago de Cuba. Most of them were killed, Castro captured. He went on trial and gave Cubans in the courtroom a first taste of his fiery oratory. Inevitably he was found guilty, and he was sentenced to fifteen years' imprisonment. But two years later came an amnesty, and the Castro brothers were released. They took themselves off to Mexico to organise a group of Cuban exiles into the 'Movement of 26 July', named after the date of their attempted coup in Santiago de Cuba. It was men of this group that the Castros led in their pathetic little invasion of their homeland in December 1956.

The Cuban people soon started to hear more of Fidel Castro. As things turned out there was nothing pathetic about that landing. In the Sierra Maestra Castro quickly attracted supporters. They responded to the hope he offered of overthrowing Batista's corrupt regime, to his daring and his oratory, and to his dreams of bringing social justice to a country that had never known it. During 1957 and 1958 Castro's irregular little army won a series of victories over the dictator's ill-equipped, ill-led and demoralised soldiers.

Finally, in January 1959, just two years and a month after Castro's invasion of Cuba, Batista threw in his hand and fled to the United States. A provisional government was formed, full of liberal good intentions, with Castro as the commander-in-chief of Cuba's armed forces. A month later he became Prime Minister. Five months after that he overthrew Cuba's new President and took the presidency for himself. Today, half a century after his landing with his eighty men, he holds it still, the last of the actors from the 1956 stage.

11–16 DECEMBER: STRIKES, ARRESTS AND AN EXECUTION

By mid-November the fighting in Hungary was over. The workers' councils remained in being, and still tried to use their industrial strength to resist the iron grip which Soviet troops and Kádár's security police trusties were imposing on the country. But it gradually became clear that the strikes which they called throughout Hungary's industrial districts were achieving nothing, while reducing the workers to penury. So on 16 November the leaders of the workers' councils called for a return to work, and looked for a matching concession from the authorities.

None came, and when on 21 November the workers' leaders gathered to establish a central representative body they found the venue they had chosen surrounded by Soviet tanks. Some managed to meet, but they lacked the authority to speak for all Hungary's industry. They called a silent demonstration for 23 November, a month to the day after the uprising began, and sure enough that afternoon the streets of Budapest emptied. Through that emptiness, as we have seen, Nagy and his companions were driven to the airport on their way to imprisonment in Romania.

The regime continued to tighten its grip on the workers' councils. It published a decree banning the umbrella organisation and workers' council organisations in cities and communities. At the same time, in an attempt to win over some groups and divide its opponents, it promised factory councils every possible support. Two prominent workers' leaders were summoned to Parliament on the pretext of negotiations and there arrested, just as Maléter had been seized by Serov on 4 November. The response was a call for a general strike, published in the workers' underground newspaper on 10 December. On 11–12 December there was a nationwide response, but the authorities struck back, with more arrests, more threats, and the occupation of some factories by Soviet army units. The new toughness aroused new resistance, which was brutally repressed, particularly in the industrial towns of northern Hungary. A whispering campaign started, 'In March we shall begin again.' It carried little conviction yet it gave the authorities a justification for yet more repression. 'Extraordinary measures' were necessary, said the Kádár regime, because 'counter-revolutionary elements' were still at work, and on 16 December a first death sentence was imposed on a rebel accused of concealing weapons.

23 DECEMBER: LAST POST IN PORT SAID

As UNEF established itself there followed a period of abrasive coexistence between it, the Allied troops, and the Egyptians in Port Said, Port Fuad and El Cap. The British and French were determined to present UNEF's arrival as the completion of the process of securing the canal which they had begun. They wanted a show of close cooperation between themselves and the United Nations. In particular, they wanted to cooperate in clearing the obstacles with which the Egyptians had blocked the canal. Already they had brought in ships and put them to work under a French admiral. Now, eager to prove themselves cooperative, they offered their services to start clearing the canal beyond El Cap. Burns, closely directed by Hammarskjöld, would have none of it. For Nasser Egyptian sovereignty was absolute; every operation on the ground must recognise that fact. For his own part, Hammarskjöld did not want the clarity of his United Nations operation to be muddied by involvement with the invaders.

So on this as on every other point he kept the French and the ever-eager British at arm's length. Tempers rose, and the same sort of criticisms that were to be aimed at the United Nations so often over the next half century resounded against the Secretary-General, the self-righteous Swede, concerned with his own prestige, intent on humiliating the allies, appeasing Nasser rather than getting the canal cleared. Other Swedes have suffered similar abuse more recently, with equally little reason: to take it and keep one's equanimity seems to be a standard requirement for Swedes who wish to serve their fellow men.

Hammarskjöld was persistent. Somehow UNEF got itself into business, and gradually, as its numbers increased to well over 1,000, it took control of more key points along the canal. Later it extended its operations to Gaza, where it remained until the 1967 war. Salvage companies under United Nations direction went to work to clear the canal. Hammarskjöld and his little team of negotiators and administrators, Burns and his scratch force of soldiers, both of them much derided, conjured up the ability to unwind the invasion of Egypt and the seizure and blockage of the canal.

In Ports Said and Fuad the British and French continued to face problems with an angry and increasingly self-confident Egyptian population. British and French troops would defend themselves if attacked, but it was obvious to even the ordinary Egyptian that as they waited, under the sufferance of Egypt and of the international community, the British in particular would never dare to take decisive action against anyone who pestered them. So abuse of the occupiers in the streets increased. So did pinprick attacks on individual servicemen, and one young British officer was taken prisoner by Egyptian freedom fighters, abandoned by his captors and hidden away in a house in a back street as British search parties combed the town, and died there.

The French brazened things out, but most of the British soldiers could see the folly and inconsequentiality of the operation on which they had been sent. They knew what the Egyptians and the world thought about their presence. Their own country, they heard, was bitterly divided. A company of UNEF troops was moved into Port Said, and its arrival only increased the eagerness of British squaddies to be gone The last weeks of British and French occupation of Egyptian soil, in the run-up to Christmas, 1956, were a miserable business, played out by demoralised men in an impossible situation. On 23 December the last of them left Port Said, seven weeks after the first had arrived. Even in their arrangements for departure the two allies handled the business differently. The British left under cover of darkness, to 'avoid awkward incidents', while the French, making a blustering show of confidence to the last, took themselves off in daylight with a show of defiance to preserve their 'prestige and honour'.[14]

WAS SUEZ TO BLAME FOR HUNGARY?

Political emotions ran very high in the autumn of 1956. It seemed as if most of the world was enraged by the Allies' attack upon Egypt. Only in France, Israel and Britain did people persist in seeing Nasser as a new Mussolini and in railing against the United States for betraying its allies. And in Britain a substantial body of liberal opinion was as enraged about Eden's folly as the rest of the world.

There was equally intense anger over Hungary. Opinion throughout the West generally saw the Soviet attack on that small country as criminal aggression, and mourned the defeat of the uprising as a tragedy. Indignation elsewhere was more muted: in the Third World by preoccupation with Suez and throughout the Communist world by censorship and raw fear.

Opinion as aroused as this naturally tended to conflate the two tragedies, and inevitably it was suggested that, one way or another, the Suez conspiracy had triggered, or at the very least licensed, the second Soviet intervention in Hungary – in brief, that the Allies' attack upon Egypt was to blame for the Russian rape of Hungary. Even today, fifty years afterwards, the few who care are still asking: was Suez really to blame for Hungary?

In 1991 I published a biography of Imre Nagy, the first written by a non-Hungarian.[15] Stephen Vizinczey, the Hungarian-born novelist and essayist, reviewed it. In a notice that was generally benevolent he turned to what he saw as my failure to address head-on the matter of linkage between Suez and Hungary. 'This is the first book by a British diplomat', he wrote, 'which at least half admits that the invasion of Suez had something to do with the crushing of the Hungarian Revolution.' He went on to assert that the linkage was obvious. He had been among the revolutionaries in Budapest during the uprising. 'We all knew that Suez meant the revolution was lost,' he wrote. 'This was so obvious at the time that when I heard the news on a transistor radio I was sick from the shock.' But in my book I had failed to acknowledge the obvious: '... alas, when it comes to the errors of British governments,' Vizinczey wrote, 'Unwin has what Stendhal described as "the habit of paying no attention to those things which are clearer than daylight".'

It may be so, but is the proposition that Suez was to blame for Hungary really 'clearer than daylight'? Vizinczey was certainly wrong in suggesting that I was the first British diplomat to examine the possibility. Long before my book, an ambassador grander and better placed than I had considered what linkage there might be between the two. In a telegram to London sent on 4 November, the very day Soviet tanks returned to Budapest, William Hayter, the British ambassador in Moscow, suggested that 'the Russians may have argued that if the United Kingdom and France ... can take the law into their own hands in the Middle East and get away with it, there is likely to be less criticism of the Soviet Union if she does the same thing in Hungary.'[16]

He returned to the question shortly after the dust had settled that winter. He then sent London a long despatch about the Russians' actions in Hungary and what had caused them to act as they did. Then, a few years later, he went public on the question, in a book about his experiences in Moscow which included a summary of the argument in that despatch.[17]

It had to be remembered, he reminded readers forgetful of the events of 1956, that there had been two separate Soviet interventions in Hungary that autumn. The first, in October, took place by invitation [however dubious, one might add, the circumstances of that invitation]. Moscow would have been bound to respond. The question was whether the second intervention, in November, 'would have occurred anyway or was influenced by the Anglo-French intervention in Egypt which occurred between the two phases'.

Hayter went on to speculate about developments within the Kremlin at the very end of October. He concluded, as I do, that a genuine decision was taken on 30–31 October to withdraw Soviet troops from Budapest – and we have seen something of the language of the Soviet declaration about a 'socialist commonwealth' in Central and Eastern Europe.[18] Then two things happened. In his struggle to come to terms with the revolutionaries, Nagy took the fatal decision to call for Soviet withdrawal from the whole of Hungary, proclaimed neutrality and announced Hungary's withdrawal from the Warsaw Pact. At the same time, on 30 October, came the Allied ultimatum to Egypt and Israel.

Opinion in the Kremlin, Hayter supposed, was divided; and Khrushchev's unctuous account of debate there bears out that supposition.[19] Khrushchev and Mikoyan might still have wanted to hold back in Hungary, Hayter believed, but 'The strong-arm party [in the Kremlin] could now use three arguments ... deriving from the Suez situation.' First, the British and French action was so alienating the Asian countries that their criticism of a Soviet attack on Hungary would be muted. Second, if Britain and France could take international law into their own hands, so could the Soviet Union. Third, the Soviet Union could not in practice [for all Bulganin's rocket-rattling] do much for Egypt, yet its prestige could not accept two simultaneous defeats, one over Egypt and one in Hungary.

These arguments, Hayter believed, had come to the support of all the other arguments for taking action against Nagy. Put them together and 'the strong-arm party had won'. The decision was taken to intervene again in Hungary, this time with an unrestrained use of force. As for the linkage between Hungary and Suez, Hayter concluded: '... the Soviet decision to go all out in Hungary was caused by Nagy and not by Suez, though the latter had contributed something.' It is a conclusion that would probably incense Vizinczey, but it seems fair enough to me. Indeed, I would go further and put numbers to it. I think that the final, fatal Soviet decision to intervene a second time was forty per cent caused by developments in Hungary itself, forty per cent by the impact of those developments on the domestic concerns of the Soviet Union, China and the satellites, and twenty per cent by Suez.

31 DECEMBER: RING OUT THE OLD

Even a desperate year like 1956, which had spread mayhem through half the world and confusion and cross-purposes in the chanceries of every member of the United Nations, eventually winds its way to its quietus. In 1956, 31 December arrived to the sound of policies being reordered, old scores settled, records set straight.

On New Year's Eve Veljko Micunovic, the Yugoslav ambassador in Moscow, was invited to a New Year's Eve party in the Kremlin. It was just a month since Khrushchev had attacked him over Imre Nagy's asylum in the Yugoslav embassy, and he expected a pretty frosty welcome. He got it. He heard Khrushchev rewriting history. In his speech he gave more time to discussing the events of the old year than to welcoming the new. He criticised 'those who divide Soviet leaders into Stalinists and anti-Stalinists, hoping in this way to cause a split in the Soviet and other Communist parties'. But they – presumably the Soviet leadership – were 'Stalinists in the consistency with which they fought for Communism and Stalinists in their uncompromising fight against the class enemy, as was Stalin, who devoted his whole life to the victory of the working class and socialism'.[20] Thus Khrushchev ate his words at the Party Congress in February, and shamelessly declared 'in the presence of about a thousand selected guests that he had grown up under Stalin's leadership and was proud of it'.[21] The guests politely applauded this temporary, short-term reinstallation of Stalin in the Communist Pantheon, but for Micunovic what was important was the phrase 'those who divide Communists into Stalinists and anti-Stalinists'. It was aimed, he deduced, at the Yugoslavs, and they were clearly still out of favour in the Kremlin.

William Hayter was still reflecting on Khrushchev's words on an earlier occasion. In mid-November Gomulka had come on a fence-mending visit to Moscow. Although they were boycotting most Kremlin events to demonstrate their disgust at the rape of Hungary, the NATO ambassadors decided to attend a party in his honour. At it, Khrushchev made a furious speech 'saying that the British and French Governments had been behaving like bandits'. Hayter, as shocked by Suez as most British diplomats, privately agreed with him; but after Hungary Khrushchev was hardly the man to cast such stones. Hayter and the French ambassador walked out, and all the NATO ambassadors, marshalled by the American ambassador, followed them.

The following night the Polish ambassador gave a return party. Again Khrushchev was in a combative mood, and this time he was clearly drunk. He used that night a phrase that dogged his footsteps ever afterwards. He was boasting of the Soviet Union's industrial achievements, and speaking as it were to the Western world he used four fatal words: 'We will bury you.' In the back of his fuddled mind must have been innocent matters like economic growth, agricultural revolutions and industrial achievements, for at that time the Soviet Union was clocking up a rate of progress that the naïve among us used to think would soon make it an economic superpower. But when his words were retailed to people in the West they thought not of abstractions like economic growth but of the Hungarian freedom fighters whom Khrushchev had buried that autumn.[22]

Most of the British and French troops withdrawn from the Suez Canal left in time to get home for Christmas. UNEF remained there, and so did the contractors working on the obstacles that still littered the canal. By 28 December, however, divers were at work and on New Year's Eve the full operation got under way, with thirty-two United Nations vessels at work, as well as eleven British and French ones clearing Port Said. On 4 January German tugs succeeded in shifting a 350-ton bridge tower from the waterway. But twelve sunken ships still blocked the canal and thirteen more were trapped in it. It was 29 March before the first ships went through the canal, and 8 April before it was open to all traffic.

In mid-December Eden returned from the Caribbean to find, in Clarissa Eden's words, 'everyone looking at us with thoughtful eyes'.[23] He felt that his colleagues had kept too much from him while he was away. But soon he was wondering as much as they were about his fitness to continue in office. Some colleagues urged him to fight on; others were silent or evasive. On 28 December he replied to a friend's Christmas letter of encouragement, and commented how very lonely it was at the top. Once again, he set out his conviction that Britain and France had been right to take action over Suez. He used words which he and many of his contemporaries still thought reasonable but which to us, with the benefit of long hindsight, seem purely fanciful: 'If we had let events drift until the spring,' he said, 'I have little doubt that by then, or about then, Russia and Egypt would have been ready to pounce, with Israel as the apparent target and western interests as the real one.'[24] A fortnight later he left Downing Street.

The Kremlin continued to watch Kádár's every move. Neither they nor he forgot that a month ago he had told Andropov that if Soviet tanks came back into Budapest he would fight them with his bare hands. On New Year's Day 1957 Khrushchev and Malenkov themselves arrived in Budapest. They were joined by the leaders of three East European countries which had gone along with the destruction of the Hungarian uprising – Bulgaria, Czechoslovakia and Romania – with Poland's Gomulka a conspicuous absentee from this gathering of jackals. But a few days later Chou En Lai himself came to Hungary to endorse the new regime. And on 5 January that regime turned the full force of repression against what was left of working class resistance. Now even 'refusal to work' and 'provocation to strike' became punishable by death.

By New Year's Eve most Conservative politicians had long gone home, intent on drowning their memories of the dying year. But Douglas Dodds-Parker, a junior minister in the Foreign Office who had been given political supervision of British publicity and propaganda directed at the Arab world, was still at work. He had found it a thankless task, and now he was considering an assessment of its effectiveness. His own conclusion was a bleak one. '... the Archangel Gabriel,' he minuted, 'transmitting with Infinite Power on The Last Trump could not sell British co-operation with France and Israel to the Arab world.'[25]

Eisenhower, triumphant in the Presidential election, was safely ensconced in power for his second term. He believed that his policy on Suez had been vindicated, and he made no apologies for the pressure he had brought to bear to force Britain and France to back down. Other Americans were less certain, and when on New Year's Eve a group of Republican leaders came to see him, they asked him about British and French attitudes to the United States. He reassured them. 'Underneath', he said, 'the governments are thankful we did what we did. But publicly, we have to be the whipping boy.'[26] It was Ike at his blandest. He could afford to be, for God was in his American heaven, and for the President, as for the United States, all was well with the world.

13
From Then to Now

In the years after Suez and Hungary, the men who had played key roles in the events of 1956 went their ways to widely differing destinies.

Eisenhower remained in the White House, more secure than ever. He served out his full second term, still benevolent, much loved by the American people, still deeply devoted to the golf course. He presided over a generally contented country, but one that remained scarred by the legacies of slavery and Jim Crow. His eye remained as shrewd as ever; very occasionally he asserted himself; and as he left office he came back to a theme he had occasionally explored during his eight years in office. It was the danger that policy could come to be dominated by a coalition on the one hand of big business and on the other of all those men, in uniform and out of it, who made their careers serving the United States' ever-increasing security needs. With the foresight of a simple man who nevertheless got to the heart of things, he warned his compatriots that what he called the 'military-industrial complex' threatened the health of the republic: 'We must never let the weight of this combination endanger our liberties or democratic processes,' he said. He lived to see Richard Nixon, his deeply suspect Vice President, become President, and died in March 1969

The fates were less kind to Anthony Eden. His physical and nervous health had been broken by the crisis. When in December he returned from his undignified flight to convalescence in the Caribbean he found his colleagues no longer the malleable creatures they had been. Now they were watching his health and measuring what was left of his political reputation. Within a month he cracked and early in January 1957 he offered his resignation to the Queen. He sailed away on a long voyage of recuperation to New Zealand, but although he lived another twenty years he never fully recovered his health, nor any position in politics. The folly of Suez dogged his once-great reputation.

Guy Mollet had come out of the Suez failure with far less political damage than Eden, but the constitution of the Fourth Republic deprived any Prime Minister of political staying-power. He remained in office until April 1957 (so clocking up a longer period in power than any other French Prime Minister in the postwar years), to be replaced by Bourgès-Manoury, the Defence Minister who had led him into conspiracy with Israel. But no conventional politician could build lasting majorities strong enough to resolve the problem of Algeria. In the end de Gaulle, recalled to office, succeeded where they had failed, bamboozling and facing down the settlers in Algeria and the French Army, creating for himself a new power base in an executive Presidency, and drawing a decisive line under the succession of constitutional crises which had plagued the Fourth Republic.

Khrushchev survived in power longer than Eden and Mollet, longer, for that matter, than Eisenhower, and through the late 1950s and early 1960s he made more than his fair share of world headlines. Hungary had strengthened his grip on the Soviet empire, while alienating sympathy for Communism in the West. He showed himself cunningly effective in one guise and dangerously impulsive in another, as when he challenged Kennedy over Cuba. In the end his colleagues concluded that he, and therefore they, were living too dangerously. They overthrew him, but spared his life. He became the first Soviet leader to lose power and yet live on in comfort and in relative personal freedom – freedom enough, indeed, to produce his remarkably tendentious memoirs.[1]

Hammarskjöld went on working, obsessive in his concern to promote what he saw as the good of mankind. His focus shifted from trouble spot to trouble spot, until he was killed in an air crash in central Africa in 1961, still intent on reconciling the irreconcilable, this time in the Congo. David Ben-Gurion entrenched himself even deeper as the father of his people, ever more mystical in his opinions, obsessed by the dignity of biblical Judaea, haunted by the vulnerability of modern Israel. He died just months after the six-day Arab-Israel war of 1967, in which, as in 1956, the Israeli army was triumphantly successful. As for Tito, he lived out an untroubled presidential existence until three days short of his eighty-eighth birthday, a patron of the non-aligned movement, only occasionally challenged by the Kremlin, his sybaritic circumstances a far cry from the life of his partisan youth. There was regret when he died, for the man himself and for the role he had played in holding Yugoslavia together – and sure enough, within five years of his death it began its slide into fragmentation.

In Poland, Gomulka tried and in the end failed to find a policy that could satisfy the conflicting demands of the Communist Party, the Soviet Union, the Polish people and the Polish Catholic Church. Gradually he lost the reputation for effective and relatively liberal Communism which had propelled him to power in 1956, power which he finally surrendered in December 1970. But he died in his bed, unlike that other Communist rebel of 1956 who had dared to challenge the Kremlin. Imre Nagy was brought back to Budapest from his Romanian exile early in 1957 and eventually put on trial for his life. The verdict was preordained: Khrushchev and Kádár needed to punish Tito for some transient offence against Communist orthodoxy and putting an end to Nagy's life, which was forfeit ever since the revolution, offered them the means of doing so. So in June 1958 he was hanged, a matter of days after his sixty-second birthday, the victim of judicial murder. He won back his reputation as a great Hungarian only in the world's year of miracles, 1989, with a reburial that reminded me, and thousands of others in the crowd that day, of that other reburial, of László Rajk thirty-three years earlier, which had lit the fuse for the revolution.

There remains Gamal Abdel Nasser. To the British and French he was the evil genius of the whole Suez story, to the Egyptian people and most of the Arab world its hero. But when particular views and prejudice on both sides of the argument are stripped away, he emerges, like Imre Nagy, as an objectively heroic figure. He had the courage to take on the second and third most powerful Western nations, accepting the risk that the most powerful of all, the United States, might join them. He had the nerve to stand up to months of political and military pressure. With enormous self-discipline he kept within the limits of international law and decent behaviour which his opponents so merrily ignored. Despite all provocations he kept his notoriously volatile people well in hand. And unlike his enemies he consistently sought a peaceable resolution of their differences. It is time for those relatively few Britons and Frenchmen who remember how their leaders loathed him to give him the credit that is his due.

THE EUROPEAN EMPIRES

Within thirty years of Suez, pretty well every trace of Britain's and France's empires vanished from the face of geography and receded into historical memory. So did the remnants of other empires, notably those of Belgium and Portugal.

By 1956 Britain, France, Portugal and the Netherlands had already shed most of their responsibilities in Asia. Within a decade after Suez they disposed of the rest (Hong Kong and Macao aside). With colonialism freshly discredited by the whole madcap adventure, the Europeans were forced also to accelerate the march to independence of colonies, particularly in Africa, which showed less promise of self-sufficiency. At every step of the way they found their hands forced by insistent demands for independence.

Colonies that were largely or entirely free of white settlement went relatively easily. We have seen Sudan entering into precarious independence on 1 January 1956. It was quickly followed by Ghana. The late 1950s and very early 1960s saw flags lowered and new ones raised in a series of independence ceremonies, throughout French West Africa, in the Belgian Congo and in Nigeria, Tanganyika, Uganda and Kenya. Within a decade colonies in which white officials from the metropolitan power ruled over black men had become rare exceptions, curious anomalies. To the extent that Britain and France had hoped that Suez would check the movement to independence they had clearly failed.

But the hopes expressed in those independence ceremonies were mostly disappointed. Freedom was no sure solvent of the stains of poverty, corruption and tribalism. To some extent all these ills were the consequences of freedom, to some extent simple inheritances from the colonial period. In Africa in particular those new nations, such as Botswana, which escaped such post-colonial problems were very few and very fortunate.

Colonies which had been largely shaped by settlers presented vastly greater problems. Rhodesia and Algeria, and the Portuguese colonies of southern Africa too, soaked up decades of United Nations resolutions, of flying visits by prime ministers and presidents, of vicious guerrilla attacks and equally vicious retaliation. In the end they too became sovereign states based, at least in theory, on the wishes of the majority.

The French had hoped that a successful blow against Nasser at Suez would bring him down. With him gone, they believed, Arab support for the Algerian nationalists would go too. France would be able to deal with the Algerian rebels and keep Algeria French. That hope, like so many others, was dashed by failure at Suez. Throughout the late 1950s the situation in Algeria steadily deteriorated. In April 1957 it brought Mollet down. The Fourth Republic drifted, holed below the waterline by a developing civil war in Algeria, with *pied noir* pitted against nationalist, French Army against freedom fighter. France's repression of legitimate national aspiration blackened its international reputation. The excesses of the fight against the nationalists stained the honour of the French Army yet failed to produce results. The strains within French democracy and society came close to breaking point. In the end they brought down the Fourth Republic and in January 1959 installed de Gaulle in the Elysée Palace.

At the time France seemed almost as near to civil war over Algeria as was Algeria itself. De Gaulle used ambiguity and chicanery to see off his opponents, and in 1962 Algeria won its bitter and resented independence. In France de Gaulle survived assassination attempts and military insurrection. Modern France still bears the marks of the events of those years – on the one hand a powerful executive presidency and self-confident, centralised government, and on the other a society still embittered forty years afterwards by what happened then to Algerians settled in France and to French settlers returning from Algeria to the mother country that had let them down.

Britain took almost twenty years longer to bring the story of Rhodesia, its own Algeria, to a conclusion. The 1979 settlement, which first re-established British authority over the rebellious colony and then launched an independent Zimbabwe, at first seemed to promise a future in which all its citizens could live together in reasonable harmony. It was years before the country, which enjoyed so much greater promise than most in Africa, sank into a tyranny extreme even by that continent's standards.

Britain's protracted failure to bring the white regime in Rhodesia to heel had embittered its relations with most of Africa and the Commonwealth, and with its traditional critics in the Arab world, particularly Egypt and Algeria. Now, in the early 1980s, the way seemed open for Britain to establish itself in the eyes of its old colonies as a reformed character. But rightly or wrongly it refused to join in effective sanctions against the Third World's new bogey, South Africa's apartheid regime. It took another eleven years before, on 11 February 1990, Nelson Mandela walked to freedom and set South Africa on the road to black-led statehood.

All these changes would no doubt have come about if the Suez war of 1956 had never happened. The demand for freedom and independence was too strong, the pressure of international opinion too insistent and the capacity of the metropolitan powers too weak to delay change indefinitely. But Suez significantly accelerated the process. It showed the world that Britain and France lacked the political, military and economic strength to resist these pressures. It eroded their moral standing. The sheer bad judgement of their leaders undermined their reputation for wisdom and cunning. Nasser's successful defiance had whetted the appetite of men like him throughout the Third World. And the United States had backed the United Nations and the Third World against Western European countries which tried to use *force majeure* to keep their subjects in order.

THE WORLD OF MARX AND LENIN

The Soviet Union had also taken a nasty tumble in the autumn of 1956, but its embarrassment was considerably better disguised than that of France and Britain. Its swift suppression of the Hungarian uprising, evil as it was, could be seen as a victory, if of a particularly brutal kind.

The world abhorred Moscow's attack on Hungary as it abhorred the British and French invasion of Egypt, but the strength of the abhorrence varied. Opinion in Western Europe and North America was outraged by the rape of Budapest, but almost everywhere else the sins of France and Britain attracted more criticism than those of Moscow. All the same, throughout Western Europe, electoral support for Communist parties collapsed, in France and Italy in particular, where it had been greatest, and it was never to be rebuilt. After Hungary the Soviet Union could no longer rely on 'useful idiots' in the West to endorse its claims to be building a new and better world. And even in the Third World, preoccupied with the sins of Western imperialism as it might be, the politically observant took careful note of what had happened in Hungary. In the words of Milovan Djilas, the Yugoslav Communist who revolted against Communism's crimes: 'The wound which the Hungarian Revolution inflicted on Communism can never be healed.'

But it was what happened within the Soviet camp that mattered most. It needs to be analysed at two different levels: what was said publicly in all those strictly ruled societies, and what was believed. That small minority authorised to speak and write in public all applauded the action which Moscow had taken to 'protect the Hungarian working people' from 'fascist counter-revolution'. Yet attentive analysts could detect differences of emphasis. The Poles, who in October had successfully defied Moscow, kept very quiet about what had happened to the Hungarians in November. The Yugoslavs, half-restored to communion with the Communist world yet fiercely criticised there for giving Imre Nagy asylum, were in a very awkward corner. They said little, but when Imre Nagy was executed their angry embarrassment was obvious. Everywhere else Communist spokesmen were categorically positive about the events in Hungary.

Yet they had to explain not just the suppression of the Hungarian uprising but also Khrushchev's rash words of condemnation of Stalin at the Twentieth Party Congress in February 1956. Those words offered some explanation of the attack on Stalinism which broke out in Budapest eight months later. Listening to Khrushchev's efforts to explain all this away at the Kremlin reception on New Year's Day 1957, the Yugoslav ambassador, Veljko Micunovic, could see how inadequate they were. The rest of Khrushchev's political career was dogged by that same embarrassment. Nagy's execution in June 1958 disposed of one of the causes of Khrushchev's embarrassment. He could not dispose of the other – his own continuing desire to rid the Soviet world of the remains of Stalinism.

But what Khrushchev and his spokesmen throughout the Communist world had to say was in the long run less important than the convictions of the masses of ordinary people who heard their words and rejected them. The suppression of the Hungarian revolution had shown how unwise it was to challenge Moscow's authority. But the revolution itself – led and sustained by ordinary working people, most of them very young – marked the political and moral failure of Communism. It showed that one should never again risk standing against Soviet tanks with sub-machine-guns and improvised grenades. As long as Moscow and its satellite leaders remained resolute, so long would their rule endure. But it showed also that there was absolutely no need to pay attention to their foolish words.

It was not just ordinary Hungarians who were saying 'Never again'. János Kádár and his regime were determined that never again would they risk provoking the Hungarian people to rise against them: the excesses of Stalinism and of Rákosi must never be repeated. So once the post-revolution reign of terror had been completed, the regime set about making Hungary 'the most comfortable barracks in the Soviet camp'. 'He who is not against us is with us' became the doctrine and the reality of politics in Hungary. At the end of the 1960s came the beginning of economic reform and by the early 1980s Hungary was reaching out diplomatically to the West and even experimenting with limited political freedoms at home. So when the year of miracles came in 1989, Hungary (with Poland, the other Eastern European country which had struck a blow for freedom in 1956) was the best prepared to exploit it.

Moscow too wanted no repetition of those pictures of Soviet tanks crushing working men and women which had played so badly in a world in which news was becoming increasingly universal. But in 1968 the Soviet leaders were confronted in Czechoslovakia with something that looked very like the challenge they had faced in Hungary. Dubcek looked like Imre Nagy, and the Czechs and Slovaks were as naïvely hopeful of change as the Hungarians had been twelve years earlier. 'Do you really not know what kind of people you are dealing with?' Kádár asked Dubcek before the Soviet tanks rolled into Prague. Taken prisoner, Dubcek was treated brutally, but spared the fate of Nagy. Moscow was learning the lesson of 1956, if with agonising slowness.

Nevertheless, neither Budapest in 1956 nor Prague in 1968 quenched the unexpressed thirst for freedom of ordinary people in Eastern Europe. When I left Budapest in 1986 after my second term there I thought that within a generation the Hungarians (and perhaps all Eastern Europeans) would win freedom for themselves. In practice, freedom came to them within three years, gift-wrapped by Mikhail Gorbachev. On 6 October 1989, thirty-three years to the day after the reburial of László Rajk, the Hungarian Communists held their last Party Congress. At it they voted for the dissolution of their party. 'The present concept of socialism, the Stalinist system,' they said, 'has exhausted all its social, economic, political and moral reserves, and has proved unsuitable for keeping pace with global developments. Thus the history of the Hungarian Socialist Workers' Party has come to an end.' All over Central and Eastern Europe Communist parties were coming to the same conclusion. The British and French empires had scarcely survived ten years after 1956, while Communist rule in Eastern Europe lasted for thirty. But in the end, Moscow's empire went like them into the history books.

In 1956 the actions of the United States were central to the defeat of the British, French and Israeli assault upon Egypt. Eisenhower saw Suez as a last spasm of British and French imperialism. He ensured that it would fail, and so helped accelerate the European powers' withdrawal from empire. He demonstrated American commitment to the rule of law and to the rights of nations, and won thereby some goodwill in the Third World and at the United Nations. The price he paid was to weaken two countries which were important to him in the long stand-off against the Soviet Union. Their support might have been particularly valuable in precisely those parts of the world from which, like a good enemy of imperialism, he had helped to chivvy them.

Very soon after Suez the United States found itself sucked deep into the crises of the Middle East. Eisenhower and Dulles had resisted Britain's every blandishment to join it in becoming a member of the Baghdad Pact. The pact's purpose was to keep Soviet influence out of the Arab world, a purpose dear to the American heart, but Washington had been content to leave Britain alone as the only power outside the region to sustain it from within. After Suez Britain's reputation in the Middle East was ruined, and the reputation of the Baghdad Pact with it. So when, in July 1958, revolution came in Iraq, with King and Crown Prince murdered and Iraq's Prime Minister, Nuri es-Said, kicked to death by the mob, no one could step in to save them. Fearful that trouble would spread, the United States landed marines in Beirut, who advanced unresisted across Beirut's beaches. Britain, pathetically eager for reinstatement as America's friend, sent parachute troops into Jordan. In 1958 only sanctity on a heroic scale prevented Britons telling Americans 'I told you so'.

From then onwards the United States became ever more closely involved in the Middle East. The Baghdad Pact was gone, leaving Turkey and Pakistan as America's associates in a new and shadowy entity called CENTO. American oil companies led the way to a close relationship between Washington and the Saudi monarchy. American sympathy for the Israelis, tested and broken in 1956, quickly revived, until by the 1970s the United States was locked in an unhealthy, quasi-colonial relationship with Israel that queered its pitch with every other state in the region. In 1979 the Islamic revolutionaries in Iran sacked the American Embassy in Tehran and held its diplomats hostage.

Washington saw the Ayatollahs as existential enemies and encouraged and supplied Saddam Hussein in a long and ultimately fruitless war against them. So in the course of the fifty years that separate us from Suez, much of the Middle East became an informal American empire, and at the same time an American quagmire.

Retrospect can trace a roughly comparable but ultimately happier story in South East Asia. French power in the region had been broken at the lost battle of Dien Bien Phu in May 1954. Two months later Vietnam was divided, the northern half of the country becoming a rigorous Communist nation, the south a client state in desperate need of Western sponsorship. Only the United States could take the lead, and only Australia joined it with some very limited military and moral support. France, the condemned ex-colonial power, was unwanted, while Britain – independent-minded for once – was determined not to embroil itself in what became, over the years, a tragic American defeat. Washington was bitter: 'All we ever asked for was a battalion of the Black Watch,' an American Secretary of State is supposed to have said, but Harold Wilson was adamant. In any case, Britain still had its hands full. Having defeated Communist insurgency in Malaya and seen that country to independence, it turned to protecting it from subversive attack from Indonesia. Wise policy kept Britain out of Vietnam, a wisdom that one cannot help suspecting (and rather hoping) was nourished by memories of other hands-across-the-Atlantic pleas for help that had been so brusquely denied at the time of Suez.

But whatever the rights and wrongs, whatever the help given and the help denied, the facts at the end of the half century that separates us from Suez are clear. The superpower which even today still piously refuses to see itself as imperial now presides over an empire as far-flung as the British empire ever was, grappling with problems which stretch even its strength to the limit. It has triumphantly seen off one rival, the Soviet Union, and cannot make up its mind to love or to loathe another, the European Union. It is just beginning to fear the rise of yet another, China, which before this century is out will probably take its place.[2]

EUROPEAN UNION...

Before Suez as ever since, the British exaggerated the intimacy and the importance of their relationship with the United States. The wartime alliance had indeed been the closest in history and until Suez British governments had subordinated all other considerations to maintaining it. But earlier chapters have demonstrated that the closeness of the relationship did not in any serious way affect American policy over Suez. Instead, Washington seemed to the British of the day to take an almost perverse pleasure in punishing their country for its temerity in presuming to act on its own. The result was that in 1956 Britain was split down the middle not just over the rights and wrongs of the Suez adventure, but in its response to America's action in breaking its slim prospect of success. Once the adventure was over, Britain could never make up its collective mind about attitudes towards the United States. A majority chose to cling to it through thick and thin, while a sizeable minority was sceptical of it and all its works. Such a divide persists to this day, in what some of us see as a fatal ambivalence that neuters British foreign policy.

For all the talk in Paris and Washington of an intimacy between France and the United States that went back to French support for the American Revolution, French opinion never presumed the closeness to America which Britain thought it enjoyed. So over Suez the French had far less sense of betrayal than the British. And France drew clearer lessons from Suez than Britain ever did. In the words of Guy Millard, Eden's private secretary, on a television programme looking back on Suez from the vantage point of 1996: 'The French simply wrote [Suez] off as a failure ... and got on with life. They went on very soon after Suez to more than thirty years of national self-confidence and national success'.[3]

They turned, moreover, with a new vigour to the prospect of building a Europe which served France's needs and followed its lead. The story for our purposes here begins at the height of the Suez crisis, on Tuesday, 6 November, and starts, like so many other aspects of the Suez drama, with a slightly mysterious conversation in Paris. Keith Kyle, Britain's most faithful chronicler of the story of Suez, provides an instructive account, which he takes from Pineau, the French Foreign Minister.

On that day Mollet and Pineau were engaged in conversations about the future of Europe with the German Chancellor, Konrad Adenauer, and his Foreign Minister. They were interrupted by an urgent call from Eden. He told Mollet that he could not go on with the assault on the canal and was going to accept the ceasefire which Hammarskjöld had negotiated. Mollet tried to persuade him to hold on, at least to play for time. He failed and returned, profoundly shaken, to the meeting with Adenauer.

Before that interruption, Adenauer had been warning Mollet and Pineau that he feared the United States might join the Soviet Union in imposing their joint will in the Middle East. It was the day after Bulganin's letter to Eisenhower, which had warned of the danger of general war in the Middle East. In full Cassandra flow, Adenauer had warned the Frenchmen that Moscow would never have suggested cooperation with the Americans if there had not been some realistic possibility that Washington might accept it. The Americans would never risk war for Europe, said Adenauer, asserting that 'American public opinion was all that was standing in the way of an American partition of the world with the Soviet Union'.[4]

Now, on Mollet's return, Adenauer tried again to convince him, with his Foreign Minister showing obvious signs of disquiet at the violence of his chief's remarks: 'France and England will never be powers comparable to the United States and the Soviet Union,' Pineau has him saying. 'Not Germany either. There remains to them only one way of playing a decisive role in the world; that is to unite to make Europe. England is not ripe for it but the affair of Suez will help to prepare her spirits for it. We have no time to waste: Europe will be your revenge.'[5]

Pineau, Kyle notes, is an unreliable witness, his memory 'sometimes demonstratively fallible'; and Selwyn Lloyd had discovered long ago that in his spare time he wrote fairy stories for children.[6] But as Kyle says, 'the flavour sounds right', and the story provides an irresistible pendant to the Suez saga.

Whatever the effect of Adenauer's words on Mollet and Pineau, it is manifest that after Suez France was never prepared to put much confidence in the United States again. Successive French leaders have shown themselves determined to trust themselves alone, ready whenever they think it necessary to pick a fight with the United States. The consequence has been decades of mutual distrust and dislike, and in times of crisis absurdities like the renaming of chips as Freedom Fries .

So France set out to make itself independent of the United States and to distance itself from the perfidious British. As John Newhouse put it, the Suez adventure 'did more damage to France's relations with the Anglo-Saxons, particularly the Americans, than any other episode in post-war history. Washington was seen to have betrayed its chief allies, and Britain abjectly deserted France and Israel at the first sign of disapproval in Washington.'[7] So France made itself a nuclear power (truly independent, as Britain never was) with at least a theoretical if highly fanciful ability to engage its enemies 'à tous azimuths'. Under de Gaulle it withdrew from NATO's integrated structure and so distanced itself from American hegemony in Western Europe. Above all France set about building a European Community in its own image, determined that it should develop into a European Union and in time a United States of Europe led by France. And for a fateful decade, France under de Gaulle kept Britain out.

...AND SPECIAL RELATIONSHIP

Britain drew very different lessons from Suez. From 6 November 1956 it turned back to the road which one British government after another had followed ever since 1940. In 1940 Churchill had then set Britain on a course of limpet-like attachment to the United States. For seventeen months he used all his guile to tempt Roosevelt into war at Britain's side. Alliance safely sealed, he made it his business to keep America sweet. Faced with a choice between the continent and the open sea, he told de Gaulle, Britain would always choose the sea. Stony-eyed, he watched Roosevelt pursue his delusion that he could charm Stalin into friendship by belittling Britain. And when (significantly in Fulton, Missouri, in the American heartland) he warned of the iron curtain that had descended across Europe he was recruiting the United States to stand firmly with Britain on the good guys' side of a continental and global divide.

This was the principle which had guided the governments in which Eden served, and he inherited it with much other baggage when he took over from Churchill. Then, at the first test, he was driven to alliance not with the Americans but with the French. Confronting Nasser he remembered that most formative of events for Englishmen of his age, Munich. At best Nasser was Mussolini, at worst Hitler, and against them Britain had stood first with France, and then alone. He allowed the crisis to tempt him away from openness with the United States until, as Dulles and Hoover, Humphrey and the President tightened the squeeze on Britain's financial position, he knew that he was beaten. Macmillan, soon to succeed him, drew the same conclusion. So immediately after Suez first Eden and then Macmillan turned once again to building bridges with the United States.

It suited the Americans that the chastened British should gradually work their passage back to favour. They lifted the financial blockade, they brought Macmillan back into the world of diplomatic courtesy. A few years later they encouraged him to try for entry to the Common Market, and helped him with nuclear weapons to clothe his political nakedness. And there, always keeping close to nurse, British ministers have remained ever since, never seriously getting out of line with American wishes.

Yet not long after Suez one man, not noted for long views, broad vision or self-assertion, tried to make them think again. He was Selwyn Lloyd, Foreign Secretary throughout the Suez crisis, his career near-fatally wounded by it, yet loyally soldiering on. On 8 January 1957 a Cabinet meeting was called to consider Britain's strategy in this so-abruptly altered world. It was to be an all-day affair and, as Foreign Secretary, Lloyd would have a central role to play. 'I had done some preparatory work for it,' he wrote. 'My theme was that, after the serious difference of opinion with the United States, we must try to make Western Europe less dependent upon America.'

Lloyd might have got support for this thesis from a Prime Minister who was still in command of his cabinet, for Eden had never shared Churchill's absolute commitment to alliance with the United States and he had been deeply disillusioned by the Americans' role in the Suez crisis. But this was Eden's last Cabinet meeting. His authority was broken, for his colleagues knew that when they dispersed he would be going to the Palace to submit his resignation to the Queen. There was no chance that day of engaging his mind in discussion of long-term strategy. Other ministers were equally distracted. 'I did not get much sympathy from my colleagues,' Lloyd recorded. 'Most of them thought that the first priority must be the mending of our fences with the United States.'[8] It is a conviction that has pervaded the Cabinet Room ever since.

ISRAEL AND ITS NEIGHBOURS

Along with Britain and France, Israel was the third aggressor in the Suez war of 1956. Unlike them, it was condemned to go on living in the heart of a troubled and dangerous region.

From the beginnings of the State of Israel, its policy has been driven by the conviction that it is in danger. The country is small, surrounded by hostile states, many of them said to be set on its destruction. The Israelis have learned the hard way, they say, that for their security they can ultimately depend only on themselves. Hence, in the phrase of a friend of mine who grew up in Israel, they have replaced the Bible's 'eye for an eye' with a doctrine of their own: 'Two eyes for an eye'; and sometimes three. Hence, too, Israel's nuclear weapons, their existence never avowed, never formally accepted by other nations but never doubted and only rarely criticised. Hence also, perhaps, an almost hysterical rejection of outside criticism of a state which, like any state, has imperfections and worse on its conscience. Hence, above all, policies which weigh Jewish and Israeli suffering far more heavily than that of Palestinians and so lock Israelis into an unending circle of conflict with their neighbours.

The story of Israel's dealings with the Arab world since 1956 illustrates all these themes. After Suez, Ben-Gurion was reluctant to see Israel's gains in Sinai and Gaza vacated. To control Sharm-al-Sheikh guaranteed freedom of passage for Israeli ships on their way to and from Eilat at the head of the Gulf of Aqaba. Eilat gave Israel an opening to the East, the more important to a country whose shipping was barred from passing through the Suez Canal. As long as Israel controlled Gaza it could prevent the kind of Egyptian-inspired Fedayeen attacks on its territory which had led up to the 1956 war. The Israelis put little faith in United Nations' supervision or buffer forces. So for a time they bitterly resisted demands that they give up the fruits of the November Sinai campaign.

By the early and mid 1960s Israel seemed to be riding high. Adolf Eichmann was brought to Jerusalem, tried and hanged. Pope Paul VI visited Jerusalem. Israel established diplomatic relations with West Germany. And in June 1967 Israeli forces won a spectacular six-day victory over the armies of three out of four of their neighbours: Egypt, Jordan and Syria. In the process the Israelis conquered territory more extensive than the diminutive State of Israel, acquiring with it problems that have haunted them ever since.

Six years later Israel was at war again after a surprise attack by Egypt and Syria. The 'Yom Kippur' war of 1973 at first went badly for the Israelis; for a day or so there seemed to be a danger of the defeat which would, Israelis are convinced, have led to their being driven into the sea. But the United States rushed arms to Israel and Israeli troops launched counterattacks: they plunged into Syria's Golan Heights and they established a bridgehead on the west bank of the Suez Canal. In a short and victorious week Israel won an aura of invincibility. From the Yom Kippur war date the beginnings of wisdom among the Egyptians and Jordanians about dealings with their doughty neighbour, and an equally significant arrogance and folly among Israelis.

In the course of the next few years Israel came to uneasy terms with Egypt and Jordan. At the same time long-term occupation of half of Lebanon and a steady erosion of Palestinian rights in the occupied territories of the West Bank and Gaza were losing Israel sympathy. Even the United States, which otherwise saw Israel as a reliable client state, almost an informal part of the American empire, grew critical. Today, fifty years after Suez, Israel's position is militarily far stronger than it was then, yet politically and morally questioned in a way unthinkable in the early years of its existence.

CENTRAL EUROPE TODAY...

Egypt and Israel have come a long way since 1956. So have Hungary and Poland. To sum up where Central Europe stands today offers a final wrap of the dramas played out half a century ago in Budapest, Warsaw, Moscow and Brioni.

Central Europe (to give Eastern Europe the name politely extended to it nowadays) is in 2006 a relatively happy place. Most of its constituent republics, Hungary and Poland included, are safely incorporated into the European Union and NATO. Most of their citizens, congenital bellyachers apart, are content that they should be. They have transformed their politics, economics and society since the Communist world fell apart in 1989. Most of their citizens are more prosperous than they were, though there are spectacular losers as well as winners from the shift to market economies and capitalist excess. Each of these countries changes the complexion of its governments every few years, which to nervous onlookers seems like dangerous instability and to me like the proper functioning of parliamentary democracy. They keep a wary eye on the inheritors of the Soviet Union's mantle, their big Eastern neighbours. As for the Russians themselves, they strive in one mode to reassert themselves as a great power, in another to reconcile themselves to a new and more limited place in the world, within which individuals can find some freedom, some security and some prosperity.

So far, that is a view of Central Europe worthy of Candide. The old

Yugoslavia, which Tito held together for so long, remains the principal exception, but even it is making progress in the wake of its neighbours. Slovenia, always the most prosperous of Yugoslav's republics, soon made its escape into Western company, the European Union and NATO. For years, Serbia and Croatia, the big boys among the South Slavs, let mad animosity and extremism consume their reputations. Now, thousands of innocent victims in Krajina, Kosovo and Bosnia later, the attraction of the European Union is making itself felt. Serbia, Croatia and the fragments of Bosnia are beginning to rebuild their positions in the eyes of the world, knowing that to despatch alleged war criminals to The Hague is the inescapable price of admission to the Union and to international respectability. Meanwhile, in Bosnia and Kosovo international viceroys and non-governmental organisations still try to root out ethnic hatreds between neighbours who, in better times, contrived to share their narrow valleys and little villages reasonably peaceably together.

...AND THE MIDDLE EAST

In the Middle East, by contrast, Candide would be hard put to discover anything even faintly resembling the best of all possible worlds. Relations between Palestinians and Israelis are quite as bitter as ever. Over the years since the formal Arab-Israeli wars of 1956, 1967 and 1973, bloodthirsty Palestinian terrorism and murderous Israeli attacks on Palestinians (put cause and effect in whichever order you prefer) have become far worse. With very few exceptions the countries of the Arab world are as far from democracy and respect for human rights as they were in 1956. And since 2001 the twin blights of fanatical terrorism on the one hand and a messianic war against terrorism on the other have come along to aggravate all these things.

To complicate matters and aggravate them still further, there is Iraq. For anyone writing about Suez in 2006 there is an irresistible temptation to draw comparisons between these two Middle East adventures. Similarities there are; but the differences between the circumstances of the two interventions are at first sight at least more striking.

The first difference is the role played by the actors in the different dramas. The Suez operation was hindered from the beginning first by American doubts and then by American opposition; and when the European Allies and Israel nevertheless went ahead the United States stepped in quickly to haul them back. The invasion of Iraq, by contrast, was led by the world's only superpower, sweeping aside all attempts to stop it. It claims to stand at the head of a coalition of the willing, but only Britain contributed much more than some slight pretence of international validation. Once the United States struck there could be no stopping a quick military victory over the Iraqis. The triumphant if repellent exercise of 'Shock and Awe' was very different from the bumbling operations of Britain and France in 1956

Secondly, the goals of intervention were different. The immediate goals were to secure international passage through the canal in the one case and the destruction of weapons of mass destruction in the other. The more long-range and ambitious goals were fundamentally different. If they had been successful in Egypt the European Allies would presumably have replaced Nasser with a politician of the old, pre-revolutionary type, a man of the kind who had served King Farouk for so long. In Iraq, on the other hand, the Americans said they were intent on something more far reaching: the creation of a democracy which, once established, would act as a model of freedom for the whole Middle East.

Finally, the international context was different. The invasion of Suez took place in a world still dominated by nation states pursuing national interests and national rivalries. Fifty years later affairs were shaped by two new salient forces in international politics: first, the threat of global terrorism and second, the United States' messianic determination to enrol the world in hunting down terrorists wherever they were to be found. Before the invasion there was no demonstrable link between Saddam Hussein and Al Qaida; but the attack played into Bin Laden's hands, provoked Iraqi resistance which, for want of other weapons, resorted to terrorist means, and fed the appetite for anti-Western terror all over the world. Now most Americans believe that Saddam Hussein was behind the terrorist attack on the World Trade Centre and many, perhaps most, Moslems believe that the United States is intent on making Iraq the central battlefield of a crusade against Islam.

Nevertheless, analysis of the two affairs reveals threads in common as well as contrasts. The attacks on Egypt in 1956 and on Iraq in 2003 are (the particular complication of Kosovo apart) the only two occasions in the last hundred years on which Britain, alone or in association with others, has attacked a sovereign state in contravention of international law. In doing so it attracted the odium of large parts of the world and in at least the technical sense committed war crimes. The same is true of its associates in both instances, but in 1956 the governments of France and Israel lost little sleep over matters of international legality and in 2003 such matters seemed to trouble the American administration relatively little. There is of course a profound irony about the American role in these two episodes. Over Suez the United States, strictly honourable or piously hypocritical as you care to see it, held international law and the will of the United Nations sacrosanct, even though that meant destroying the policies of its two closest allies. Over Iraq by contrast its determination to protect its own absolute freedom of action has consigned international law and the United Nations to irrelevance.

It would be a brave man who said with any confidence today, in January 2006, that he knew what the outcome in Iraq would be, but all of us can read the writing on the wall. Coalition troops will gradually come home, the timetable largely dictated, whether avowedly or not, by domestic political considerations. They will leave behind them some kind of rough-and-ready government in Iraq. It rule will be challenged daily by terrorist atrocities and in places by something close to civil war. To maintain itself it will be tempted to resort to the kind of repression that will remind the world of some of Saddam Hussein's less heinous crimes. There will be a show of democracy, and some Iraqis will be willing to die for it. But religious, tribal and ethnic differences are likely to play a more salient part than democracy in shaping the future of Iraq.

Iraq will not become a shining model of democracy to inspire the Middle East nor a centre of stability in the region. Instead, religious and tribal links will give Iran, Iraq's old enemy and America's continuing bugbear, a kind of oversight over several Iraqi provinces. After its experiences in Iraq, the United States will surely stop short of military sanctions against Syria and Iran, but action to isolate them will bring yet another cause of discord to the Middle East. Only the changing facts of demography may, in time, persuade Israel to let the Palestinians make a reality of Palestine. The Middle East will go on mattering to the West's interests and it will attract continuing commercial and diplomatic intervention. But Iraq has taught the Anglo-Saxon world no end of a lesson, just as Egypt taught Britain and France in 1956.

The elements of that lesson are several. For a superpower to win battles against an ill-armed enemy is straightforward, but winning hearts and minds is infernally complicated. Getting in is easy, getting out difficult. Other peoples' interests, other peoples' prejudices are as dear to them as ours are to us, for a nation's history leaves a deep if only subconscious imprint on it. Arabs and Moslems remember the Crusades and many another incursion into their homelands: they resent being told what to do by Anglo-Saxons, Franks, Christians, post-Christians and born-again Christians. 'Never again' is an aspiration, not a promise; but it will be a long time before the Middle East experiences again the casually brutal intervention which Iraq suffers today and to which Egypt was subjected half a century ago.

Source Notes

CHAPTER TWO (pp. 9–17)

1 Quoted in Tony Judt, *Postwar*, London: William Heinemann, 2005, p. 163.

CHAPTER THREE (pp. 27–43)

1 Quoted in Stephen Unwin and Carole Woddis, *A Pocket Guide to Twentieth Century Drama*, London: Faber & Faber, 2001, p. 149.
2 Quoted in Frank Giles, *The Locust Years, London: Secker & Warburg,* 1991, p. 273. The description of *Les Taxis de la Marne* which follows is drawn from Giles's book.
3 Arthur Miller, *Timebends*, London: Minerva, 1990.
4 Colin Clark, *My Week with Marilyn*, London: HarperCollins, 2000.
5 Rupert Croft-Cooke, *The Verdict of You All*, London: Secker & Warburg, 1955.
6 *Report of the Departmental Committee on Homosexual Offences and Prostitution*, London: HMSO, 1957.

CHAPTER FOUR (pp. 44–72)

1 Anthony Nutting, *No End of a Lesson*, London: Constable, 1967, p. 22.
2 Quoted in Patrick Cosgrave, *R. A. Butler: An English Life*, London: Quartet, 1981, p. 12.
3 Attlee to Gaitskell, on Eden's succession to Churchill, quoted in Peter Hennessy, *The Prime Minister: The Office and Its Holders since 1945*, London: Allen Lane, 2000, p. 212.
4 Quoted in John Colville, *The Fringes of Power: Downing Street Diaries 1939–1955*, London: Hodder & Stoughton, 1985, p. 708.
5 Quoted in Evelyn Shuckburgh, *Descent to Suez, Diaries 1951–56*, London: Weidenfeld & Nicolson, 1986, p. 327.

6 Ibid., p. 326.
7 Alex Danchev, ed., *War Diaries of Field Marshal Lord Alanbrooke*, London: Phoenix Pres, 2002, p. xvii.
8 Shuckburgh, p. 329.
9 Ibid., p. 330.
10 *The Times*, London, 8 February 1956.
11 Quoted in Frank Giles, *The Locust Years*, London: Secker & Warburg, 1991, p. 264.
12 Ibid., p. 267.
13 Ibid., p. 266.
14 Quoted in Jean-Pierre Rioux, *The Fourth Republic, 1944–1958*, Cambridge: Cambridge Unversity Press, 1987, p. 273.
15 John Glubb, *A Soldier with the Arabs*, London: Hodder & Stoughton, 1957, p. 423.
16 James Morris, *Farewell the Trumpets*, London: Faber & Faber, 1978, p. 250.
17 Quoted in Trevor Royle, *Glubb Pasha*, London: Little, Brown, 1992, p. 137.
18 Ibid., p. 492.
19 General Sir John Hackett, quoted in Royle, p. 183.
20 A former colleague of Glubb, quoted in Royle, p. 451.
21 Quoted in Royle, p. 448.
22 Ibid., p. 452.
23 Quoted in Keith Kyle, *Suez*, London: Weidenfeld & Nicolson, 1991, p. 90.
24 Ibid., p. 90.
25 Selwyn Lloyd, *Suez 1956*, London: Jonathan Cape, 1978, p. 47.
26 Nutting, pp. 34–5.
27 Anthony Eden, *Full Circle*, London: Cassell & Company, 1960, p. 352.
28 Robert Rhodes James, *Anthony Eden*, London: Weidenfeld & Nicolson, 1986, p. 432.
29 Quoted in ibid., p. 432.
30 Shuckburgh, p. 346.

CHAPTER FIVE (pp. 73–97)

1 Stephen E. Ambrose, *Eisenhower, The President*, London: George Allen & Unwin, 1984, p. 330.

2 Quoted in Keith Kyle, *Suez*, London: Weidenfeld & Nicolson, 1991, pp. 125–6.

3 Ibid., p. 132.

4 Ibid., p. 133.

5 Ibid.

6 Ibid.

7 Ibid.

8 Ibid., p. 134.

9 Ibid.

10 Evelyn Shuckburgh, *Descent to Suez, Diaries 1951–56*, London: Weidenfeld & Nicolson, 1986, p. 327.

11 Kyle, p. 136.

12 William Clark, quoted in Robert Rhodes James, *Anthony Eden*, London: Weidenfeld & Nicolson, 1985, p. 454.

13 Ibid.

14 Quoted in Anthony Nutting, *No End of a Lesson*, London: Constable, 1967, p. 46.

15 Rhodes James, p. 456.

16 Cabinet records quoted in Rhodes James, p. 459.

17 Ibid., p. 461.

18 Ibid.

19 Quoted in Alistair Horne, *Macmillan: 1894–1956*, London: Macmillan, 1988, p. 405.

20 Quoted in Rhodes James, p. 463.

21 Quoted in Ambrose, p. 330.

22 Selwyn Lloyd, *Suez 1956*, London: Jonathan Cape, 1978, p. 87.

23 As summarised in Kyle, p. 146.

24 Lloyd, p. 89.

25 Quoted in Kyle, p. 155.

26 Ambrose, p. 331.

27 Ibid.

28 Recorded in Nicholas Elliott, *Never Judge a Man by His Umbrella*, Norwich: Michael Russell, 1991.

29 Kyle, p. 210.

30 Quoted in Kyle, p. 176.

31 See above p. 61, and Kyle, p. 90.

32 Quoted in Kyle, p. 222.

33 Ibid., p. 246.

34 Quoted in Nutting, p. 62.

35 Quoted in Lloyd, p. 130.
36 Quoted in Horne, p. 424.
37 Quoted in Kyle, p. 249.
38 Ibid., p. 254.
39 Quoted in Rhodes James, p. 617.

CHAPTER SIX (pp. 99–115)

1 Nikita Khrushchev, *Khruschev Remembers*, London: André Deutsch, p. 559.
2 Quoted in William Taubman, *Khrushchev, The Man and His Era*, London: Free Press, 2003, p. 273.
3 Khrushchev, p. 617.
4 Quoted in Taubman, p. 283.
5 Veljko Micunovic, *Moscow Diary*, New York: Doubleday, 1980, p. 11.
6 William Hayter, *The Kremlin and the Embassy*, London: Macmillan, 1966, p. 127.
7 C. L. S. Cope, HM Legation, Budapest to E. F. Given, Foreign Office, 27 January 1956, National Archives.
8 Published after the 1956 revolution, but before Nagy's execution in 1958, under the title *Imre Nagy on Communism*, London: Thames & Hudson, 1957.
9 Ibid., pp. 43–65.
10 Ibid., pp. 20–42.
11 Quoted in Taubman, p. 355.
12 Peter Wright, *Spycatcher*, quoted in Taubman, p. 356.
13 Khrushchev, pp. 405–6.
14 Hayter, p. 135.
15 Khrushchev, p. 403.
16 Quoted in Alistair Horne, *Macmillan, 1894–1956*, London: Macmillan, 1988, p. 368.
17 Anthony Eden, *Full Circle*, London: Cassell & Company, 1960, p. 355.
18 Ibid., p. 357.
19 Ibid., pp. 360–1.
20 Khrushchev, p. 404.
21 Ivone Kirkpatrick, *The Inner Circle*, London, New York: Macmillan, St Martin's Press, 1959, p. 262.

22 Selwyn Lloyd, *Suez 1956*, London: Jonathan Cape, 1978. p. 64.
23 Khrushchev, p. 407.
24 Ibid., p. 405.
25 Quoted in Brian Bravati, *Hugh Gaitskell*, London: Richard Cohen Books, 1996, p. 313.
26 Ibid., p. 311.
27 *The Times*, London, 5 May 1956.
28 Philip Ziegler, *Mountbatten*, London: William Collins, 1985, p. 535.
29 Conversation with András B. Hegedüs.
30 Stephen Vizinczey, *Truth and Lies in Literature*, Chicago: University of Chicago Press, 1988, p. 322.
31 János Berecz, *Counter-Revolution: Words and Weapons*, Budapest, 1986, p. 88.

CHAPTER SEVEN (pp. 116–134)

1 Ferenc Nagy, *The Struggle Behind the Iron Curtain*, New York: Macmillan, 1948, p. 190.
2 Ferenc Váli, *Rift and Revolt in Hungary*, Cambridge, Mass.: Harvard University Press, 1961, p. 1980.
3 Ibid., p. 438.
4 Tamás Aczél and Tibor Méray, *The Revolt of the Mind*, London: Thames & Hudson, 1960, p. 402.
5 Veljko Micunovic, *Moscow Diary*, New York: Doubleday, 1980, pp. 76–7.
6 Norman Davies, *God's Playground, a History of Poland*, vol. 2, Oxford: Oxford University Press, 1981, p. 585.
7 United Nations, *Report of the Special Committee on the Problem of Hungary*, New York, 1957, para. 52.
8 Sándor Kopácsi, *In the Name of the Working Class*, Toronto: Lester & Orpen Dennys, p. 101.
9 Ibid.
10 Tibor Meray, *Thirteen Days That Shook the Kremlin*, London: Thames & Hudson, 1958, pp. 74–5.
11 Kopácsi, p. 103.
12 Meray, pp. 75–6.
13 UN Report, para. 467.
14 Kopácsi, pp. 104–5.

15 From *Harmincad utca 6: A Twentieth Century Story of Budapest*, quoting the late Sir Mark Russell.

CHAPTER EIGHT (pp. 135–151)

1 Keith Kyle, *Suez*, London: Weidenfeld & Nicolson, 1991.
2 Quoted in Anthony Nutting, *No End of a Lesson*, London: Constable, 1967, p. 87.
3 Quoted in Kyle, p. 295.
4 Quoted in Nutting, p. 89.
5 Robert H. Ferrell, ed., *The Eisenhower Diaries*, New York: Norton, 1981, p. 331.

CHAPTER NINE (pp. 152–167)

1 Quoted in Keith Kyle, *Suez*, London: Weidenfeld & Nicolson, 1995, p. 412.
2 Ibid.
3 Quoted in A. J. Barker, *Suez: The Seven Day War*, p. 102.
4 Ibid., p. 127.
5 Quoted in Kyle, p. 454.
6 Ibid., p. 452.
7 Quoted in Kyle, p. 450.
8 Quoted in Richard Weight, *Patriots*, London: Macmillan, 2005, p. 288.
9 Ibid., p. 463.
10 Stephen E. Ambrose, *Eisenhower the President*, London: George Allen & Unwin, 1984, p. 357.
11 Ibid., p. 358.
12 Ibid., p. 360.
13 Ibid., p. 361.
14 Ibid., p. 364.
15 Ibid., p. 369.
16 Quoted in Selwyn Lloyd, *Suez 1956*, London: Jonathan Cape, 1978, p. 152.
17 Quoted in Kyle, p. 402.
18 Ibid., p. 403.
19 Ibid.
20 Douglas Hurd, *Memoirs*, London: Little, Brown, 2003, p. 133.

21 Ambrose, p. 359.
22 Hurd, p. 137.
23 Ibid., p. 139.
24 Ibid., p. 140.

CHAPTER TEN (pp. 168–183)

1 Reproduced in full in Tibor Meray, *Thirteen Days That Shook the Kremlin*, London: Thames & Hudson, 1958, pp. 144–8.
2 Sándor Kopácsi, *In the Name of the Working Class*, Toronto: Lester & Orpen Dennys, 1986, p. 152.
3 Nikita Khrushchev, *Khrushchev Remembers*, London: André Deutsch, 1971, p. 417.
4 Ibid., p. 418.
5 Ibid., p. 419.
6 Veljko Micunovic, *Moscow Diary*, New York: Doubleday, 1980, p. 131.
7 Khrushchev, p. 421.
8 Micunovic, p. 144.
9 Khrushchev, p. 418.
10 Micunovic, p. 144.
11 Khrushchev, p. 418.
12 Ibid., p. 421.
13 Micunovic, p. 133.
14 Ibid., p. 132.
15 György Litván, ed., *The Hungarian Revolution of 1956*, London: Longman, 1996.
16 United Nations, *Report of the Special Committee on the Problem of Hungary*, New York, 1957, para. 76.
17 Litván, p. 125.
18 Ibid., p. 103.

CHAPTER ELEVEN (pp. 184–195)

1 Cited in Ferenc Váli, *Rift and Revolt in Hungary*, Cambridge, Mass.: Harvard University Press, 1961, p. 365.
2 Douglas Hurd, *Memoirs*, London: Little, Brown, 2003, p. 138.
3 The full text is reproduced in György Litván, ed., *The Hungarian Revolution of 1956*, London: Longman, 1996, p. 105.

4 James Michener, *The Bridge at Andau*, London: Secker & Warburg, 1957.
5 *The Times*, London, 23 November 1956.
6 Veljko Micunovic, *Moscow Diary*, New York: doubleday, 1980, pp. 144–6.
7 Ibid., p. 150.
8 See p.109 above.
9 Litván, p. 107.
10 Ibid., p. 108.
11 Micunovic, p. 169.
12 Ibid., p. 170.
13 Recollection of one of Nagy's companions, recorded in Peter Unwin, *Voice in the Wilderness*, London: Macdonald, 1991, p. 237.

CHAPTER TWELVE (pp. 196–219)

1 Mark Amory, ed., *The Letters of Evelyn Waugh*, London: Penguin, 1990, pp. 477–8.
2 Hansard, 22 November 1956, cols. 1943–4.
3 Quoted in Anthony Howard, *Rab: The Life of R. A. Butler*, London: Jonathan Cape, 1987, p. 241.
4 Ibid.
5 Ibid.
6 Quoted in ibid., p. 248.
7 Quoted in Alistair Horne, *Macmillan, 1894–1956*, London: Macmillan, 1988, p. 448.
8 Quoted in ibid., p. 429.
9 Quoted in ibid., p. 449
10 Quoted in ibid.
11 Quoted in ibid., p. 459.
12 Quoted in Stephen E. Ambrose, *Eisenhower the President*, London: George Allen & Unwin, 1984, p. 373.
13 Quoted in Peter Hennessy, *The Prime Minister: The Office and Its Holders since 1945*, London: Allen Lane, 2000, p. 217.
14 Kyle, p. 522.
15 Peter Unwin, *Voice in the Wilderness*, London: Macdonald, 1991.
16 Moscow telegram to Foreign Office no. 1547 of 4 November 1956, National Archives FO371/122381.

17 William Hayter, *The Kremlin and the Embassy*, London: Macmillan, 1966, pp. 152–3.

18 P. 168 above.

19 Nikita Khrushchev, *Khrushchev Remembers*, London; André Deutsch, 1971, pp. 416–18.

20 Veljko Micunovic, *Moscow Diary*, New York: Doubleday, 1980, p. 187.

21 Ibid., p. 188.

22 Hayter, p. 151.

23 Quoted in Robert Rhodes James, *Anthony Eden*, London: Weidenfeld & Nicolson, 1986, p. 591.

24 Ibid., p. 593.

25 National Archives FO953/1714/P1011/3.

26 Quoted in Ambrose, p. 373.

CHAPTER THIRTEEN (pp. 220–239)

1 Nikita Khrushchev, *Khrushchev Remembers*, London: André Deutsch, 1971.

2 For a brilliant analysis of the American empire, its strengths and weaknesses, and for reasons why it may not last, read Niall Ferguson, *Colossus*, London: Allen Lane, 2004.

3 Quoted in Richard Weight, *Patriots*, London: Macmillan, 2001, p. 275.

4 Keith Kyle, *Suez*, London: Weidenfeld & Nicolson, 1991, p. 466.

5 Pineau, cited in Kyle, p. 467.

6 Selwyn Lloyd, *Suez 1956*, London: Jonathan Cape, 1978, p. 54.

7 John Newhouse, *De Gaulle and the Anglo-Saxons*, New York: Viking Press, 1970, pp. 77–8.

8 Lloyd, p. 236.

Index